HOPEFUL TRAVELLERS

In this exploration of the nature of social reality in a mid-nineteenth-century Upper Canadian farming community, Professor Gagan employs the techniques of historical demography to reconstruct the population of mid-Victorian Peel County — specifically the histories of those families who occupied the county between 1845 and 1875. The evidence will be familiar to anyone who has tried to trace nineteenth-century Canadian family roots, but in this analysis the material is used to answer a broad range of questions related to the central problems of land availability and social change.

The author argues that in Peel County, as in the rest of Upper Canada, immigration, settlement, and population growth rapidly changed the previously agrarian frontiers of cheap and abundant farm land into mature agricultural communities. Patterns of inheritance, the timing of family formation, the size and structure of families, the life-cycle experiences of men, women, and children, chances for social betterment, and patterns of vocational and geographical mobility were all linked to the problem of land availability and all underwent subtle changes as rural society attempted to adjust to the new realities of life in the clearings.

This book is both a significant contribution to the social history of Ontario and to the growing corpus of comparative, international scholarship on the history of the family.

DAVID GAGAN is a member of the History Department at McMaster University.

DAVID GAGAN

Hopeful Travellers:
Families, Land, and Social Change
in Mid-Victorian Peel County,
Canada West

A PROJECT OF THE BOARD OF TRUSTEES
OF THE ONTARIO HISTORICAL STUDIES SERIES
FOR THE GOVERNMENT OF ONTARIO
PUBLISHED BY UNIVERSITY OF TORONTO PRESS
TORONTO BUFFALO LONDON

ISBN 978-0-8020-2435-0 (cloth)
ISBN 978-1-4875-9886-0 (paper)

Canadian Cataloguing in Publication Data

Gagan, David, 1940–
    Hopeful travellers
    (Ontario historical studies series, ISSN 0380-9188)
    "A project of the Board of Trustees of the Ontario
    Historical Studies Series for the Government of
    Ontario."
    Bibliography: p.
    Includes index.
    ISBN 978-0-8020-2435-0 (bound)   ISBN 978-1-4875-9886-0 (pbk.)
    1. Rural families—Ontario—Peel—History—19th
    century. 2. Peel (Ont.)—History—19th century.
    3. Peel (Ont.)—Social conditions. 4. Peel (Ont.)—
    Economic conditions. I. Title. II. Series.
    FC3095.P43G33   971.3'53502   C81-094441-3
    F1059.P25G33

This book has been published with the assistance of funds provided by the
Government of Ontario through the Ministry of Culture and Recreation.

FOR SARAH, JAMIE, BECKY, AND ABBY

The notion of superior dignity will always be attached in the minds of men to that kind of property with which they have most associated the idea of permanence.

Samuel Taylor Coleridge

(*Lay Sermons* 1852)

Contents

Tables

Figures

The Ontario Historical Studies Series

When discussions about this series of books first arose, it was immediately apparent that very little work had been done on the history of Ontario. Ontario has many fine historians, but much of their work has been focused on national themes, despite the fact that the locus of many of the important developments in the history of Canada — as recent events remind us — was, and is, in the provinces. While other provinces have recognized this reality and have recorded their histories in permanent form, Ontario is singularly lacking in definitive works about its own distinctive history.

Thus, when the Ontario Historical Studies Series was formally established by Order-in-Council on 14 April 1971, the Board of Trustees was instructed not only to produce authoritative and readable biographies of Ontario premiers but also 'to ensure that a comprehensive program of research and writing in Ontario history is carried out.'

From the outset the Board has included both professional historians and interested and knowledgeable citizens. The present members are: Margaret Angus, Kingston; J.M.S. Careless, Toronto; Floyd S. Chalmers, Toronto; R.E.G. Davis, Toronto; Gaetan Gervais, Sudbury; D.F. McOuat, Toronto; Jacqueline Neatby, Ottawa; J. Keith Reynolds, Toronto; and J.J. Talman, London. E.E. Stewart and Raymond Labarge served as valued members of the Board in its formative period. The combination of varied interests and skills of Board members has proven useful. A consensus was soon reached on the need for research in neglected areas of Ontario history and for scholarly and well-written works that would be of interest and value to the people of Ontario. We trust our work will satisfy these criteria.

After much careful deliberation the Board settled on six major areas in which to pursue its objectives: biographies of premiers; a bibliography; a historical atlas; a group of theme studies on major developments (social, economic, and cultural, as well as political) in the province; the recording on tape of the attitudes, opinions, and memories of many important leaders in Ontario; and, as a culmination of these studies, a definitive history of Ontario.

The first edition of the bibliography was published in 1973. Since it was well received, the Board sponsored the preparation of a second, comprehensive edition prepared by Olga Bishop, Barbara Irwin, and Clara Miller, entitled *Bibliography of Ontario History, 1867-1976.* This volume was published in 1980. Our first major publication was *G. Howard Ferguson* by Peter Oliver (1977), followed in 1978 by *Ontario since 1867,* a general history of the province, by Joseph Schull. *The Pre-Confederation Premiers: Ontario Government Leaders, 1841-1867,* edited by J.M.S. Careless, the second volume in the biographies series, was published in 1980. The first of the theme studies, *The Politics of Federalism: Ontario's Relations with the Federal Government, 1867-1942,* by Christopher Armstrong was published in 1981. *Hopeful Travellers: Families, Land and Social Change in Mid-Victorian Peel County, Canada West,* by David Gagan is the second of the theme studies. We hope it will find a large and interested reading audience and that it will be followed each year by one or more equally interesting books, the total of which will inform and illuminate Ontario history in a new and lasting way.

The Board is greatly indebted to its editors, Goldwin French, Editor-in-Chief, Peter Oliver, Associate Editor, and Jeanne Beck, Assistant Editor, for their assistance in the selection of subjects and authors and for their supervision of the preparation, editing, and publication of works in the Series.

Murray G. Ross
Chairman, Board of Trustees
Ontario Historical Studies Series

24 April 1981

For many years the principal theme in English-Canadian historical writing has been the emergence and the consolidation of the Canadian nation. This theme has been developed in uneasy awareness of the persistence and importance of regional interests and identities, but because of the central role of Ontario in the growth of Canada, Ontario has not been seen as a region. Almost unconsciously, historians have equated the history of the province with that of the nation and have depicted the interests of other regions as obstacles to the unity and welfare of Canada.

The creation of the province of Ontario in 1867 was the visible embodiment of a formidable reality, the existence at the core of the new nation of a powerful if disjointed society whose traditions and characteristics differed in many respects from those of the other British North American colonies. The intervening century has not witnessed the assimilation of Ontario into the other regions in Canada; on the contrary, it has become a more clearly articulated entity. Within the formal geographical and institutional framework defined so assiduously by Ontario's political leaders, an increasingly intricate web of economic and social interests has been woven and shaped by the dynamic interplay between Toronto and its hinterland. The character of this regional community has been formed in the tension between a rapid adaptation to the processes of modernization and industrialization in western society and a reluctance to modify or discard traditional attitudes and values. Not surprisingly, the Ontario outlook is a compound of aggressiveness, conservatism, and the conviction that its values should be the model for the rest of Canada.

The purpose of the Ontario Historical Studies Series is to describe and analyse the historical development of Ontario as a distinct region within Canada. The Series as planned will include approximately thirty-five volumes covering many aspects of the life and work of the province from its original establishment in 1791 as Upper Canada to our own time. Among these will be biographies of several prominent political figures, a three-volume economic history, numerous works on topics such as social structure, education, minority groups, labour, political and administrative institutions, literature, theatre, and the arts, and a comprehensive synthesis of the history of Ontario, based upon the detailed contributions of the biographies and thematic studies.

In planning this project, the Board and its editors have endeavoured to maintain a reasonable balance between different kinds and areas of historical research, and to appoint authors ready to ask new kinds of questions about the past and to answer them in accordance with the canons of contemporary scholarship. Ten biographical studies have been included, if only because through biography the past comes alive most readily for the general reader as well as the historian. The historian must be sensitive to today's concerns and standards as he engages in the imaginative recreation of the interplay between human beings and circumstances in time. He should seek to be the mediator between all the dead and the living, but in the end the humanity and the artistry of his account will determine the extent of its usefulness.

Hopeful Travellers: Families, Land, and Social Change in Mid-Victorian Peel County, Canada West, the second theme study to be published, is a detailed examination of the 'nature of ordinary social experience' in a rural community. The author has used the concepts and methods of historical demography, quantitative microanalytical social history, and family history, developed by British, European, and American scholars, to fashion a 'collective biography' of the people of Peel County in the mid-nineteenth century. In this he has described and analysed the forces of change which influenced families, households, and individuals, their responses to altered circumstances, and the effects of this process of adjustment. We hope that this work will enlarge our understanding of the social history of Ontario and that it will encourage historians to undertake similar studies of other Ontario counties or regions.

Goldwin French
Editor-in-Chief
Peter Oliver
Associate Editor
Jeanne Beck
Assistant Editor

Toronto
24 April 1981

Preface

This book is about the people of an Upper Canadian community in the years immediately before and after Confederation. It is not, except incidentally, a piece of local history. The reader who wishes to discover the facts about skunk hunting (a not altogether unimportant pastime in rural Ontario) in nineteenth-century Peel County will have to refer to the several volumes of anecdotal history written by that most eccentric of Ontario's local historians, William Perkins Bull. This study uses the population of Peel County from 1850 to 1870 as a generous, but nevertheless restricted, sample of rural society generally in nineteenth-century Ontario. The purpose of the analysis is to inquire into the nature of ordinary social experience in order to resolve two questions in particular: what were the strategies which ordinary families devised to promote their long-range social and economic objectives in an era of rapid social change; and what larger forces of change determined the form and function of those strategies? Secondarily, the study seeks to identify the principal outlines of individual social experience within the context of the family and its goals. The book deals, in short, with the facts of life in a mid-nineteenth-century agrarian society as they pertain to the making of livings, the material circumstances in which people lived, their domestic arrangements, the stages of life through which they passed, the structures and functions of the families and households in which they lived, and, finally, the sources of discontinuity which forced them, from time to time, to adjust their expectations and to reconsider the facts of their lives.

The evidence presented throughout this book reflects the fact that familial and individual experience must be reconstructed from the only recorded 'events' in the lives of ordinary people, events such as birth, education, employment, marriage, parenthood, home ownership, widowhood, and death. These 'events' now, as in the past, tend to take the form of social statistics. Consequently, much of the evidence presented in this book is numerical rather than anecdotal or textual. I have attempted to present it, however, in a manner which will inform the general reader and the scholar alike without unnecessarily confusing either.

Whatever his methods, the historian's task must remain constant: to frame the results of his research in a descriptive account which reconstructs, as plausibly as possible, an actual, not a theoretical world of historical reality. In short, the numerical evidence presented here has the same function as more traditional documentation, to illuminate the issues and events being discussed.

Whether the people of mid-Victorian Peel County are acceptable surrogates for rural society in Canada West, whether the 'microcosmic' approach to social history is an effective one, is a matter of some debate among social historians. Certainly this is not the only way in which to reconstruct the social past. But in so far as the characteristics of real people related to demonstrable processes of social change and continuity in finite periods of time can shed light on a level of historical experience so far impenetrable by scholars accustomed to working at higher levels of aggregation, microanalysis is an indispensable new tool for the social historian. In a series of historical studies which take in the broad sweep of Ontario's historical development from the earliest times to the present, it seems especially important to inquire, at critical intervals and with as much intensity as possible, into the dynamics of those historical processes which shaped the characteristics of Ontarians and moulded their expectations. The thirty years between 1845 and 1875 were a demonstrably critical period in the history of the province of Canada and the early history of Ontario. This book takes a closer look at the historical circumstances of life, as it was experienced by ordinary Canadians, during this important era.

Happily, although the theories and methods of historical demography, of quantitative microanalytical social history, and of family history are not well developed as branches of Canadian historiography, British, European, and American scholars have explored these new avenues of historical research with benefit for all social historians. Consequently, this study is at least implicitly comparative in scope in so far as I have attempted to utilize both the theory and the substance of their research as reference points for my analysis, especially where the historiography deals with the problem of societal change and continuity among eighteenth- and nineteenth-century North American rural populations and their European antecedents. But, of course, nineteenth-century Canada West was not eighteenth-century Massachusetts or seventeenth-century England. The circumstances of time and place are necessarily the most crucial ingredients in this study of families, land, and societal change in mid-Victorian Canada West.

In the course of reconstructing the history of more than 10,000 families I have been fortunate in the assistance, support, and encouragement that I have received from so many quarters. My research assistants, Robert Leitch, Ruthanne Buckner, Laura Foley, John Stonehouse, and Helmut Manzl, undertook a monumental task—coding the data—with great tenacity. In the early stages of the research Herbert Mays, now of the University of Winnipeg, helped me to grapple with the project's methodological and theoretical problems. The programming skills of Barbara Deal and Christine Feaver resolved the conundrums of record linkage and data processing and curbed the worst excesses of a scholar new to the world of computer technology. In this regard, all of us owe a debt of gratitude to the forbearance of the staff of the Academic Computing Services unit at McMaster University.

I must acknowledge also a particular debt to several of my colleagues for their advice and criticisms. Peter George, Peter Pineo, John Weaver, and Frank Denton, all McMaster scholars, offered useful comments about the analysis and methods at various stages of my research. Richard Rempel lent his editorial skill and his knowledge of mid-Victorian British society to the manuscript at a critical stage in its evolution. Professor Marvin McInnis of Queen's University has been an unfailing source of stimulating counter-arguments to the hypotheses explored in the earlier published reports of the Peel County History Project. Finally, Michael Katz, now at the University of Pennsylvania, shared his theoretical and technical expertise with me at the outset of this project and in so doing shortened its duration and sharpened my appreciation of the pitfalls ahead.

Goldwin French and Peter Oliver, editors of the Ontario Historical Studies Series, have been generous to a fault in their patient encouragement of the project. The Board of Trustees of the OHSS provided substantial financial support. In this regard, I owe a very special debt, as many Canadian scholars do, to the Canada Council and to its successor the Social Sciences and Humanities Research Council of Canada which provided the initial research grants and a leave fellowship that made this project possible.

It is customary as well for scholars to thank their wives for everything from muzzling the dog to massaging the ego while scholarship pursued its inevitably tortuous path. I am pleased to say that my wife, Rosemary, did neither. She read microfilm, coded data, reconstituted families (including our own), corrected computer output, edited and typed reports, and spent vacations in places like Grand Rapids in order to get the job done. She deserves a full share of the credit for its completion.

It remains for me to accept full responsibility for whatever shortcomings this finished product may have.

DPG
Burlington, Ontario
31 December 1980

HOPEFUL TRAVELLERS

1 Continuity, Change, and Ordinary Experience

West of metropolitan Toronto the suburban frontier is a ragged salient of subdivisions pushing north from Lake Ontario beyond Port Credit through the old orchards of Toronto Township and the once bountiful wheatlands of Chinguacousy (see Maps 1, 2). At Highway 7, the regional planners' Hadrian's Wall which establishes the line of demarcation between developed and underdeveloped territory, suburbia retreats eastward, past Brampton and Bramalea, then southward to converge again with the outer limits of the metropolis. Behind this crabgrass frontier, the new city of Mississauga, sprawling, unfocused, slashed by freeways, and pummelled by the endless din of Toronto International Airport, has obliterated every physical vestige of southern Peel County's rural origins. Beyond the line of subdivisions, however, country estates, handsomely restored mid-Victorian farmhouses, picturesque villages, and 'Century Farms' sustain the image of a way of life nevertheless long lost to remembrance, longer still to experience.

In much the same way, Ontario's social past has been buried beneath successive layers of the rubble of modernization, surfacing occasionally in memory or imagination like a restored Georgian mansion whose outward solidity, simple elegance, and structural orderliness bespeak a world less complex, more stable, and more easily comprehensible than our own. But just as architectural conservancy frequently preserves merely the shell of an otherwise gutted, sanitized, and functionally modernized structure, so, too, memory and imagination have a habit of confusing appearance and reality in our social past. Life as it was becomes life as we observe it, at a great distance, to have been: a simple round of daily activities attuned to seasonal rhythms in a social environment whose enduring characteristic was continuity, not change. All of this can be seen, and understood, in a Sunday afternoon's walk around one of Ontario's 'pioneer villages' whose stock-in-trade is a social past cleansed of all complexity save the mastery of redundant manual skills. To a resident of such a place in the 1840s or 1850s, possessing one of those skills, indeed which particular skill, among many,

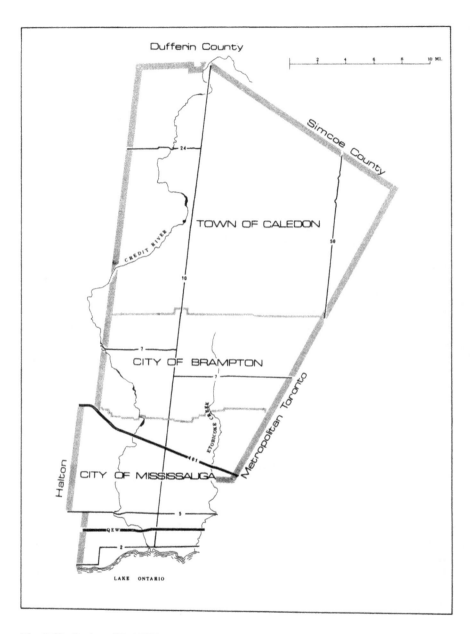

Map 1 The Region of Peel 1975

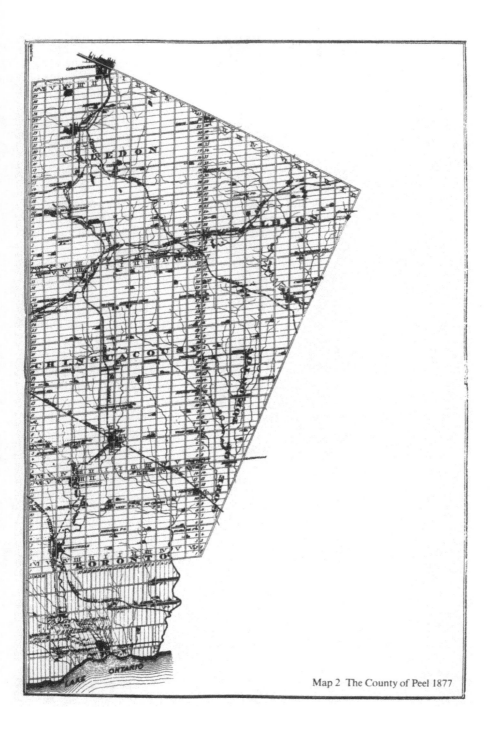

Map 2 The County of Peel 1877

he did possess was a matter of social survival. It might determine the age at which he could get married; how large his family would be; whether he would be able to educate his children; when they would eventually leave home and start families of their own; what kind of house he would occupy; how large a household he would have to support; whether he and his wife would have enough to live on in their old age; how he would divide his estate among his children; above all else, whether he would be a resident of that community for only a few months, for a few years, or for his entire life; and, finally, whether he would ever save enough capital to acquire what he truly aspired to have, land — enough for himself and at least some of his sons, because owning it or speculating in it was the proven road to security. In mid-Victorian Upper Canada, the skill that a man possessed was one of a whole catalogue of characteristics which not only set some men apart from or made them similar to other men, but also revealed how far each had advanced, or might expect to advance, in what was a highly competitive, complex society, however backward and simple it may appear in contrast to our own.

The society of mid-nineteenth-century Peel County, Canada West, is a case in point. Families moved into and left the community at an astonishing rate, so high in fact that only one-quarter of the families enumerated at census time would have been there since the previous census and would stay until the next enumeration ten years later. In their own way, the concession lines and sideroads of Peel were as busy as the freeways which carry people into and out of the region today. All of this coming and leaving then, as now, had to do with the making of livings, securing land or employment adequate first to sustain life and then to provide economic security, material comfort, and social standing. It was not an easy row to hoe. Some groups — those with a little capital, marketable skills or commodities, the native-born, Protestants, and the earliest wave of settlers — enjoyed greater success than others — the professional man, the unskilled, the newly arrived immigrant, and especially the Irish Roman Catholic. But time was also a vital factor. If a man, whatever his background, had not succeeded in acquiring some reasonable level of security by the time he was forty, his chances of improving his position thereafter were slim; hence the persistent distinction between the relative stability of the older, established generation of residents and the restlessness of the aspiring younger men in this community in which the young, in the 1850s and 1860s, were the objects of much concern.

After two decades of intensive settlement and unprecedented prosperity rooted in a vigorous market for the staple of local agriculture, wheat, land was much in demand and, consequently, increasingly expensive and difficult to acquire. By the 1860s farmers' sons could no longer be assured that they had a future as farmers, and farmers' daughters could no longer be certain that they would be mistresses of their own households as early as their mothers had been.

Educating both sons and daughters for a future in which neither farming nor perpetual domesticity would be their immediate preoccupation was one alternative. Another was to move once again to some new agricultural frontier where the emigrant farmer's expectation of relentless improvement might be fulfilled, and where the established attitudes and structures of the farm family.would continue to shape and inform individual social experience. By the 1860s these questions were all the more pressing because rural society throughout Canada West was in the midst of a difficult era of economic transition. Inflation, depression, falling commodity prices, blight, and market dislocation, one following hard upon the heels of the other after 1857, conspired to create a crisis of confidence in the promise of Canadian life. Whatever course was taken, these altered circumstances of material life in mid-Victorian Upper Canada required action if the objectives of the rural family, especially the expectations of its children, were to be met.

How the people of Peel responded to these events is the subject of this book. On the surface, their behaviour appears to have been remarkably 'modern' judging by the subtlety of the strategies which this society adopted in response to the forces of social change: a new system of transferring wealth from one generation to another, a system that forced parents to make difficult choices among the legitimate expectations of all their children; restricting the size of the traditionally large farm family in order to serve better the interests of all the children of a marriage and the economy of the family; curbing the desire of mature children to be independent proprietors by discouraging the formation of new farm families through delayed marriage; trimming domestic establishments to their essential proportions — parents and children living alone rather than in the company of the relatives, hired hands, and domestic servants who once populated the farm household. These strategies were not invented, however, by the families of Peel County; nor were the circumstances in which they were applied entirely unique. In pre-industrial England, in colonial Massachusetts and Pennsylvania, in nineteenth-century Europe and America, similar concatenations of events engendered remarkably similar responses from local populations. The sources of threatened discontinuity and the effects of popular responses to it in a Canadian context are the primary concerns of this analysis.

In a much broader sense, however, the book is a collective biography of all those very ordinary people who resided, however briefly, in this corner of mid-Victorian Upper Canada in the two decades before Confederation. Like conventional biographies which deal with the lives and times of highly visible historical characters, this biography treats familial circumstances, childhood, education, work, marriage, family life, motivation, success, failure, pride, and prejudice. Unlike traditional biographies, however, this is not the record of unique encounters with unique historical circumstances which can be fashioned into a revelation of equally unique actions. This biography is the record of shared encounters with the common circumstances of life in a society in which the nature of individual experience was defined by the events that took place within the limited worlds of the family, the household, and the community. At this very elementary level, historical 'events' are neither as grand nor as decisive as, say, Disraeli's Second Reform Bill or, closer to home, the Quebec Conference which paved the way for the Confederation of the Canadas. But as the 'lives and times' of the people of mid-Victorian Peel County, Canada West, illustrate, the family, the household, and the individual were as subject to the forces of change and as compulsive in their search for order and continuity as any larger society ever was.

This collective biography, then, is also a 'case study,' a microanalysis limited, in space and time, to the people of a single locality during two decades of its history. The analysis strives to find the general in the particular and then to argue that what appears to have been peculiar to these people, in this place, at that time, may have meaning and significance in terms of a much broader spectrum of popular experience in mid-Victorian rural Upper Canada. The objection is sometimes raised that conclusions derived from a microanalysis of historical social experience in one limited little world cannot be imputed to a wider population. But even if the larger importance of events viewed in a severely restricted context remains to some extent speculative, the difference between the sharp focus that emerges when the historian works at the level of individual experience and the lack of delineation when social history is filtered through several layers of aggregated impressions makes the exercise well worth the risk. There is simply no other way to understand how life was actually lived in the past than to reconstruct, stage by stage, the lives of actual people as they went about the very ordinary business of getting on with life itself.

Thus, this societal analysis necessarily relies particularly on the sources from which ordinary lives can be reconstructed. A few letters and personal memoirs survive, but in terms of the sources from which history is traditionally written these people are historically invisible. Their letters and diaries, if they ever existed, obviously were not considered worth saving for posterity. It is unlikely that they had much to say for themselves in any case. As one pioneer's son remarked, his parents had too much of the 'prose of life' to be interested in prose of any other sort.[1] In short, the historian intent on reconstructing the lives of ordinary Canadians must begin with the only records that most of us will ever leave to posterity. These are the official and semi-official records which we routinely generate as we make our way through life. The most important of those records, for the mid-nineteenth century, are the returns from the decennial censuses. They report, for each individual in each community, age, sex, marital status, occupation, religious affiliation, and place of birth. For children, school attendance is recorded, and for adults levels of literacy. The 1851-2 and 1861 returns noted the relative quality of residential accommodation; and the 1861 and 1871 returns reported land occupancy and property ownership (for heads of household) as well as information on farm production and (for 1861) farm values. Apart from this explicit information, much is implicit in these records: family size and structure, household size and structure, and births during the year are some especially important examples.[2] These manuscript census returns are the most important, but not the only kind of routinely generated records from which the social past can be reconstructed. For example, then as now, all legal transactions involving real property had to be recorded at county registry offices. Local abstracts and copy-books of deeds are available for most nineteenth-century Upper Canadian communities. The abstracts, one for each lot in each township, list in chronological sequence each transaction — sales, mortgages, deed polls, quit claims, discharges of mortgages, and transfers by will or gift — involving all or part of any lot. Each abstract is, in itself, a legal history of a piece of ground; and the copy-books provide the details of that history as they relate to the individuals who owned or occupied each lot. Another set of legal documents now widely available, the records of County Surrogate Courts, come closest to being literary sources. They contain copies of last wills and testaments deposited with the court for probate. By their very nature these wills, most of them apparently written without professional advice, are reflective, even philosophical documents which, in addition to describing the accumulated rewards of a life's work, review past family relationships, anticipate the future, and strive to create order and harmony in a little world shortly to be threatened with calamity.

Four other types of records are of particular importance to this study. In spite of their rather spotty distribution, the surviving marriage registers for Peel, some official and some denominational, have been useful in resolving certain questions about age at marriage. Similarly, municipal assessment rolls (also badly preserved for this county), though not entirely appropriate substitutes for census returns, nevertheless contain enough information to be useful in the pre-census period particularly with regard to land ownership, occupation, and geographical mobility. The same may be said for the county directories which appeared at fairly regular intervals. Last but not least, the Crown Lands Papers which contain the pre-patent history of each lot in each township are an invaluable source of information on the settlement process.

As useful as all this individual information is, in its disaggregated form it is essentially unusable. That is to say, the censuses yield a file of information for, in this case, about 13,000 families on three census returns referenced only by name, township of residence, and census date. Similarly, the abstracts of deeds represent, for three coterminous census dates, a file of information representing approximately 13,000 different landowners referenced by lot, township, and owner's name. But if his purpose is to reconstruct all the important characteristics of historical individuals *across* time in order to document the nature and timing of changes that take place in individual experience, the historian requires a file for each individual or each family which pulls together all available routinely generated documents. In this case, that means a file which first links all of the records of a particular individual or family together at each of the three census dates (1851, 1861, and 1871), then links the three decennial files to each other to create a continuous record of historical experience. And it must be done without the aid of the social insurance numbers which follow modern Canadians and allow them to be followed, wherever they go, from birth until death.

Happily, even historians have become automated enough to put computers to work doing at least some of the more tedious tasks associated with historical research. An automated record-linkage procedure created the principal multivariate family and household files which form the basis of this study. In effect, the computer became an electronic genealogist programmed to identify people by their constant characteristics (name, age, place of birth, and sex), occasionally running afoul of (and then berserk from) the infinite varieties of John Macdonald in a predominantly Scots-Irish community. Beyond this stage of marshalling discrete files into continuous, comprehensive family histories, however, electronic data processing has played a still more significant role. What the historian can discover about the lives of most ordinary individuals in the past is meaningful only to the extent that their lives can be compared to and contrasted with the characteristics and the experience of other individuals who shared their social, economic, demographic, and cultural environments from time to time. Moreover, since these individuals did not articulate their attitudes and their aspirations or comment on the quality of their lives or the circumstances which affected it, the historian must infer, from records which are essentially numerical in form, the substance of individual experience and the apparent sources of variation on its main themes. Again, the computer makes it possible for the historian to sort through 10,000 possible variations on a theme and to identify the principal outlines of a common past. Thus, most of the documentation employed in the analysis that follows consists of numerical data presented in tabular, but sometimes in graphic form, which serve to illustrate, describe, and explain the comparative condition of groups of individuals in this society and the circumstances which seem to account for their relative condition most precisely.

The routinely generated records of historically invisible and inarticulate common people, record-linkage, computer generated numerical evidence, and the microcosmic level of inquiry constitute the methodology employed in this search for the meaning of individual experience in our social past. This is sometimes described as the 'new' history; but in fact it is an established and now highly refined variation[3] on the historian's traditional mandate: to employ new and old sources alike in new ways in order to rediscover the past, to understand it, and to interpret its meaning to the present. If there is something 'new' about the new history it is that British, European, American, and now Canadian scholars have rediscovered a lost world of individual experience, the conditions of life in pre-industrial western societies. Because the contrasts between our own time and this not too remote past seem so great we have assumed, mistakenly one historian suggests, that knowledge about how people lived in that world can tell us nothing about ourselves.[4] It is a false assumption. History, whatever else it may be, is a process in which society's natural preference for continuity must contend intermittently with dynamic agents of change. Change takes place, but the momentum of continuity is not lost.[5] Social experience, consequently, is never the product of wholly new circumstances. At any point along the continuum of history the conditions of life represent, though not necessarily equally, the elements of both old and new worlds of social reality. Thus, to know ourselves, to understand the realities of our own social condition, it is necessary to comprehend the cumulative effects of this on-going process in which change is never absolute and absolute continuity is never guaranteed. Since we are always in the midst of that process, the present can never be completely distinguishable from the past.

We have dared to presume that industrialism, 'progress,' development, 'modernization' — the terms, as used by sociologists, are interchangeable — have disrupted the continuum of history. Yet discontinuity is not the preferred pattern in history. It is precisely at the level of 'the behaviour of concrete human beings in specific areas in finite periods of time'[6] that it is possible to test these alternative hypotheses. The shape of social reality becomes particularly magnified and meaningful when it is fixed in time and place and related to the experience of actual people. In that context it is possible to understand the nature and the effects of those observable processes which determined the meaning of social reality from time to time, and consequently to understand the strategies and mechanisms of social survival which individuals, families, and societies have employed in order to cope with change in their social environments. All of this is a necessary prelude to the more important task of comparing social experience and its determinants across cultures and through time in order to relate life in one age, one region, or one culture to life in any other time and place. The rediscovery of that lost world of the family and of individual experience in the age immediately preceding our own is therefore of considerable historical importance. But the historian who enters it may appear 'at times to resemble ... the archeologist, who seeks to breathe life into a long-dead civilization.'[7]

The contours of individual experience in the Canadian past are virtually unmapped. Yet Victorian Canadians thought that they, too, lived in an age such as our own, an age apparently characterized by a sharp break with a dead past. 'THANK HEAVEN! we live in the nineteenth century ... Never before did such glorious days as these dawn upon the human race ... How shall we contrast the darkness of former ages with the meridian splendour of modern times?'[8] The source of this wonderful pride (and of its close relative, fearful anxiety) was the idea that progress and improvement had elevated the human condition to new standards of social, moral, and intellectual perfection. What was particularly remarkable about these developments, from a mid-Victorian Canadian perspective, was that they had been accomplished so swiftly by a largely immigrant population whose only assets were their ingenuity, their willingness to work, the cohesiveness of their families, and the inestimable richness of the land. Familial labour converted to land, land to capital, and capital to social improvement was the elementary formula infinitely repeated by a million and more poor emigrants who had raised themselves to 'affluence and independence' in the shortest possible time. That was the essence of perhaps the most widely quoted contemporary essay on life in mid-Victorian Upper Canada,[9] and most other commentators concurred with both the substance and the spirit of this interpretation. The progress of society was simply individual improvement writ large.[10] Both were foreordained by an environment which placed no restrictions on human inventiveness, especially the ability to devise 'hitherto unknown or unthought of' solutions to the problems of social survival and economic progress.[11] The society which emerged from this process was heralded as something new in the world, fluid, egalitarian, and progressive in a way that its less enlightened European parents never had been and never would be.

The world of individual social experience in mid-nineteenth-century Upper Canada has already yielded striking evidence that urban society, at least, did not conform to these popular notions. In his book *The People of Hamilton, Canada West*, Michael Katz has demonstrated that in fact the hallmarks of Upper Canadian urban society in the age of progress were inequality of opportunity, unequal rewards, and social structural rigidity which condemned the vast majority of people to live in perpetual uncertainty about their social survival, at best to anticipate only marginal improvements, after a life of labour, in the conditions into which they were born. It remains to be seen whether the facts of life in the countryside of this preponderantly agrarian province were more or less propitious than the unfulfilled promises of life in the city.

Viewed in the long term and with the advantage of hindsight, the economy of mid-Victorian rural Upper Canada might reasonably have justified a degree of cautious optimism in spite of the sometimes fearful consequences of its short term fluctuations. The 1850s were ushered in by a series of events which at least one historian has described as a revolution.[12] The Irish famine emigrations of 1847-8, the advent of responsible self-government in 1849, the completion of the St Lawrence canal system, a reciprocal trading agreement with the United States of America, and an expanding imperial market for Canadian wheat all contributed, in less than a decade (1846-54), to the definition of a new era in Canadian history. Whether these developments indeed constituted a 'revolution' is debatable.[13] But there can be no doubt about the apparent potential for a great leap forward in the confluence of a vast new pool of unskilled labour, the commercial opportunities presented by expanding domestic and export markets, the completion of an efficient transportation system, and, withal, the legislative independence to turn these new opportunities to the province's advantage. Certainly that was how Upper Canadians chose to interpret these developments,[14] and in the years before 1857 their optimism was amply rewarded. By the end of the decade the province had indeed undergone a significant transformation. Railways spanned the length and breadth of Canada West, further enhancing the Laurentian system's natural advantages as the province's commercial lifeline. Freed by the railroad from the tyranny of the riverine system, commerce and industry expanded into the hinterland to become the catalysts of the first great age of urban development in Canada West. With the diffusion of technology and capital came new opportunities for employment on the 'urban frontier' which first rivalled, and eventually replaced, the rapidly receding backwoods as the focus of demographic growth and of popular faith in the inevitability of individual social improvement. These new manufacturing, distribution, and service centres flourished, however, largely by virtue of the steel umbilicals that connected them to the province's two great commercial metropolises, Toronto and Hamilton, the source of the life-giving nourishment — goods, investment, taste, ideas, and people — which flowed from parent to progeny in return for wealth flowing in the other direction. At the heart of this delicate symbiosis lay the interdependence of commerce and agriculture.[15]

Commercial agriculture — producing surplus food for exchange in the market-place — was always the principal characteristic of Upper Canadian agriculture, the myth of the self-sufficient pioneer notwithstanding.[16] What distinguished the Canadian farmer of the early nineteenth century was the nature of the market economy in which he functioned. It was a staples economy focused on a few highly prized natural commodities which were paid for in cash and drained off through the lake ports to the United States, Great Britain, and Europe. Among these commodities, wheat and its by-products already constituted the substance of rural prosperity when accelerated foreign demand after 1846 produced a bonanza for those with land and labour enough to capitalize on these unusual circumstances. Consequently, between 1850 and 1860 surplus farm production (measured in caloric units) increased by 100%[17] as previously uncultivated land was cleared and cropped, as new agricultural frontiers (for example, Bruce County) were opened to a rapidly expanding agricultural population, and as the benefits of modern technology were applied to the problems of cultivation. In 1861, the farmers of Canada West produced nearly 25 million bushels of wheat, a crop that would not be equalled for another 15 years and then only by the combined production of all Canadian farmers.[18]

From this perspective, the events of the early 1860s represent a serious setback for agriculture in Canada West. The contraction of the imperial market at the end of the Crimean War was followed, in succession, by a severe commercial depression (1857-60), a rapid decline in wheat prices (47% in four years), a series of severe crop failures, and, finally, at the end of the American Civil War, the disruption of the American market for Canadian livestock, dairy products, cereal, and forage crops.[19] In the end, much of the ground gained in the 1850s was lost. Between 1860 and 1870 surplus farm production in central Canada declined by 100%.[20] In the eyes of contemporary observers these and certain other circumstances of life in rural Canada West had the makings of a genuine crisis. First, Upper Canada's frontier of cheap and abundant land had disappeared in the 1850s under the pressures of immigration and natural demographic increase. Consequently, the province's ability to assimilate more immigrants was severely constrained, all the more because the commercial depression of 1857-60 choked off the prospect of increased urban employment opportunities. As a result, not only new arrivals but the province's burgeoning native-born population had begun increasingly to drift across the border in search of land or employment. The threat of demographic stagnation, particularly in the rural areas, convinced many observers that only a new frontier of free or cheap land could reverse this drift and, in so doing, preserve the fundamental equation between agrarian improvement and commercial prosperity. Worse, perhaps, it was equally apparent that, whatever the state of the staples trade, wheat production, the province's life-blood, was in serious difficulty by 1864. Rust, midge, and soil exhaustion, especially in south-central Ontario, had taken their toll, as they had in every other community where wheat mining was not tempered by science.[21] The crisis in agriculture, then, compounded the economic and demographic problems which threatened to stifle progress and delay Upper Canada's appointment with destiny. 'I have no hesitation in declaring that there never was a period in the history of Canada when the people suffered more than they do at present,' complained one legislator whose colleagues readily supplied a catalogue of trials and tribulations. The province, they alleged, was no longer a field for immigration; rural property values had plummetted; agrarian indebtedness had increased drastically; sons could no longer afford to inherit the family homestead; and farmers were leaving the province by their thousands. Politicians talked of the 'general gloom which hangs like a pall on the land.'[22]

Upper Canada's interest, after 1864, in the scheme to unite the British North American provinces in a political confederation was not wholly the product of these factors. Constitutional, political, and cultural considerations contributed equally, perhaps primarily, to the leadership that Canadian politicians willingly assumed in the negotiations which laid the basis for political union. But in so far as the proposed new Dominion government would be empowered to annex a western frontier of free land and commercial expansion immediately adjacent to Ontario, economic and social factors obviously loomed large in Ontario's hopes for the success of the experiment. The history of Ontario's subsequent sense of 'mission' in the west, its hysterical reaction to the strident nationalism of the Red River Métis who rebelled against the terms of annexation in 1869, and the westward migration of Ontario farm families after the passage of the Dominion Lands Act (1872) served notice that Manitoba was Ontario's colony, an outlet for restless energy yearning to realize its full potential.[23]

If, after 1870, Manitoba or the American mid-west replaced Ontario, at least at the level of popular wisdom, as the new garden of Eden, there is nevertheless considerable evidence that in the 1870s Ontario's economy substantially recovered from the rude shocks to which it had been subjected between 1857 and 1865. In retrospect, the 1860s represent not so much a watershed as a sometimes painful return to normality, to orderly if less spectacular development, after a decade of erratic swings between boom and bust; and when the air had cleared there was still a future for agriculture in the province. In the next decade, agricultural production regained most of the ground lost in the 1860s, partly through the recovery of export markets, but particularly as the result of increased domestic demand for wheat, flour, and, more especially, meat, poultry, and dairy products. Farm prices remained fairly buoyant throughout the decade while production costs, especially freight rates, declined.[25] In other words, the farmer who successfully weathered the effects of the economic, demographic, and natural elements which buffetted him in the 1850s and 1860s might have emerged from that experience with his faith shaken but with his hopes for the future substantially intact. Since most of those elements were beyond his power to control, however, much depended on the strategies which he was able to devise to palliate their immediate effects and to promote his long-range objectives.

This study is concerned with the effects of those factors of change and uncertainty on the rural population of Peel County during this critical period of Canadian history, and with the strategies which these historical farm families devised to mitigate, or perhaps in some cases to capitalize on, the altered circumstances of rural life in mid-Victorian Ontario. Peel County lies between Toronto and Hamilton in what is now the 'Golden Horseshoe' of suburban development which rims the north shore of Lake Ontario (see Map 3). After thirty years of active settlement Peel, in 1850, embraced an agrarian society on the threshold of social and economic maturity promoted by the vigour of its agricultural economy. Wild land was still available from the Canada Company in the more remote corners of the county — and from speculators in every township. Log houses were still more common than the frame, brick, or stone residences of the 'improving' farmer. And at least one of the county's five townships, Caledon, was considered to be 'beyond the verge of civilization' by all but 'divil-me-care' backwoodsmen.[26] Nevertheless, in 1851 Peel ranked seventh among the wheat producing counties of the United Province of Canada and second only to York County among the south-central and eastern counties of Canada West.[27] The value of trade — principally wheat and flour going out and consumer goods coming in — moving through Port Credit, Peel's entrepôt, exceeded three-quarters of a million dollars in 1851, a volume surpassed only by

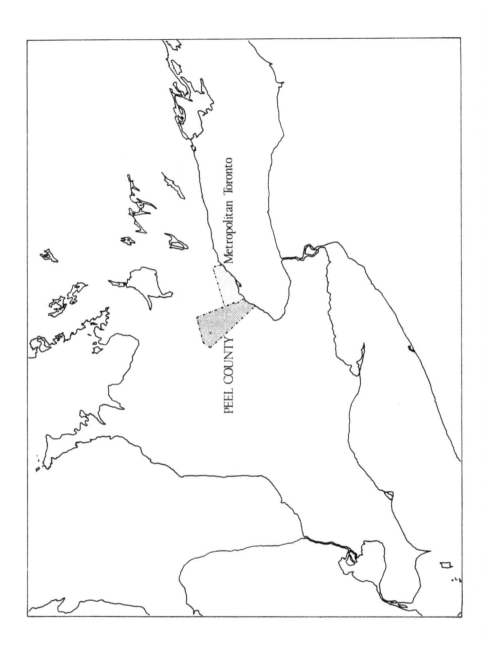

Map 3 Peel County, geographical location

Toronto, Kingston, and Whitby.[28] Only five other counties in Canada West (Brant, Wentworth, Halton, Prince Edward, and York) had as high a ratio of cropped to occupied land as Peel did in 1851; only one county (Grey) exceeded Peel's ratio of wheat land to cropped acreage.[29] Thus, on the eve of the wheat boom of the 1850s Peel County was admirably suited to capitalize on the full flowering of commercial agriculture; and its position was further enhanced as the decade progressed when first the Grand Trunk Railway, then the Great Western, traversed the county linking it with Toronto, Hamilton, Montreal, and the American mid-west.

These natural and man-made advantages were not lost upon the newly arrived immigrant, the speculator, the merchant, or the artisan with enough capital put by to get a start in farming. They flocked to Peel in the late forties and early fifties in such numbers that, by 1860, after less than two decades of very intensive population growth, Peel County was already overpopulated, at least in the sense that the rural economy could assimilate more families only through the death or outmigration of established farmers or through the subdivision of existing farms. Brampton, the county town and creature of the railroad, briefly (1856-70) provided a new source of economic opportunity in the retail trades; but by 1870 it, too, had reached the limits of its growth as a service centre. Consequently, if for no other reason than demographic pressure, the 1860s for Peel as for the larger regional universe of which it was a part represented an important watershed. Only three counties east of Hamilton (Ontario, Hastings, and Stormont) increased their rural populations during the decade. Of the others which experienced demographic stagnation or decline, Peel suffered the greatest losses. Finally, in the wake of commercial failure, falling commodity prices, and the ravages of nature — midge, rust, and soil exhaustion — Peel with York, Brant, and Dundas counties led the retreat in the 1860s from wheat as the centrepiece of agricultural production in Ontario.[30]

Thus, in many respects — patterns of demographic change, urban development, the growth of transportation networks, the biases of local agriculture, and the timing of a crisis of confidence in the promises of rural life — the thrust of developments in Peel County and in the province ran parallel courses in the 1850s and 1860s. We must assume that within Peel's restricted world of social and economic activity, populated, nevertheless, by a generous sample of the province's rural population, the immediate reality of individual experience was also much the same as it was throughout rural Canada West. More to the point, precisely because it is difficult, if not impossible, to comprehend the nature of change and continuity in the lives of the vast majority of ordinary Upper Canadians, it is necessary to assume that the effects of the principal sources of change can be observed, with equal meaning, within the narrower boundaries of the microcosm. It is only in this fashion, at any rate, that we can begin to understand how families and individuals responded to the forces of discontinuity which alternately promised or threatened to change the quality of their lives.

In mid-Victorian Peel County, Canada West, there is unmistakable evidence of a rural society in transition. Delayed ages of marriage among the youngest generation of adults, declining marital fertility, a greater propensity on the part of parents to educate children, a lengthening period of youthful dependence between childhood and adulthood, and the contraction of household structures constitute a related set of adjustments in the attitudes and behaviour of Peel's rural families. These adjustments were implemented between 1850, which marks the end of the pioneer stage of Peel's historical development, and 1870, the beginning of a half century of relative stasis in the demographic characteristics of the region. If it could be traced to its original sources — the external stimuli which promoted these adjustments, this discontinuity — this transition undoubtedly would be found rooted in the larger historical processes characteristic of the metropolitan economy, transcontinental and transoceanic in its scope but nevertheless an important determinant of the nature and timing of change in localized societies drawn into its orbit. Thus both the price of wheat in Toronto in the mid-1860s and the decision to link Montreal and the American mid-west by a railway in the mid-1850s coincide with major social and economic developments in Peel County. But if it is theoretically possible to account for discontinuity in the behaviour of concrete individuals with reference to the macro-processes of history, the actual links cannot be empirically demonstrated. Instead, we must rely on surrogate explanations drawn from the changing realities of material life in this limited locale.

Here, demographic and social change accompanied, or shortly followed, changes in the nature of economic opportunity as defined by the ability of this local economy, from time to time, to absorb new families, farm and non-farm alike, and to promote their material aspirations. The availability of land, the relative fluidity of Peel's vocational structures, the drop-out rate among the county's established families and individuals, and the appearance of wholly new sources of employment (the town, for example) each contributed to the definition of economic opportunity here, to the potential for material improvement, and, consequently, to the relative sway of continuity and change in the attitudes and behaviour of the people of Peel between 1850 and 1870. Among these factors, however, it was the historical interaction of families and land which promoted the most fundamental alterations in this rural society at mid-century.

In rural Peel County after 1840 economic security and social betterment apparently were predicated on favourable family/land ratios associated with the extensive, continuous cultivation of a preferential cash crop, wheat, and when necessary its less rewarding substitutes, oats, barley, peas, and hay. By 1860, however, excessive competition for land, especially competition resulting from intragenerational demographic pressure and from the expansion of established farms to increase production, had greatly escalated the social and economic costs — real and potential — of land ownership. It became necessary, therefore, to initiate strategies designed to protect the rural way of life rooted in this particular variant of agrarian capitalism and its promise of social betterment from the predictable consequences of too many people competing for too little land. Restricting intergenerational access to land and its rewards, delaying the formation of new families, relieving intragenerational pressure on land through family limitation and by training children, through education, for non-farm employment were all essential elements of this partially voluntary, partly pre-scribed preservationist movement.

The result is the appearance of social discontinuity in this rural society, especially in the realities of individual expectations. But appearances can be deceiving. In fact, such alterations as were effected in the attitudes, behaviour, and expectations of families and individuals here were intended, in the end, to promote continuity, to preserve the generic character of rural life in Ontario in an era of uncertainty.

2 *Genesis*

The five townships — Albion, Caledon, Chinguacousy, Toronto, and the Gore of Toronto — which constituted Peel County were integrated into Upper Canada's frontier of agricultural settlement in 1820. Until 1806, the area between Etobicoke Creek and Burlington Bay was the preserve of the Mississauga Indians, who had resisted successfully the Crown's efforts to purchase their land. An initial surrender was arranged in 1806 and at least part of the region, including what was to become the Old Survey of Toronto Township, was opened to settlement. The War of 1812-14 brought immigration to a standstill, however, and it was not until peace in Europe and America and the consequences of peace in Britain — massive social dislocation — opened the floodgates of emigration that the expansion of Upper Canada's settlement frontier became urgent. Consequently, in 1818 the Crown and the Mississaugas at last came to terms for the purchase by the government of the rest of the Mississauga Tract, and in 1819 tenders for surveying the new townships were let.[1]

Compared to most of the other forty-six counties carved out of southern Ontario, Peel was relatively small. Its 293,000 acres extended from Lake Ontario nearly forty miles northward, at first narrowly confined by the Credit River and Etobicoke Creek, then broadening to encompass the upper reaches of Mimico Creek and the Humber River. Inside this spatial rhombus, concession lines running at right angles to the lake and sideroads spanning the creeks and rivers from east to west scored the landscape in four of the five townships into perfect parallelograms, roughly three-quarters of a mile wide (66 chains) by nearly two deep, each containing five 200-acre lots. These would be divided into half lots, each fronting on a concession road. In the southern half of Toronto Township, however, the survey had squared the grid. Here, on the 'front,' long narrow lots four to the mile and more than a mile deep ranged along the sideroads in blocks of five, gave the appearance of a succession of seigneuries awaiting the pleasure of a landed gentry and the labour of their tenantry.

Initially, John Graves Simcoe's military road, Dundas Street, and the lake were the region's only arteries of trade, commerce, and communication with the town of York. It was the centre not only of provincial, but of regional government, for in the beginning Peel had no political identity of its own. Until 1851 the county was governed from York, later Toronto, as part of the Home District which included the counties of York, Peel, Simcoe, and Ontario. For the purposes of political representation Peel was in the West Riding of York until 1833, when its five townships were designated as the second riding of York entitled to one seat in the provincial legislative assembly. Its first representative was the future rebel, William Lyon Mackenzie. Before 1851, in any event, Peel County was merely a geographical expression for the purposes of registering property and establishing electoral districts. After 1851, when the county replaced the district as the basic unit of local government in Canada West, Peel was recognized by statute as a separate administrative unit; but in practice it was governed by a common council for the United Counties of York and Peel until 1866 when popular agitation won for Peel political independence from York.[2]

This political relationship with York/Toronto during the first half of the nineteenth century was fraught with serious implications for the social and economic development of the county in the age of settlement. If Peel was a new frontier of free or cheap land after 1819 it was, in the first place, York's frontier, and the master-servant relationship which quickly developed between the government and the vested interests at 'muddy York' on the one hand, and the natural resources of Peel on the other, had a profound effect on the nature and pace of the community's growth. Land, after all, was at once the province's most bountiful asset and its most important commodity. To colonial administrators land was the vital catalyst of social and economic development, the essential source of public revenues, a sound foundation (in the form of endowments) for the principal institutions of provincial society, and even the fountain of both the imperial and the Canadian governments' largesse in rewarding their servants. To the speculator Upper Canada's backwoods offered windfall profits from a limited investment of capital if the growth of population fulfilled the predictions of the essayists and the dreams of the politicians. To the immigrants, land held the promise of independence, an existence free from the social and economic constraints of the old world which placed the private ownership of a thousand, five hundred, or even one hundred acres of land and the opportunities it afforded beyond the reach of ordinary men.[3] In Peel, as in every community in Upper Canada, the conflicting interests of government, speculator, and immigrant settler quickly surfaced to plague the orderly development of society.

Crown land could be alienated into private hands by sale, by free grants with or without the payment of fees, and by 'privileged' grants to military claimants and to United Empire Loyalists or their children. Before 1826 free grants as well as military and Loyalist land grants represented the thrust of government policy

TABLE 1

Alienation of Crown land in Upper Canada and Peel County 1810-40

	Upper Canada	Peel County
Total acres alienated	3,500,000*	230,200
(a) Alienated by sale	–	73,568†
Percentage of total	–	31.9
(b) Alienated by grants	3,039,000*	156,632‡
Percentage of total	85.8	68.8
(c) Free grants	1,338,800*	83,977*
Percentage of (b)	44.0	53.6
(d) Military grants	346,900*	16,855†
Percentage of (b)	11.4	10.7
(e) UEL grants	1,125,300*	43,050†
Percentage of (b)	37.0	27.5
(f) Surveyors' grants	228,000*	12,720
Percentage of (b)	7.5	8.1

* 1804-24   † 1826-40   ‡ 1810-40
Source: Paterson, p 153; Public Archives of Ontario [OA], Crown Land
Papers [CLP] RG 1, C-I-8, Vols XI and XII, Land Grants, A-M, N-Z, 1810-35

in Upper Canada. But the need for more revenue coupled with the evident failure of scores of patentees to improve their property let alone take up residence on it prompted the administration in 1826 to abolish free grants and to introduce the New South Wales system of alienation by sale at auction. The government established an 'upset price,' in effect a reserve bid, for each lot in advance of regularly held auctions. Successful bidders then were permitted to pay for their land in annual instalments, but they were required to take up residence within six months and to provide, within three years, a sworn affidavit testifying that settlement duties (clearing half the roadway on their frontage and erecting a dwelling) had been performed. This system obtained until 1837 when land policy was again changed by removing the option of instalment buying in favour of cash purchases only.[4]

Under these various schemes (catalogued in Table 1) approximately 230,000 acres or nearly 79 per cent of the land in Peel County was transferred from the Crown into private hands between 1810 and 1840. In effect, all of the land which could be alienated was. The remaining 20% represented either Crown Reserves or, particularly after 1824, Clergy Reserves which normally were leased rather than sold. (In 1824, the Crown Reserves were transferred to John Galt's Canada Company.) Of these 230,000 acres more than two-thirds were alienated by direct grants of one sort or another. Thirty-two *per cent* of Peel's lands designated for settlement were alienated, in the first instance, by sale. Of the more than 156,000 acres ordered for granting after 1810, 83,977 (54%) were awarded as free grants to 627 unofficial petitioners; 43,500 (27%) were assigned to 115 children of Loyalists; 16,885 acres (11%) went to 90 military claimants; and 12,720 (8%) were used to discharge the government's obligations to the five men who surveyed the county. The result of this system in Peel, as elsewhere in Upper Canada, was the distortion of the settlement process to the detriment of the ordinary settler and his aspirations.

In the first place, neither the military claimants, who received on the average 187 acres each, nor the sons and daughters of Loyalists, whose grants averaged 375 acres, were as likely to be legitimate settlers as the first generation of Loyalists or the discharged Revolutionary War veterans had been. Elizabeth Ferris Henderson is a good example. The daughter of John Ferris, UE, she resided with her father and husband David in Kingston Township. She received a location ticket for 200 acres in Caledon Township in 1828, two years later submitted an affidavit of settlement duties performed, and then retained title to the property for the next fifteen years, finally selling it in 1845 for £100.[5] She never occupied her land. It sat, idle and barely developed, an obstacle to improvement in the township. It is difficult to know precisely how many of these grantees, 'privileged' and otherwise, followed Elizabeth Henderson's example; but it is certain that of the 842 individuals who received grants of Crown land in Peel between 1810 and 1835, only 161, less than 20%, were residents of the county in 1836.[6] It is entirely probable that most of the remaining four-fifths never set foot in the county.

If the total amount of land taken out of circulation by absentee grantees is a matter of speculation, the acreage deliberately closed to private ownership as a matter of policy is more definite. By statutory requirement, one-seventh of the land in each township was assigned to the Clergy Reserves Corporation as an endowment for the support of a protestant clergy. In Peel these reserves consisted of more than 40,000 acres concentrated in Albion, Caledon, Chinguacousy, and Toronto Gore townships, which had to absorb a greater than normal percentage of reserved land because the old survey of Toronto Township had none. The extent to which these reserves were a hindrance to the settlement of Upper Canada or agents of a 'dynamic process' of settlement has occasioned much debate.[7] Such evidence as exists for Peel County scarcely supports the view that these reserves eventually provided the means for integrating late, inexperienced immigrants into highly developed agricultural communities. For example, an official inspection of Albion's 5,000 reserved acres as late as 1845 revealed that after a quarter of a century of settlement in the township, nearly 40% of the Clergy Reserves were in the hands of absentee owners or lessees and still unimproved and unoccupied. Of the 2,900 occupied acres a little more than 50% (1,500 acres) were occupied by the owner or lessee; the remainder had been sublet and in several cases broken up into very small plots. The twenty-three families on these lots had managed to clear a mere 500 acres, less than 20% of the acreage they occupied.[8]

The government of the day also set aside 10,500 acres of land in Peel as part of the endowment for yet another institution, King's College. To be administered by and for the Church of England, the proposed college was intended as a

TABLE 2

Distribution of land, Peel County 1820-40

	1820	1830	1840
No. of acres alienated	56,530	131,524	229,140
Percentage of alienated acres held by proprietors of 500 acres or more	27.4	19.8	10.0
Total no. of proprietors of 500 acres or more	8	14	16
No. of non-resident proprietors of 500 acres or more	7	12	13
Total no. of different proprietors	245	855	1542
Proprietors of 500 acres or more as percentage of total	3.2	1.7	1.0
Absentee proprietors of 500 acres or more as percentage of total	2.9	1.4	0.84

nursery where young professionals — the future leaders of the province — could be imbued with correct political, moral, and spiritual attitudes. The scheme quickly encountered stiff political opposition, especially from the proponents of a common schools system, and had to be abandoned; but the endowment was perpetuated (and fell to King's College's successor, the University of Toronto) and together with the Clergy Reserves before 1840 effectively restricted more than 15% of Peel County's total acreage to occupation by lease only.

Finally, and most significantly, between 1810 and 1840 the vacant lands of Peel County attracted the attention of a group of men, some of whom acquired their land as free grants, others by sale, who constituted a class of great, powerful, and more or less permanent absentee landlords. They are not to be compared with the Elizabeth Hendersons, the little speculators who sought security in one or two hundred acres of bush. These men, as a group, never represented more than 3% of the total number of proprietors in the community; yet they sat, at any time between 1820 and 1840, astride a minimum of 10% of the county's vacant land (Table 2). Moreover, as Table 3 illustrates and as contemporaries recognized, these speculators, whose lands were one of the principal sources of distortion in the orderly social and economic development of the county (see Map 4), not only were, for the most part, residents of Toronto, but were often the very men responsible for defining and policing the land policies of Upper Canada.

This class of speculators made its appearance almost immediately after the first surveys of Toronto Township were completed, that is, before 1812. John Beikie, clerk of the Executive Council, patented 800 acres, as did Duncan

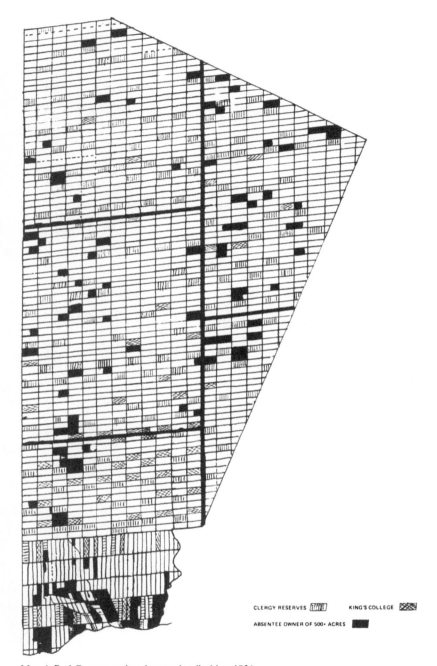

CLERGY RESERVES   KING'S COLLEGE

ABSENTEE OWNER OF 500+ ACRES

Map 4 Peel County, major absentee landholders 1836

TABLE 3

Principal absentee proprietors of land,* Peel County 1820-40

Name	Occupation	Residence	Highest office	Acreage	Grant or purchase
Reuben Sherwood	surveyor	Leeds Cnty	Commandant, Leeds County Militia	[900]†	grant
James Chewett	surveyor	York	Deputy Surveyor General	5,770	grant
Samuel Ryckman	surveyor	Flamborough		1,600	grant
Timothy Street	surveyor	Niagara		3,295	grant
Richard Bristol	surveyor	Bayham Twp		800	grant
Michael Sloot	gentleman			1,800	grant
John Beatty	gentleman	New York		1,100	grant
Cawthra family	merchants	York		800	purchase
W.A. Baldwin	gentleman	Etobicoke		2,625	purchase/gift
Jarvis Family		York	Sheriffs, etc.	1,000	grant
John Strachan	clergyman	York	Bishop, Exec. Council	2,400	grant
John McGill	gentleman	York	Receiver-General	600	purchase
Peter McGill	banker	Montreal	Legis. Council		
D'Arcy Boulton, sr	gentleman	York	Solicitor-General		
D'Arcy Boulton, jr	gentleman	York	Auditor-General	1,200	grant
Samuel Smith	gentleman	York	Administrator of Upper Canada	1,950	grant
John Robinson	lawyer	York	Chief Justice	1,000	grant
Adam Ferrie	merchant	Hamilton	Exec. Council	1,100	purchase
Peter Adamson	gentleman	Esquesing	Legis. Council	900	purchase
Andrew Mercer	magistrate	York	Clerk of Exec.	850	purchase

TABLE 3 (cont'd.)

Name	Occupation	Residence	Highest office	Acreage	Grant or purchase
John Radenhurst	Public servant	York	First Clerk, Crown Lands Dept	700	grant
Levi Lewis	gentleman	Lincoln Twp	Legis. Assembly	800	grant
William Proudfoot	banker	York	President, Bank of Upper Canada	2,325	purchase
King's College		York		10,500	grant

* 500 acres or more

† Included in total for W. A. Baldwin. It should be noted as well that both Robinson and Adamson had (as one English emigrant described them) 'country seats' in Toronto Township.

Cameron, member of the Legislative Assembly for Glengarry, and Roger Loring, aide-de-camp to Sir Roger Sheaffe, who succeeded Isaac Brock as commander of the British forces in Upper Canada. Their 2,400 acres, about 8% of the old survey (excluding the Indian reservation), established the pattern that was to become a permanent characteristic of Peel after the War of 1812. Indeed, the very act of surveying the four new townships after 1818 created the first of Peel's most persistent absentee landlords — the surveyors Richard Bristol, Timothy Street, James Chewett, Samuel Ryckman, and Reuben Sherwood. They were paid in land, more than 4% of the county's total area, and still held most of their lots as late as 1840. Similarly, the King's College endowment produced what was, by any other name, a major absentee landlord controlling another 4% of the county's total acreage between 1820 and 1850.

But Peel's absentee proprietors of particular historical interest are eighteen men and their families whose names are inextricably linked to the mainstream of Upper Canadian history between 1820 and 1840. The list (Table 3) includes five executive councillors: John McGill, Samuel Smith, John Beverley Robinson, John Strachan, and Adam Ferrie. Ferrie, a Scottish merchant who moved his interests to Canada where he and his sons rose to prominence as entrepreneurs in the Hamilton and Galt areas, became active in provincial politics only after 1837. The others held some of the most powerful appointed offices in Upper Canada before the rebellion. Smith had been the Administrator of the province in 1819 (in effect, acting lieutenant-governor). Robinson had been Attorney-General, and was Chief Justice in 1837. 'Captain' John McGill, who died in 1834, had served as Inspector-General, then Receiver-General. The D'Arcy Boultons, father and son, one sometime Solicitor-General and the other Auditor-General of Public Accounts, were members of the same privileged circle. Two bankers, William Proudfoot and Peter McGill, were directly connected to this political establishment. Peter McGill, President of the Bank of Montreal, was John McGill's nephew and himself a member of the Legislative Council after 1840. William Proudfoot was a Scottish emigrant who enjoyed the patronage of the Boultons and through them rose to become the president of the Bank of Upper Canada on the eve of its fateful collapse in 1836. The Jarvises, too, held appointed positions of public trust in the affairs of the Home District, most notably as successive sheriffs. James Chewett, the surveyor, also falls within the compass of this colonial establishment. He was Strachan's pupil and the son of a surveyor-general of Upper Canada. Chewett soon became Deputy Surveyor-General, and his subsequent commissions included the construction of the provincial legislative building. Finally, Andrew Mercer, whose fortune endowed the Mercer Reformatory for Women, held appointments as Clerk of the Executive Council, Paymaster of the Militia, King's Printer, and Magistrate; and John Radenhurst, First Clerk of the Land Patents Office, processed, with a good deal of arbitrariness, all petitions for land to and from the Executive Council.

Not all Peel's great absentee landowners were cut from the same cloth. The Cawthra family held no offices and even tended toward neutrality in their political sentiments. Their real interest was money. Merchants and private bankers, their landholdings paled into insignificance beside the indentures of mortgage which they held against property throughout the province. W.A. Baldwin was a member of another prominent York family which produced the architect of responsible government in Upper Canada, his brother Robert. William Augustus shared his father, William Warren Baldwin's, interest in land speculation and farming, and in addition to his handsome estate in Etobicoke had extensive holdings in Peel which developed from a wedding present of 900 acres from his father-in-law, James Buchanan, the British Consul in New York.

The Cawthras and the Baldwins are the exception which prove the rule that land speculation on a grand scale in Upper Canada united the rich and the powerful, whatever their political affiliation, in a common interest. But it seems clear that in Peel County, at least, the families who played the game for the highest stakes were synonymous with York's Tory establishment of power, place, and privilege, the so-called 'Family Compact.' Indeed, even among the less grand speculators in this county, excluded here only by virtue of the size of their holdings in this place, the names of several more of York's leading families predominate: Denison, Carfrae, Ridout.[9] William Lyon Mackenzie coined the epithet 'Family Compact' to identify an apparent conspiracy to use family connection, executive authority, and legislative supremacy to control the economy, society, and politics of Upper Canada in the interests of an oligarchy of Tory families. He singled out the Boultons, Robinsons, Sherwoods, Macaulays, Hagermans, Allens, Powells, Jarvises, Joneses, and the McGills as the tallest heads in this conspiracy led by John Strachan. The Denisons, the Carfraes, the Ridouts, Proudfoot, the Streets, and others all fell into the category of henchmen.[10] Their specific improprieties, which Lord Durham repeated in his famous *Report*, were that they allegedly possessed and controlled the highest offices in the province and therefore most of the powers of government; that they maintained their power by dispensing patronage through the Legislative Council, the judicial system, and the Church of England; and that they sought to achieve their social and economic objectives through their manipulation of the banks and the vacant lands of the province.[11] In particular, their open disdain for the commercial and entrepreneurial classes in the province and their readiness to promote the interests of the landed classes have been interpreted as evidence of the extent to which they identified public policy with private interest, in spite of their altruistic defence of their actions.[12]

The record of absentee landlordism in Peel County during the first twenty years of the region's history of settlement leaves little room for doubt that, whatever ideological and familial bonds held the 'Family Compact' together, they shared at least one material interest — the profits to be made from the vacant lands on York's frontier of economic development. In this they were not different from their constituents for whom gambling in land, as one historian has remarked, had become a 'national pastime.'[13] But the acreage under their control and the way in which they acquired it are remarkable even by contemporary standards; and when their unofficial activities are linked to the results of the land policies which were their official responsibility, their effect on the social landscape of colonial Upper Canada comes into sharp relief. Toronto Township, especially the southern half, is a case in point. In the other four townships of Peel, Crown and Clergy Reserves and the lands of the largest speculators together represented, on average, about 20% of the land available for settlement. In Toronto Township they constituted about 30%. But in the southern half of the township, which attracted the most attention from speculators, their holdings alone, on the eve of the uprising of 1837, represented more than 30% of the area. As late as the 1850s much of it was still undeveloped.

Ironically, William Lyon Mackenzie, too, was an absentee proprietor in Peel in the 1820s and 1830s, albeit the owner of a very insignificant lot. It was Mackenzie who first made a public issue of the inability of legitimate settlers in Peel to secure Crown deeds to their land, while government officials openly flouted the regulations. Strachan, according to Mackenzie, had been given patents for his 2,000 acres on the pretext of defraying the costs of a journey to England on official business in 1828, land which Strachan still held, unimproved, a decade later. Meanwhile, ordinary settlers could not get patents for their lots precisely because their land remained unimproved as the result of the economic stagnation, created in part by the distortion of the settlement process by the holdings of the absentees, which in turn prevented them from acquiring the capital necessary for improvements.[14]

The facts seem to be on Mackenzie's side. Most of the public officials among the speculators do not appear to have petitioned for their grants but rather acquired their patents simply by executive order. Moreover, all the great absentee proprietors seem to have been able to secure deeds and to retain ownership of their vacant property for fifteen or twenty years before taking their profits. Ordinary settlers who were slow to improve their lots, who failed the exercise, or who were unable to meet their monetary obligations each January either waited interminably for a satisfactory inspection report or had their property auctioned out from under them. In Chinguacousy Township, which Mackenzie knew best, the elapsed time between locating and deed registration averaged thirteen years; and as late as 1842 more than 60% of the occupants of land who had been in the township at least five years still had no legal title to their farms.[15]

Some simply squatted on lots which they assumed to be rightfully theirs and defied the authorities to evict them. Others swore false oaths, with the assistance of sympathetic neighbours or larcenous magistrates, attesting to the performance of settlement duties. The practice apparently was widespread as early as 1824.[16] For most, the court of last resort was the Commissioner of Crown Lands.

Thus, in June 1833, David Long, a settler in Albion Township, begged for more time to complete his settlement duties and to raise more cash. His land, he said, had already cost him

$23 five journeys to York & back making 180 miles ... with loss of my toe nails & three weeks idelness it is a pity if I lost it I being prepared to go on direct, having some utensils a yoke oxen 3 cows & what is better four sons ... who are all desirous of being their own servants ... I hope you will pardon me, theres [sic] now [sic] man a greater object for land than I am at present ... I beseech you for Godalmightys [sic] sake to assist me ...[17]

The petition fell on deaf ears and Long's land was put up for auction.

Ultimately, of course, these inequities, added to his infinite list of grievances against the injustices of his times and the imperialism of York's political and social élite, drove William Lyon Mackenzie to rebellion in 1837. Though relatively few of them joined his rebellion, many of the settlers of Peel counted themselves among Mackenzie's most ardent supporters, returning him as their representative in spite of repeated attempts to expel him from the Legislative Assembly. Indeed, Peel became a battleground of the contending Tory and radical factions. Mackenzie had been forced to campaign in 1836 with an armed escort, and several meetings threatened to degenerate into full-scale riots.[18] A year later Mackenzie was in exile and the fortunes of his constituents and their causes which he championed were left to the palliative effects of time and improved circumstances. Still, for the next thirty years at least the main elements in the social history of Peel County remained those which had been indelibly implanted during the first forty years of the community's development.

'What is capital but property unequally distributed?' asked Upper Canada's Chief Justice, John Elmsley, during one of the many early debates on land policy.[19] The idea that Upper Canada's public land should be used to create a society characterized by political, social, and economic inequality in the interests of stability and progress continued to inform official policy until the middle of the nineteenth century.[20] In Peel County, the practical effects of this design are to be seen in the diversion of thousands of acres of land into the hands of speculators, and especially into the control of a few highly placed families at Toronto before 1840. From this original distortion of the land-hungry immigrant's high expectations flowed the ineluctable facts of the ordinary settler's experience in the community during the next thirty years. Wave upon wave of prospective farmers pursuing the dream of equal opportunity encountered, instead, a very unequal struggle for individual and familial security.

They came — from England, Scotland, the United States of America, the older counties of Upper Canada, and especially from Ireland — until, by 1851, 3,700 families representing nearly 25,000 men, women, and children were settled in Peel County. As Figure 1 indicates, however, the flow of migrants was not relentless. In 1828 the population stood at about 4,300, an increase of only 20%

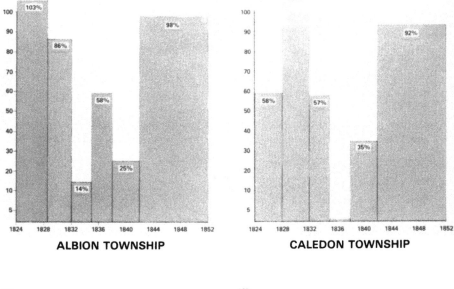

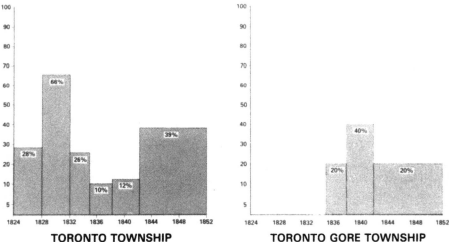

1 Percentage increase in population by township, Peel County 1824-52

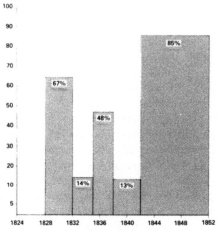

CHINGUACOUSY TOWNSHIP

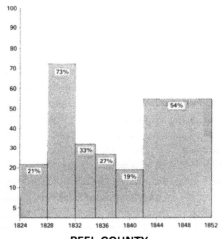

PEEL COUNTY

after a decade of settlement. The great migrations from the British Isles after 1828 hastened the growth of population in the county; but by the end of the troubled thirties the rate of growth had noticeably slowed and in two townships, Caledon and Toronto — one the most remote and the other with the highest levels of absentee ownership — it had come virtually to a standstill. No census data are available for the years between 1842 and 1852, but the startling increase in Albion, Caledon, and Chinguacousy townships which nearly doubled their population, and an overall increase of 54%, were almost certainly the direct or indirect result of the Irish migrations of the late forties. In short, the relative speed with which the county was filled up had much to do with the pressures placed on Upper Canada's frontier of settlement generally by patterns of transatlantic migration throughout the period, and by domestic social and economic conditions.

An equally cogent reason for this pattern of growth is suggested by Table 4. By 1835, more than three-quarters of all the land that would be privately owned in 1852 already had been taken up. In Toronto Township, more than 90% of the land had been alienated into private hands by 1835, in Toronto Gore nearly 85%, in Chinguacousy more than 78%, and in Albion and Caledon better than two-thirds. In all, 196,000 acres — two-thirds of the county's entire acreage — were privately owned by 1835. When the Clergy Reserves are added to this figure, to all intents and purposes there remained less than 60,000 acres — the equivalent of six hundred 100-acre farms, much of it in the least attractive townships of Albion and Caledon — open for settlement through the public auction system after 1835. (In 1840, according to the registry records, fewer than 46,000 acres remained unpatented.) These 196,000 acres were owned by approximately 1,200 landholders; yet the population of the county stood at 10,000 in 1835, perhaps 1,700 families in all.[21] With allowances for the non-agricultural population of the principal towns and villages (Streetsville, Port Credit, and Springfield) it seems plausible, then, that at least one of every four rural householders (400/1,600) was a tenant or squatter on someone else's land by 1835, either because they could not afford the upset price of unpatented land, or because they were unable to purchase land held for speculation at any price. In either case, the inference to be drawn is clear. By 1835, unless he was content with leased land, the prospective farmer in Peel required capital to get land. Even if he had capital, his ability to acquire good land was dependent on the willingness of an established owner, more often than not a speculator himself, to part with his property. Peel County, with only 50% of its 1852 population in place on the eve of the Rebellion of 1837, was no longer, if indeed it ever had been, a frontier of cheap land awaiting the poor, but industrious immigrant.

These developments can be illustrated best with reference to Chinguacousy Township, for which the 1842 assessment roll exists. The roll lists 741 owners or occupants of land. Of this number, 568 (77.8%) were actually residents of the township; the rest (22%) were absentee proprietors. Of the resident occupants of

TABLE 4

Rate of land alienation by township, Peel County 1830-52

Township	Before 1830	1830-5	1835-42	1842-5	1845-52
Albion	46.7	23.8	17.9	0	11.6
Caledon	31.8	34.9	14.7	8.0	10.6
Chinguacousy	51.9	26.2	16.5	0.9	4.4
Toronto Gore		83.3	8.8	4.5	3.4
		(by 1835)			
Toronto	90.9	1.3	5.4	1.3	1.0
Peel County	52.3	25.9	13.1	2.6	6.0

* The figures represent the percentage of the total acreage held in 1852 which was alienated during the period given at the top of the columns.
Sources: PAC, Provincial Secretary's Papers, RG5, B26, Vols I-VII; Province of Canada, Legislative Assembly, *Journals*, Vol. III, 1843, Appendix L and Vol. V, 1846, Appendix H; *Census of the Canadas, 1851-2* (Quebec 1853)

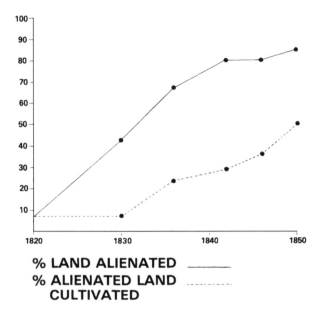

% LAND ALIENATED _____
% ALIENATED LAND ------------
CULTIVATED

2 Comparative rates of land alienation and cultivation, Peel County 1820-52

land, 39% owned the farms they occupied; another 24% were in the process of securing titles (which they eventually received) by completing settlement duties. The remaining 215 (37%) were effectively tenants, although they may have been in the process of buying land on the instalment plan, a common practice, through annual quit rents plus interest.[22] In any event they did not have, and never acquired, titles to the lands they occupied. Finally, in 1842 only 13% of the landowners, resident or non-resident, were the original locatees and Crown patentees of their land. The vast majority had purchased their lots from some former private owner at whatever price the traffic would bear. Most of the activity had taken place before the rebellion of 1837; less than 25% of the residents of these concessions were recent arrivals.

Thus, in just twenty years this township had undergone a complete transformation. In 1820 it had been a vast reserve of wild land freely open to settlement. In 1842, 95% of its land was in private hands (see Table 4) and two-fifths of those private landholders were non-residents. Consequently, new arrivals increasingly faced the prospect of tenancy or, if they had capital, of using it to purchase expensive land rather than to improve cheap land. In either case, the results were the same. In Chinguacousy, as in the rest of the county, development proceeded slowly, and sometimes not at all.[23]

Figure 2 compares the rate of land alienation in Peel County to the rate at which land was improved, as reported in the annual assessment returns, which distinguished between cultivated and uncultivated land. The distinction seems to have been based on rather crude assumptions about the nature of land improvement and use, but it was vital nevertheless. As the result of legislation passed in 1819 uncultivated — that is, unimproved — land was valued for assessment purposes at four shillings per acre, improved land at £1. Taxed at the rate of one penny per pound of assessed value, 100 acres of wild land paid less than two shillings per annum when it was taxed at all, 100 acres of improved land more than four times as much.[24] Thus speculators could maintain vast tracts of unimproved land for years at little cost. Surrounded by underdevelopment, isolated from markets, and with little capital to improve his holdings, the so-called 'improving' farmer's performance often belied his reputation.

By 1830, when more than 40% of Peel's land had been taken up, less than 10% of it had been improved. Five years later, nearly a quarter of the alienated acreage had been improved, a reflection of the flurry of settlement activity in the early thirties. But over the next decade the rate of improvement abated considerably. Between 1836 and 1842, although land alienation proceeded apace, the rate of improvement remained nearly constant. Ultimately, it was the advent of better economic prospects with the appearance, first, of an American market for local wheat shipped through Port Credit, and then of a burgeoning imperial market for Canadian wheat and flour which spurred Peel's emergence after 1846 as a developed, agrarian society. In the meantime, as late as 1845, for every 600 acres of improved land in Peel County there were a thousand more of wild land awaiting the axe, the plough, and the labour of many hands.

The shock wave of Irish immigrants which struck the Canadas with full force between 1848 and 1850 was the catalyst which propelled population toward Peel County. Few of these most recent arrivals actually appeared in Peel. In 1852 as in 1842 the population of the county was predominantly native-born and steadfastly Protestant; Irish Roman Catholics never accounted for more than 10% of the families in the community. The fact that nearly 90% of the heads of families in Peel in 1852 nevertheless were foreign-born suggests that Peel's new population consisted of first-generation immigrant families with previous Canadian experience, enough at least to have produced native-born children (see Table 5) and to have accumulated a little capital with which to buy land or launch a business. Whether they came from older farming areas with capital raised from the sale of improved farms or from established towns and villages with capital acquired through a trade, a profession, or merely day labour is impossible to know. They represented an amazingly diverse range of skills — more than 200 different trades, professions, and avocations (see Table 6); yet vocational labels

TABLE 5

Distribution (%) of population by place of birth and by religious affiliation 1842-52

	Total pop'n 1842	Total pop'n 1852	Heads of families 1852
Place of birth			
England	11.9	12.7	21.7
Ireland	26.4	29.6	50.0
Scotland	8.5	6.2	13.1
USA	2.9	1.8	2.9
Upper Canada	} 50.0	} 49.4	11.6
Other BNA provinces			0.5
Other	0.2	0.2	0.2
(N)	(14,983)	(24,816)	(3,700)
Religious affiliation			
Church of England	39.9	31.1	31.8
Roman Catholic	8.8	11.0	11.1
Wesleyan Methodist	2.9	17.7	15.7
Episcopal Methodist	2.7	4.3	4.2
Other Methodist	11.8	5.5	5.5
Baptist	0.9	2.9	2.9
Free Kirk		9.8	8.3
Church Of Scotland	16.8	9.7	8.5
Other Presbyterian	5.8	9.8	8.4
Other	1.1	2.1	2.3
Not given	18.1	0.9	1.3

TABLE 6

Distribution (%) of heads of families by occupational classification 1852

Agriculture	63.6
Manufacturing of textiles	2.0
Manufacturing of apparel	3.8
Manufacturing of wood products	1.9
Manufacturing of metal products	0.1
Manufacturing of food products	1.0
Manufacturing of luxury goods	0.01
Miscellaneous manufacturing	0.3
Construction	3.5
Manual labour	11.4
Commerce	2.9
Transportation services	2.6
Domestic service	0.2
Professional services	0.8
Education and public service	1.2
Others	4.6

reveal little about them, if their subsequent experience in Peel is a reliable guide. What a man called himself from time to time was never definitive. In mid-nineteenth-century Upper Canada nothing was permanent except, of course, the land.

Each plot of it represented a private world of experience to be gained, of problems to be resolved, of rewards to be reaped or lost, of aspirations to be fulfilled, and perhaps even of traditions to be established. The varieties of individual experience were potentially infinite. But the lowest common denominators — land, families, and the historical rhythms of rural life — remained constant from one little world to the next. Thus, they inevitably melded into a universe of common experience, common solutions to common problems, common aspirations, and, eventually, common traditions. What remained private was the nature, degree, and consequences of individual success or failure.

3 Families and Land: The Mid-Century Crisis

In 1851 the population of Peel County was 24,816. A decade later it had increased by 9.8% to 27,240. When the next census was taken in 1871 it revealed that in the preceding decade Peel had lost 5% of its 1861 population, in spite of the skyrocketing growth of the county's new town, Brampton, whose population had increased 65% in the 1860s. Put another way, the *rural* population of Peel County in 1871 (23,331) was not only significantly smaller, by 10%, than it had been a decade earlier, there were actually fewer rural dwellers in the county in 1871 than there had been in 1851 when Peel was still considered a field for immigration, and when there was still vacant land in two of the five townships. Moreover, the population of the county — rural and urban — continued to decline for the remainder of the nineteenth century. In 1890 the total population of Peel was essentially what it had been in 1850.

These are the elementary facts of Peel's demographic history in the middle decades of the nineteenth century. They invite, indeed require, analysis. Why is it that, at a time when Upper Canadians were exercised over the annexation of a new agricultural frontier in the west as an outlet for population, there is striking evidence in Peel and elsewhere in the heartland of Upper Canadian agriculture (see Table 7) not of rural overpopulation but rather of demographic decline? What combination of circumstances transformed the frontier of pioneer settlement of the late 1830s and early 1840s into the apparently stagnant community of the 1860s? How did it transpire that an area which was demonstrably underpopulated, in terms of the availability of vacant land, at any time between 1819 and 1855, could move from underpopulation to depopulation in less than two decades? These are questions which might equally be posed in relation to the general pattern of the ebb and flow of population in mid-Victorian Ontario. As Table 7 suggests, demographic decline or stagnation was prevalent among the south-central and eastern lakeshore counties of Canada West in the 1860s, perhaps confirming the gloomy auguries of the politicians. But this trend was clearly offset by a northwestward moving line of demographic growth which evidently had not run its course by 1870. What factors and processes account

TABLE 7

Net population change (%), selected Ontario counties 1850-70

	1850-60	1860-70
Bruce	+869%	+76%
Grey	+193	+57
Essex	+ 49	+30
Kent-Lambton	+ 98	+42
Huron	+171	+27
Middlesex	+ 48	+37
Elgin	+ 26	+ 5
Perth	+145	+22
Oxford	+ 42	+ 4
Norfolk	+ 34	+ 8
Waterloo	+ 46	+ 4
Brant	+ 19	+ 6
Wentworth	+ 12	− 3
Halton	+ 24	− 1
Peel	+ 10	− 5
York	+ 22	nil
Ontario	+ 36	+10
Northumberland	+ 30	− 2
Hastings	+ 41	+ 8
Prince Edward	+ 10	− 3
Lennox-Addington-Frontenac	+ 31	− 2
Dundas	+ 36	nil
Stormont	+ 24	+ 5
Glengarry	+ 20	− 3

Source: *Census of the Canadas, 1851-2*, Vol. I, p 311; *Census of the Canadas, 1860-1*, Vol. I, pp 521-7; *Census of Canada, 1870-71*, Vol. I, Table 1.

for this dichotomy, these paradoxical aspects of growth and stagnation in a rural society in which the oldest communities, in 1860, were barely sexagenarians?

At the simplest level of explanation it might appear that, with some anomalies, these demographic trends merely reflect the much-discussed operation of the 'frontier' as a force in North American history. Attracted by the opportunities for social and economic improvement represented by undeveloped territory, the theory assumes, populations routinely vacated established communities, moving to new frontiers where the unique social and economic processes inherent in the interaction between men and virgin land were initiated once again. In their wake, these migrant populations left a succession of mature societies in which economic success and social improvement were dependent on techniques of conservation rather than exploitation.[1] No longer attractive to immigrants who equated prosperity with production as opposed, for example, to the greater availability of goods and services in, or the cultural benefits of an established society, these communities attained a state of equilibrium, demographic, social, and economic, and there they rested until technological change, industrialization for example, once again altered the nature of opportunity there.

As appealing as this scenario is, it nevertheless fails to account for the anomalies that inevitably arise in real, as opposed to hypothetical historical circumstances. One of those anomalies is self-evident in Table 7. Some of the oldest settled rural communities in Canada West continued to add to their rural populations long after they had passed the frontier stage of development and long before either industrialization or urbanization became an important factor there. A more interesting variant is represented by Peel County and, I suspect, other communities in Canada West. Simply put, by the mid-1850s the assimilation of new farm families into the economy of rural Peel County was possible only through the death or displacement of established farmers, or the subdivision of existing farms. Subdivision was unacceptable because it undermined the theory and practice of agrarian capitalism as it had developed under the aegis of the wheat economy. More, not less, land was what the improving farmer thought he required. Thus, established farmers themselves, as much as recently arrived migrants, represented a constant source of pressure on land available for cultivation, land for their own requirements and for their maturing, soon to be independent, children. The upshot of the subsequent mania for land amid unstable economic conditions 1856-65 was a period of rapid social change as the problem of too many people competing for too little land promoted, equally, a major redistribution of land in Peel County as well as a search for alternative strategies to promote the social and economic security of the farm family as the problem of land availability became more intractable. In effect, the roots of demographic and social change in Peel County 1850-70 can be traced, in the first instance, to the economic self-interest of the county's improving farm families.

In America, the farmers' frontier lasted until 1890. In parts of Canada, northern Alberta for example, land for homesteading was still available in the late 1960s. In Ontario, the agricultural frontier, if it ever existed as a 'frontier' in the classical sense of the term — an area adjacent to a settled region in which a low ratio of population to cheap and abundant land favoured the social and economic objectives of the small agrarian capitalist[2] — came to an end when Bruce County was opened to settlement in 1854. If Peel ever was a frontier in that sense it had moved beyond the frontier stage of its development very quickly. The average price of an acre of Peel's land in the 1840s, $12, was no bargain. Immigrants were taught that they could buy the best farms in developed townships for just $2 an acre more.[3] Nor, as we have seen earlier, was land abundant in Peel in the 1840s. By 1842 nine-tenths of the county's arable acreage was in private hands, however unimproved it might have been. Finally, by 1851 the population per 1,000 occupied acres in Peel, 99, was already higher than for some of the earliest settled counties of the province, for example Lennox-Addington and Frontenac (85), and significantly greater than for areas of more recent settlement such as Huron (68), Grey (59), and Perth (67) counties. In short, judged by those measures which define the frontier as a place, Peel had ceased to enjoy that status after twenty years of active settlement.

If, however, we characterize the frontier in terms of the social and economic processes which take place there, there is something to be said for defending Peel's image, even in the 1850s, as a frontier environment. The economics of frontier agriculture consisted in the extensive, rather than intensive, use of land to produce a cash crop for exchange in the market-place. The crude equation of ample land and labour with productivity and prosperity, and a casual disdain for the scientific farmer's conservationist techniques on the assumption that exhausted soil could always be abandoned for fertile virgin land elsewhere, were the hallmarks of the frontier farmer. In Upper Canada they were called 'wheat miners'[4] and the farmers of Peel's till plain were no exceptions. They followed the system of continuous cropping of cereal grains, especially wheat, and were warned as early as 1856 by one of their own, John Lynch of Brampton, who was a recognized authority on agriculture in the province, that 'the time will come ... when the present rich and productive land of Canada will not only fail to produce a heavy crop of wheat ... but will become incapable of producing wheat at all to any profitable amount.'[5] Nevertheless, as late as 1870, when the transition to mixed farming was well under way in Ontario, the single characteristic of agricultural production which set Peel apart from every other county in the province was Peel's significantly higher ratio of cropped to occupied acreage.[6] Thus, throughout the period, land in Peel continued to be evaluated by the pioneer's rule of thumb — 'a farm incapable of producing [wheat was] practically valueless'[7] — and was bought and sold on the strength of its natural productivity. For example, in Caledon Township in 1860 reported farm values varied directly and significantly in relation to land capability, that is to soil quality, and bore no significant relationship to any other factor.[8]

This wheat culture, rooted in the extensive cropping of naturally fertile soil by little familial armies of cultivators whose collective labour was at once the motive power and the working capital of the frontier farm, was firmly fixed in place when the wheat boom and the railroad mania of the 1850s conspired to focus the attention of speculators, immigrants, and improving farmers from outside the county on Peel's productive capacity and its new-found agricultural prosperity. Population growth, the appearance of a new commercial town, and the disappearance of the county's remaining vacant lands were all symptomatic of the advent of this new era. So too was the behaviour of Peel's established farm families. Between 1850 and 1860 their ratio of cropped to occupied acreage increased by 22%, while the proportion of their cropped acreage devoted to wheat increased by 10%. More significantly, they began to expand their farms, enlarging the territory available for cultivation in response to a buoyant market. As Table 8 indicates, in 1851 approximately 16% of land occupiers in Peel held more than 100 acres. Their acreage represented about 37% of all land held. Two decades later, more than 25% of Peel's occupiers held at least 101 acres and their lands comprised 54% of the county's occupied land. It is clear that these expanding farmers gained at the expense of families who occupied between 11 and 100

TABLE 8

Distribution of families by percentage of total land occupied, Peel County 1851, 1871

| | 1851 | | 1871 | |
	Pop'n (%)	Land (%)	Pop'n (%)	Land (%)
10 acres or less	10.4	0.7	13.8	0.8
11-50 acres	21.3	8.0	15.2	5.0
51-100 acres	52.4	54.0	45.4	40.2
101-200 acres	13.7	29.0	20.7	37.0
Over 200 acres	2.7	8.0	4.7	17.0
Total	100.0	100.0	100.0	100.0

acres, many of whom were reduced, apparently, to the level of small-holders. Moreover, it is also clear that this transition was virtually complete by 1861.[9] The result, in any case, was a substantial alteration in the rural landscape. Average farm size increased, in twenty years, by about 40% — from 98 to 140 acres. Among the most established group of families (see Chapter 5) farm size increased by more than 60% (see Table 14 below). In 1850 Peel County had contained only 56 holdings larger than 200 acres and merely 5 of these exceeded 500 acres. Two decades later, of the 136 farms over 200 acres, 18 encompassed more than 500. Land, lots of land, apparently was still the prescription for economic success and social improvement in this community in spite of the critics who thought that 'one of the great banes of the Canadian farmer consists in the occupancy of too much land.'[10]

There remained a still more profound reason for the expansion of farm territory in the 1850s, a reason also related to the exigencies of land extensive, labour intensive pioneer agriculture. In the 1840s and 1850s the motive power of the family farm was the farm family, especially its children. Their contribution to the social and economic improvement of the cash-poor immigrant family in a period of chronic labour shortages was universally praised by nineteenth-century commentators. Satisfying children's, especially sons', legitimate expectations of future compensation commensurate with their contribution to the economy of the family was an equally compelling reason to assemble additional property. Indeed (if the memoirs of immigrants are trustworthy reflections of parental motivation) Canadian parents seem to have been anxious to promote the independence and security of their children as a reward for their long subordination to the family's common goal, improvement. Patrick Shirreff, who toured the province in the 1830s, marvelled at the tenacity of a man who systematically acquired 1,000 acres, having started with a hundred, so that his nine sons might share his own sense of independence.[11] A hundred acres for each son was a patrimony more readily acquired in the 1830s than in the 1850s or 1860s when the press of population, native-born as well as immigrant, was rapidly eroding the province's frontier of uncultivated land. But such a patrimony was

TABLE 9

Summary data for male population, Peel County 1851-71*

	1851	1861	1871
No. of males over 15 years	7,285	8,252	6.735
Males 15-30 years as percentage of all males	54	52	54
Males 15-30 years per 1,000 males 40-60 years	2,433	2,741	2,203
Males 15-30 years per 1,000 acres available land†	29	41	29

* From published aggregates
† 'Available land' is calculated as the sum of uncultivated land held by occupiers, all land freed through mortality (20/1000 among males 30-70 years), and land freed through outmigration of occupiers (5% of total annually).

the historical promise of the Canadian backwoods; and the culture of the Canadian farm family, symbolized ultimately by the transmission of property from one generation to the next, bound it to the values and expectations of successive generations of farm children nourished on the promise of security and improvement through the possession of landed property.[12]

In the middle decades of the nineteenth century, half the male population over the age of 15 consisted of men not yet 30 (see Table 9). These were the youths whose labour fuelled the farm economy in the late forties and early fifties and who stood ready, in the late fifties and early sixties, to launch their own enterprises. And like the 'boomies' of the 1950s who appeared, like a demographic aneurism, in the arteries of education, employment, and social security in the 1960s and 1970s, this rising generation made its presence felt in the 1850s, especially in terms of the ability of Peel's rural economy to fulfil their social aspirations. Between 1851 and 1861 the number of males aged 15-30 for every 1,000 acres of available land in Peel increased by more than 40%. Their numbers, in relation to the size of the next oldest cohort (their fathers), increased 13%. Few alternatives were available to satisfy this generation's desire for land. Eighty miles to the north, in the 'Queen's Bush,' land was still plentiful and cheap, and in 1861 the census takers noted that some of Peel's young men were clearing farms in Grey and Bruce counties. Another possibility was to subdivide existing farms into smaller economic units; but the market-place and his own goal of improvement through extensive cropping clearly led the Canadian farmer to reject this European custom. Instead, some of Peel's farmers chose to compete with their neighbours, with speculators, new immigrants, and, in some cases undoubtedly, their own sons, for new territory which would increase their productivity in the short term and, in the end, perhaps provide patrimonies for more than one of their children. Others, unwilling or unable to compete with what became a rapidly escalating battle for land, turned to the laws of inheritance to resolve the problem of too many men competing for too little land in an economy that favoured the opposite principle. In either case, this problem was essentially homegrown, and it could be resolved only by the application of home remedies.

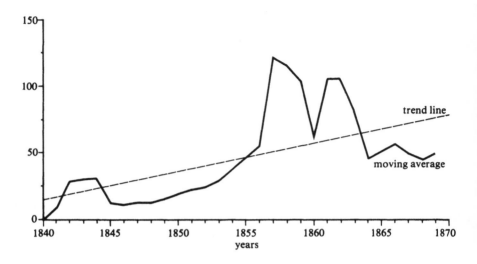

3 Trend line and three-year moving averages for cost of land per acre, Peel County 1840-70

The effects of the economic and demographic pressures on Peel's finite supply of rural land are graphically illustrated in Figure 3, which describes both the long-range trend (trend line) and the short-term fluctuations (moving averages) of land prices in Peel between 1840 and 1870.[13] As the trend line predicts, land worth less than $15 an acre in 1840 would more than quadruple in value by 1870. Inflation, devaluation, and variable conversion rates from sterling to decimal currency during the period may account for some of this startling appreciation. Nevertheless, the trend of prices adequately reflects the ever increasing pressure on land in the community as a result of the two most important factors, supply and demand. The situation benefitted established owners in the long run, just as it was detrimental to tenant farmers whose rents were tied to the market value of land (2%-4% of current value) and to aspiring farmers lacking capital or credit. But the behaviour of land prices in the long term was scarcely cause for alarm. Men of property invested a good deal of faith, after all, in the predictability of rising land prices. It was the unpredictability of the market from year to year, its short-term behaviour, which severely tested the average farmer's faith in land as good security for himself and for his children.

By 1853, at the height of the wheat boom, the mania for land at any price was clearly in full flight, driving the cost of an acre to astronomical levels in just four years. Neither the collapse of the railroad bubble nor the commercial depression of 1857-60 had sustained effects on the price of land. Not until the mid-sixties,

TABLE 10

Mortgaged indebtedness, Peel County 1850-70

	1851	1861	1871
Percentage of total acreage mortgaged	11.3	38.0	16.2
Value of mortgages ($)	228,708	1,915,029	812,271
Mean debt per mortgaged acre ($)	27.38	64.87	49.54
Debt per acre of county land ($)	1.00	7.00	3.00
Per capita debt, total population ($)	9.00	70.00	30.00
Average interest rate last 10 years (%)	7	8.3	7.4
Average term (years)	4	5	5

after a decade of inflation punctured only by a brief plunge in 1859-60, was some semblance of rationality restored to property values. That development coincided, not surprisingly, with a sudden fall in wheat prices — from $1.40 per bushel in 1859 to $1.15 in 1861, then to 95¢ and 96¢ in 1863 and 1864 respectively — and with the first of a succession of poor harvests as wheat rust and midge increasingly plagued Peel's crops. Farmers were clearly unwilling to risk additional capital at a time when it was more prudent to tighten their belts. Moreover, farmers were speculators too, notwithstanding the fact that they worked their investments, and many of them had already taken a beating in the scramble for land.[14] The value of property acquired at the height of the expansionist movement plummetted 60% in just two years. Its owners would not recover their investment quickly, and in the meantime they had the added burden of repaying the expensive borrowed capital with which many of them had financed their transactions.

In 1850, about 11% of the county's acreage was mortgaged, representing a communal debt of approximately $1 per acre or $9 per capita (see Table 10). Ten years later, the proportion of indentured acreage had more than tripled and the community's level of indebtedness stood at $70.00 for each man, woman, and child. Furthermore, the decennial average rate of interest cited in Table 10, 8%, obscures the more important fact that during the years of highest land prices (1857-61) the effective mortgage interest rate was 11%, while rates of 15, 18, and even 20% were not uncommon.[15] In short, the costs of more favourable family/land ratios, for whatever purpose, included an unprecedented level of mortgaged indebtedness in a community of farmers who historically had shunned indentures against real property as a means of financing improvements and additions.[16] The farmers of Peel were not unique in this regard. Commenting in 1871 on the land craze of the fifties and its subsequent repercussions, the editor of the Canadian Farmer wondered at the otherwise 'sober and sedate' people who 'spent all their ready cash ... nay even mortgaged the homestead' with 'often fatal' results because they 'thought of nothing but additional land.'[17] He was also convinced that this phenomenon had been particularly acute in the rural districts west of Toronto. At any rate, as Table 10 implies, the Peel farmer who mortgaged his future in the fifties redeemed his notes in the sixties under much altered economic circumstances which had a demonstrably sobering effect on both real estate and mortgage markets throughout the decade.

Who, then, indulged in this costly enterprise? By observing changes over time in the landholding patterns of Peel's rural proprietors it is possible to distinguish those who expanded their holdings from those who did not, and to compare their characteristics. Because of the difficulties of creating continuous data for the entire county from incomplete records, however, a sample is employed here representing those *permanent* families who resided in Chinguacousy Township from before 1850 until after 1870 and for whom continuous data exist. The sample is small but revealing. One-third of the permanent families of Chinguacousy increased their territory, two-thirds did not. The expansionist families added, on the average, 95 acres to their original holdings which in turn had averaged about 95 acres compared to the slightly larger farms (averaging 115 acres) of those families who did not enter the land market for additional acreage. What is of particular importance, at any rate, is that half of the 'improving' families added the equivalent of at least one farm (ie, 100 acres) to their holdings between 1850 and 1870. Moreover, with a single exception all of those struck by the land fever were farmers. Only one apparent 'speculator,' a merchant, was among them.

More to the point, as Table 11 indicates, men who were between the ages of 25 and 34 in 1852 were significantly overrepresented among the heads of the expansionist families, just as men on the verge of retirement in 1852, that is, aged 55-64, were particularly visible among those whose farms did not increase in size. In short, additional land seems to have become especially important to men whose families, from the vantage-point of 1852, would predictably increase and grow to maturity in the next twenty years. This conclusion is borne out by the data for family size in relation to farm expansion (Table 12). The improving families were represented by a disproportionately large number of men with no children in their households, while men whose families were substantially completed (4-6 children living at home) by 1852 were overrepresented among those who were content with the status quo. Put another way, in a community in which 5 or 6 children of the 8 or 9 normally produced by a marriage survived to maturity, nearly half (47%) of the families requiring more land in the 1850s and 1860s were still quite small in 1852. From this perspective, farm expansion anticipated the needs of growing families both for a rising standard of living and for land for their sons.

Michael Perdue and Thomas Holtby were typical of the men who felt in need of more land during this critical period. Perdue was a tenant farmer on 100 acres worth $300 when he bought it in 1845. At the time he had one son and another was on the way. By 1861 his family of five children, four of them sons, was complete, and in the meantime Perdue had acquired an additional 150 acres at a cost of $42 an acre, twelve times the cost of his original farm. Holtby was also a

TABLE 11

Distribution of heads of family by age cohort, 1852, and farm extension, Chinguacousy Township 1850-70

Age of head of family, 1852 (years)	Farm size increased 1850-70 (%)	Farm size did not increase 1850-70 (%)	Total pop'n (%)
15-24	4.7	4.6	4.6
25-34	27.9	19.5	22.3
35-44	37.2	37.9	37.7
45-54	25.6	27.6	26.9
55-65	4.6	9.2	7.7
65 and over	0	1.2	0.8
Total	100.0	100.0	100.0

$N = 130$ $\chi^2 = 11.4620$ $DF = 5$ Sig. $= 0.05$

TABLE 12

Distribution of heads of family by number of children at home, 1852, and farm expansion, Chinguacousy Township 1850-70

Number of children at home 1852	Farm size increased 1850-70 (%)	Farm size did not increase 1850-70 (%)	Total pop'n (%)
0	16.3	2.3	6.7
1-3	30.2	27.6	28.5
4-6	27.9	45.9	40.0
7 or more	25.6	24.2	24.6
Total	100.0	100.0	100.0

$N = 130$ $\chi^2 = 10.5615$ $DF = 3$ Sig. $= 0.02$

tenant farmer who worked 100 acres in 1852 to support his wife and three daughters. By 1860 his family had grown to eight, and there were two more additions in the seventies. In 1856 Holtby bought for $4,000 the 100 acres he had rented, then paid an equal sum for 50 acres more at the height of the land boom. He evidently had second thoughts about his investment, however, because he divested himself of 50 acres, at a loss, in the mid-sixties. John Snell's situation was not quite so common. In 1852 he was 41. Eight of his eventual family of 11 children were living at home, all of them under the age of 14. The Snell farm consisted of 100 acres acquired between 1838 and 1845 at a cost of $1,300. In 1854, and again in 1863, Snell added 100 acres to his farm. This new land cost an average of $60 an acre. With an additional 125 acres which Snell rented during the wheat boom, his land must have provided the standard of living that so large a family demanded; yet Snell's land promised security, in the long term, for only two of his four sons.

The evidence, then, suggests a regime in which the need to compete for arable land did not affect all families equally. Demographic pressures emanating from within the families of the generation of men who established their households at mid-century and whose families grew in size and maturity over the next twenty years created the most visible group of expansionists. They were part of a distinct minority among the farmers of Peel, but a minority large enough to have exacerbated the increasingly critical shortage of land in the county. This crisis abated only after it became apparent that there were real limits to demographic and economic continuity premised on a finite resource in an overpopulated society dependent on a staple economy. In this respect, the actions of those farm families who either would not or could not indulge in this costly competition are equally central to an understanding of the processes by which this little universe of social activity was transformed.

Even under the most favourable circumstances — cheap land and the absence of demographic pressure — few farmers could afford to satisfy the desire of all their sons to be 'their own servants,' in David Long's words, by providing them with land. In this sense, the economic and demographic constraints which restricted the availability of land in Peel County and in the region at mid-century simply brought into sharp relief a problem historically common to North American farmers since the beginning of settlement. In response to the competing claims of so many young men, Peel's newest families, those with the freedom to anticipate the expectations of their children in the 1860s and to amortize the costs of meeting those expectations, adopted the strategy of entering the land market to acquire additional land in the 1850s. But it is apparent that not all of the farm families in the community were willing to hazard their new fortunes, and that among the least willing were men whose families were already completed (Tables 10 and 11), men faced with making an immediate choice between the equally legitimate expectations of several mature children and the old age security represented by an unencumbered, improved, productive farm. Their strategy, in short, was dictated by their need to balance conflicting and even contradictory objectives[18] represented by the contentment and well-being of deserving children on the one hand, and on the other by a historical attachment to a favourable man/land ratio and to the standard of living associated with it, a cultural bias that militated against the alternative to farm expansion — subdivision. Dividing the indivisible, in short, was the dilemma of those proprietors who were unable or unwilling to risk the rewards of their own labour to satisfy their obligations to their children.

'It is certain,' Susanna Moodie complained in the 1850s, 'that death is looked upon by many Canadians more as a matter of ... a change of property into other hands than as a real domestic calamity.'[19] But the vocational aspirations of sons (an average of 4 in families completed before 1870), the legal rights of wives, the social expectations of daughters, and even the sentimental attachments that informed and motivated familial relationships were inevitably linked to the possession of property, its rights, its obligations and, in a society where landed property was a finite resource, its limitations. Mrs Moodie might have reflected, more accurately, that under such circumstances death and the subsequent transmission of property into other hands created the potential for domestic calamity. Choices had to be made. Justice had to be seen to be done. Calamity had to be avoided if possible. This was the problem facing the rural landholders of Peel who turned, in the 1850s, to the laws of inheritance to resolve their dilemma of dividing the indivisible among all those who perhaps deserved, but could no longer expect, to be men of property. The immediate effects of their strategy included varying degrees of 'domestic calamity.' In the long run, it produced a permanent alteration in the culture of the farm family.

There are as many ways to devise estates as there are minds to devise them; but in terms of first principles, at least, testators who are survived by more than one dependent face essentially two choices — a single heir or multiple heirs. In a single heir, or impartible, system of inheritance all real and personal property of consequence is assigned to one survivor to the exclusion of all other claims on the estate. The rule of primogeniture (abolished in Canada by law in 1856) simply defined that principal heir as the eldest male heir in order to guarantee the historical continuity of landed property, its perquisites, and obligations. But any number of inheritance systems can promote the same objective.[20] Conversely, multiple heir systems tend toward more or less perfect partibility, that is, the equal distribution of wealth among all of the legitimate claimants. As Table 13 indicates, both systems — and a third — were employed by the farmers of Peel County throughout the nineteenth century. More to the point, the third system, the 'Canadian' system of inheritance, in one decade became the most common vehicle for transmitting property from one generation to the next.[21]

The 'English-Canadian' system of inheritance was a hybrid, a preferential system which deliberately attempted to combine the economic conservatism of the impartible system with the social and sentimental egalitarianism of the partible. (The Canadian social historian A.R.M. Lower employed the term 'English-Canadian' in contrast to French-Canadian practice, although preferential systems are, in fact, universal.) It involved devising the estate upon a single heir, usually a son, who in return for his patrimony was obligated to provide, out of his own resources, more or less equitably for all of the residual heirs and legatees as they would have been provided for had the estate been settled in a perfectly partible fashion. In this way land, as much land as one man needed to secure his future could be passed on, undivided: its proven productive capacity, in turn, would bear the costs of compensating the legitimate heirs who had been denied their birthright. Clearly, the system was advantageous to the farmer whose substance, increasingly after 1850, took the form of a single asset — land (Table 14).

Thus, for example, a farmer who died in 1867 leaving his farm and a mere $54 in personal property instructed that his son, James, was to inherit the 100 acre farm, its crops, stock, and implements, providing that:

TABLE 13

Percentage distribution of estates devised by farmers by inheritance system employed and year will written, Peel County 1845-99

System	1845-55	1856-65	1866-73	1874-90	All estates
Impartible	32.1	17.3	11.9	18.2	17.1
Partible	28.6	11.5	8.4	6.5	8.7
'Canadian'	39.3	71.2	79.7	75.3	74.2
Total	100.0	100.0	100.0	100.0	100.0

$N = 515*$ $\chi^2 = 49.9088$ DF = 6 Sig. = 0.001

* These cases represent estates which were not probated as intestate and in which the testator had to choose between at least two possible heirs in devising his estate.

TABLE 14

Principal probated assets of deceased farmers, Peel County 1840-90

	1840s	1850s	1860s	1870s	1880s
(a) Mean acreage	105	112	163	217	150
(b) Average personalty	–	$2,000	$2,500	$2,500	$2,600

1st He shall find and furnish all the Flour, Pork and Butter and milk, potatoes and other vegetables with plenty of good firewood ready for use and ... keep 1 horse [and buggy] ... the above shall be found and supplied during ... the life of ... his mother.

2nd He shall pay ... annually ... the sum of $100 as part of [her] subsistence which payments shall be continued until the end of [her] natural [life].

3rd He shall pay ... to his brother William ... the sum of $1,200 ... I give and bequeath to my daughter Jane ... the sum of $200 which sum her brother James above mentioned shall pay ... I give and bequeath to the [5] children of my late daughter Rachel ... the sum of $200 ... which sum shall be paid ... by the said James ... in equal sums when they severally attain their 20th year. And further the said James ... shall pay all debts due by us ... and defray all our funeral expenses.[22]

The minimum cost to James of inheriting his farm, assuming that his mother lived for another ten years, was $3,400, half the market value of the farm. Obviously, this farmer counted heavily on his son's willingness to accept these obligations, on his family's willingness to become James's dependents, and on the land's continued ability to provide adequately for James so that he, in turn, might provide security for his mother and brother.

This farmer's actions, wittingly or not, conformed to the attitudes of the vast majority of his peers who drew up their wills after 1855. Whether they acted independently, sought advice from their neighbours, or had professional counsel (few did), the result was the definition of a common solution to a common problem. As the correlations in Table 15 suggest, partibility, equity, was the traditional objective of testators. Impartibility was the resort of men with small

TABLE 15

Correlation of selected variables with inheritance system preferred by testators choosing between at least two possible heirs, Peel County 1845-90

Variable	Canadian	Impartible	Partible
Will written before 1845	no	no	no
Will written 1846-55	yes (−)	no	yes (+)
Will written 1856-65	no	no	no
Will written 1866-72	no	no	no
Will written 1874-90	no	no	no
Farmers	yes (+)	no	yes (−)
Manufacturers	no	no	no
Construction	no	no	no
Labour (unskilled)	no	no	no
Commerce	no	no	no
Transportation	no	no	no
Professional	no	no	no
Retired	no	no	no
Value of personal property	yes (+)	yes (−)	no
Amount of land owned	yes (+)	no	no
Total no of surviving children	yes (+)	yes (−)	no

Note: This table excludes intestates. Significance levels reported are for r_c at 0.01 or better where t_c is for a two-tailed test. Coefficients are derived from the regression matrix.

estates and small families. But as it became more difficult to acquire land, men with land and large families conspired to protect their investment and still honour their legal, moral, and sentimental obligations to all those who survived them. Most stopped short of entailing their estates to provide livings for all of their heirs; but they effectively achieved the same goal by making their land and its new masters contractually responsible for the continued well-being of all their surviving dependents.

Thus, the generation of young farmers whose farms were the spoils of the land mania of the late fifties and sixties was the first to bear the new burdens of inheritance in an overpopulated rural society. In return for their land, approximately half of these farmers became responsible for fulfilling bequests to an average of four surviving legatees and providing an annuity to at least one other; a further 25% were obligated only to pay annuities to a minimum of two relatives. The remainder, though freed from monetary obligations other than debts and funeral expenses, normally were entrusted with the direct care or support of the deceased's family. The average total value of direct bequests was $1,600, but half those responsible for these gifts paid more. Annuities averaged $160 per annum. What these figures meant to the principal heirs is more readily comprehended from their perspective. An average annuity represented the annual wages and board of a farm labourer in the 1850s.[23] The total average cost of direct bequests to a principal heir represented 1,200 bushels of wheat, the produce of 66 acres in the best of times, at the 1871 price for fall wheat delivered in Toronto.[24] It is probably not too wide of the mark to suggest that the real costs of inheritance under this system represented, on the average, the equivalent of at least three years' cash income from a hundred acre farm. Whatever the actual costs, they were often more, in any case, than the now land-poor second generation could afford out of its own meagre assets. An analysis of all the mortgages against farm property in Toronto Gore Township from 1860 until 1890 reveals that 5% of all indentures, and 4% of the total debt represented by those indentures, were incurred as the direct result of inheriting property.[25] Indeed, farmers sometimes gave mortgages to principal heirs who took over the farm before their parents' death. These mortgages effectively replaced a will in so far as they stipulated similar contractual obligations, but in addition bound the heir to provide old age security for both the surviving parents. Thus, the cost of inheritance ultimately depended on how long one or both parents survived.[26]

The residual heirs, three out of every four survivors mentioned in these wills, evidently were compensated according to a complicated formula, part tradition, part legal and sentimental considerations, and, clearly, part impulse to promote continuity in the domestic arrangements of the family at the time of the head of household's death. Thus, sons who did not inherit land were most frequently rewarded with cash bequests, rarely less than a year's income, sometimes a substantial down payment on a farm of their own, more usually $450. Fathers who recorded their aspirations for these secondary male heirs seldom envisaged farming as a possibility. One son was enjoined to learn a trade before receiving his legacy which would buy him a set of tools; another was simply admonished to 'betake himself to work as a man should'; and a third was expressly instructed to use his $600 to pursue 'some honourable profession.'[27] Moreover, it seems certain that many parents had attempted to assist some of their sons, especially elder sons, during their lifetime and therefore did not feel compelled to treat them equitably as heirs. As one man explained, 'having previously ... assisted [four of his five sons] by sums of $ and settlements to such an extent as I could afford' they could not expect to share equally with his five daughters and his youngest son.[28]

The succession of one son as head of the household almost certainly meant the exodus from the household of his brothers, who were rarely conceded further claims, including rights of domicile, on the farm. Not so wives and daughters whose domestic arrangements were usually carefully, sometimes elaborately spelled out, for obvious reasons. By law, wives held dower rights (a one-third interest) in their husband's real property, rights which had to be conveyed to the new owner in return for adequate compensation. Thus, testators took care, at the very least, to see that dower rights were formally discharged by their principal heirs in a combination of cash payments, goods, and housing provided for widows. Most husbands' generosity did not end there; but dower rights commuted to goods and services ensured a minimum standard of old age security for widows whose husbands could not leave them cash incomes. How that security was to be delivered by the principal heir was always a matter of careful deliberation, then, for legal as well as sentimental reasons. Unmarried daughters, too, were the objects of special attention. Their only security lay in the extent to which the new head of household acted, or was required to act, *in loco parentis* until they established households of their own.

How actively deceased fathers expected their direct heirs to fulfil this role may be judged by the nature of the strictures under which some of them were empowered to act. Thus, 'if any of my three daughters do contract any immoral or vicious habits or be disobedient to their mother,' read one testament, 'my executors may divide [her legacy] ... between the other two daughters.'[29] More commonly, daughters' choice of husbands had to be acceptable to their brother-parents. In return for this obedience they continued to be housed, fed, clothed, and, eventually, provided with a dowry. It consisted of the same goods their mothers had brought to their husbands: a feather bed and bedding, a cow, clothing, and a sum of money ($100-$500 was the usual range). In this way, life for surviving daughters continued as before, in a familiar setting, but in the same condition of dependence which had characterized their relationship to their fathers, awaiting the opportunity to begin their own families.

For wives, the death of a husband ended a partnership and signalled the advent of a new stage of life; but in less than a quarter of the 'Canadian'-style wills, compared to the vast majority of the partibly or impartibly devised estates, were wives recognized as mistresses of their own futures. They became the dependents of their sons, grandsons, sons-in-law or their husbands' executors, their standard of living and even their future conduct prescribed or proscribed literally from the grave. Thus, more than 20% of the deceased husbands who devised their estates according to the 'Canadian system' explicitly forbade their wives to remarry or cohabit as a condition of inheritance. The penalties ranged from loss of income and / or rights of domicile to losing guardianship over her own children.[30] Most husbands were not so explicitly restrictive; yet the very nature of the settlements they made for their wives nevertheless had the same effect. 'As long as she behaves herself prudently and remains my widow'[31] — one man's expectation — seems to have been the universal hope of husbands contemplating death.

The source of this concern, in part, was sentiment. Few men willingly accept the possibility that they can be replaced, in their wives' affections, by another after a long and successful partnership. It was also a question of practicality. Once his wife's future security became the contractual obligation of a third party, her only guarantee of security was to continue in the circumstances which required her son, grandson, or son-in-law to fulfil those obligations, particularly the requirement — normal in these cases — to house, feed, convey, and minister to the physical and spiritual needs of surviving widows within a familiar domestic environment. In some instances, principal heirs were instructed to build a small house on the farm where the widowed mother and a female companion could live privately. But in the great majority of cases, the new householder was enjoined to set aside specific rooms and furniture within the family's home, to provide prescribed amounts and types of food, heat, and transportation, and to guarantee the widow continued access to the family garden and to the barn if she wished to keep a cow. These arrangements clearly ensured that the widow's annual income from her trust or annuity, considerably less than if she had received dower rights as either capital or land which could be converted to capital, enabled her to provide herself with amenities over and above her basic requirements of food, shelter, and domestic services. In short, a modest private income nevertheless insufficient to afford independence, and a guaranteed minimum standard of living provided in what was once her own household, effectively bound widows to these contractual arrangements and ensured their 'prudent' behaviour.

These provisions were meant, as well, to give the husband assurance that his widow would continue to enjoy the familial setting and the domestic arrangements to which she had become accustomed. No longer mistress of her own household, she would be surrounded nevertheless by familiar people and objects, an environment which would help to ease her reversion to single status. 'It is my particular injunction,' wrote one man who left his wife in better than average circumstances, 'that my children and wife shall remain in love and friendship to each other ...'[32] Evidently it was a condition more easily willed than carried into effect. Susanna Moodie fretted that widowhood in a daughter-in-law's household meant 'ironing the fine linen, or boiling over the cook-stove, while her daughter held her place in the drawing room.'[33] Frances Stewart, in her reminiscences, described widowhood as a state of being 'bewildered, weak and confused,' a continuation of a lifetime of never being 'allowed ... to think or act but as ... guided or directed ...'[34] Such were the perceptions and the experience of widowhood among gentlewomen.[35] Nevertheless, the contractual arrangements made by their deceased husbands undoubtedly guaranteed most women at least a tolerable existence as widows. In any event, as long as capital invested in land remained landed property, these were the only arrangements they could confidently anticipate.

The transmission of property from one generation to the next under this preferential system of inheritance, then, inevitably altered the circumstances and expectations of those affected by it in a variety of ways. Principal heirs inherited a legacy of debt and familial obligations, additional burdens to bear at a time when their own young families' needs already strained their resources. Over the long term their patrimony would compensate them, but in the short term they would begin their lives as independent farmers at some disadvantage to their own security. Sons who were residual heirs fared better than they would have under an impartible system, worse than they might have under a system of partible inheritance. Travelling money, capital to invest in a farm, trade, business, or profession, in short, a modest start in life in some other place, was the usual extent of their legacies. Wives and daughters were perhaps justified in equating death and inheritance with 'domestic calamity.' The sense of personal loss was accompanied, or was shortly followed, by a real loss of status within their households in return for a guaranteed minimum level of continued social security. But the land-poor farmer and his equally land-poor heir had little else save food, shelter, and pocket money to offer without jeopardizing their investment. By the 1860s, protecting it had become an art, skilfully and commonly practised by an entire generation, an entire community, of farmers. Their sons, as Table 13 illustrates, followed their example. The impartible-partible system of inheritance persisted until the twentieth century.

The wholesale adoption of a new system of inheritance, in this case one which was neither impartible nor partible but attempted to achieve the objectives of both in response to a crisis, is of great importance. Any system of inheritance, as two scholars have recently argued, 'sets limits, creates problems and opportunities, and evokes certain types of behaviour which conform to it or avoid its consequences.'[36] It has been suggested, for example, that in rural societies single heir systems of inheritance and their variants tend to retard population growth by restricting the availability of land to a relatively fixed number of households. This in turn promotes delays in the age at which young couples anticipating a patrimony may marry and limits the number of new families to those who can expect such a patrimony. Children denied access to land will either remain celibate or emigrate in search of new economic opportunities. Fewer marriages, later marriages, celibacy, and emigration slow the rate of population growth, protect favourable family/land ratios, and promote particular types of family structures — extended families — in which parents and still-dependent married children, or married children and their celibate brothers and sisters, share the same roof. Conversely, it is supposed that perfect partibility, distributing land equally among surviving children, encourages higher rates of marriage, earlier family formation, rapid population growth, and the proliferation of relatively simple family structures consisting of parents and young children.[37]

These examples greatly oversimplify the impact of either system and ignore entirely the subtle effects which both patterns, or any of their variants, are capable of producing. The two extremes merely illustrate the widely held assumption that in societies where family formation presupposes an economic foundation of real property, any alteration in the circumstances under which land becomes available to new families necessarily provokes changes in the other direction: earlier or later ages at marriage; more or fewer children (larger or smaller families) depending on the age at marriage; higher or lower rates of emigration, particularly among the young; changes in the structures of households and families as children remain home-bound longer awaiting land, or leave home early to occupy land of their own. Clearly the implementation of the 'Canadian' system of inheritance in Peel County after 1850 represented a permanent alteration in the conditions under which land became available to subsequent generations of children. Moreover, in spite of its egalitarian intent, it was a system of preferential inheritance[38] which restricted access to land in order to maintain customary man / land ratios in the face of mounting demographic pressure. Its consequences — inequality, insecurity, deprivation, and 'domestic calamity' for some survivors, for others debt, prolonged dependence, and protracted familial obligations — were far-reaching. In theory, and in fact, the men and women of the next generation were bound to conform to these limitations. They could not avoid the problems which this new system of inheritance created for them, but they could attempt to protect their own children from repeating their experience.

One last example from the experience of a Peel County family will perhaps underscore these generalizations by placing events in a broader historical context. The history of the Leslie family, as reconstructed by Richard Houston in his brilliant genealogy of the Standish family of Esquesing Township,[39] illustrates the intergenerational effects of land availability in Peel County. John Leslie of County Tyrone, Ireland, arrived in Upper Canada in 1818 and acquired a grant of land on the western limits of Chinguacousy Township. In time, the prolific Leslie clan's holdings exceeded 1,100 acres. John Leslie's three sons were all freeholders in Peel or Esquesing. The five sons of his eldest son George (all born between 1827 and 1846) all became freeholders in Peel. But of the five sons of George Leslie's eldest son John (b. 1827) only two became freeholders of family lands. The other three, and two of their four sisters who were married to farmers, took up farming, but in Manitoba and, subsequently, in British Columbia and Alberta. Among the Standish family and their close relatives in Peel, the Leslies, the Reeds, and several others, family farms were never subdivided into units of less than 100 acres, the proceeds of the sale of land to sons were the customary sources of daughters' legacies, and prolonged dependencies in their fathers' houses were the traditional lot of sons fortunate enough to be able to anticipate, as land became scarcer, a farm amid the other homesteads of the clan. The Leslies were exceptional in the duration of their commitment to Peel. But who would carry on the family's traditional loyalty to Chinguacousy Township in a narrowing sphere of economic opportunity became a matter of hard, practical decisions given the force of contractual obligations binding parents and children to the dictates of limited space.

Unquestionably, the loss of rural population experienced by this community in the 1860s had much to do with the attraction, elsewhere, of new or better economic opportunities associated directly with the availability of cheaper and more abundant land, or with non-farming opportunities created by the movement of population to those areas. Similarly, it would be unwise, in attempting to explain this loss of population, to ignore the climate of uncertainty, however fleeting, which the operation of external forces created in this local economy. But as the history of land occupancy in mid-nineteenth-century Peel County clearly demonstrates, the circumstances which propelled population out of rural

Peel on the eve of Confederation had less to do with economic stagnation than with a considerable act of faith in the local economy on the part of established farmers. Anticipating a rising standard of living not only for themselves but for their sons, they either expanded their homesteads or placed legal restrictions on the availability of land in order to maintain man/land ratios which they had come to associate with prosperity. These actions were largely responsible for that movement of population — those who could not acquire land, those displaced off of it, and those to whom land was denied — away from Peel's rural townships between 1860 and 1870.

Thus, Peel's farm families emerged from the 1860s with a more favourable population/land ratio (84 per 1,000 acres) than had existed two decades earlier (99 per 1,000). Fewer people cultivating more acres meant that even though yields of wheat per acre declined by 16% between 1850 and 1870, and the total volume of wheat produced in 1870 was 90,000 bushels (14%) short of the 1851 harvest, surplus production remained virtually the same in spite of the ravages of nature. Per capita production of wheat in 1870 (24 bu.) was only marginally less than in 1851 (27 bu.). In the short run, of course, some ground was lost. The wheat crop of 1870 represented only 60% of the bumper harvest of 1860 — 934,000 bushels. It is clear that income losses resulting from declines in wheat production were offset by the continuing demand for the county's other field crops — hay, oats, barley, and peas — and by alternative areas of farm production, especially livestock and dairy produce which had already begun to play an important role in this farm economy (see Table 16). Moreover, lower freight rates and the introduction of mechanized implements[40] represented just two of the factors of the costs of production which had become more favourable to the producer.

For all these reasons, the outlook for Peel's rural economy at the outset of the 1870s must have been an optimistic one, but one tempered by the memory of recent events. To the extent that this rural society was prepared for the new circumstances of agrarian prosperity or mere survival, as the case might be, in post-Confederation Ontario, its hopes lay in the strategies of social and demographic adjustment adopted during the two preceding decades. Farm expansion and its corollary, limiting accessibility to land among the rising generation of men, were not the only measures necessary to bring about this transition. But they were critical. First, they established the purpose of the exercise: to maintain family/land ratios historically associated with rural prosperity in Ontario. Then they created the conditions which made a secondary, though equally vital set of adjustments necessary. The land and demographic squeeze which beset one generation of these farm families became the inheritance of the next, literally as well as figuratively. One generation solved the urgent problem of too many people competing for too little land by applying financial and legal solutions suited to the immediacy of the problem. But neither debt nor domestic calamity were permanent solutions to the problem of economic opportunity and social security in a

TABLE 16

Selected summary statistics for agriculture in Peel County 1850-70

	1851	1861	1871
Total acreage improved (%)	51	65	73
Improved acreage in wheat (%)	29	32	18
Total acreage cropped (%)	30	49	60
Total cropped acreage in wheat (%)	49	42	27
Total acreage in wheat (%)	15	20	17
Wheat production (bushels)	659,575	934,139	569,126
Wheat concentration index*	0.404	0.462	0.282
Milch cow population	8,107	9,809	10,500
(% increase)	–	21	7
Butter production (lbs)	491,882	741,100	728,720
(% increase)	–	51	–

Sources: *Census of the Canadas, 1851-2*, II. Table 6; *Census of the Canadas, 1860-1*, II, Table 11; *Census of Canada, 1870-1*, III, Table 11, 13.

*The wheat concentration index is the ratio of wheat acreage per 1,000 cropped acres to the acreage of other field crops per 1,000 cropped acres.

mature, established society. It remained for the next generation to sort out the permanent social implications of these events and to act accordingly.

4 Household, Family, and Individual Experience

Canniff Haight, in his sentimental memoir of country life in Upper Canada during the 1830s, recalled growing up in a very large household. It consisted of his parents and their six children, two uncles, two nieces, and his father's parents. Their homestead had been the grandfather's farm before it descended to Haight's father, who assumed responsibility not only for the management of the farm but for the collective welfare of the fourteen people sheltered in his household. In demographic terms, this household consisted of a *conjugal family unit extended upwards* by the presence of aged parents and *extended laterally* by the presence of the head of household's celibate brothers and nieces, all supported by their common labour on the land attached to the household. This *houseful* was of a particular type recognized by historical demographers as an *extended multiple family household*.[1] The italicized definitions conform to the most recent scheme for classifying households and families in past time according to their structures; but for the moment the terminology is much less important than the problem of whether or not this large and complicated household was ever typical of the domestic environments within which most nineteenth-century rural Upper Canadians lived out their lives.

It is an important question on several levels. At the simplest, we cling to the belief that one of the principal distinctions between the lives and times of our great-grandparents' generation and our own is that they grew up in or were the progenitors of large families commonly and happily augmented by assorted relatives — grandmothers, maiden aunts, homeless cousins. More to the point, there is a substantial body of historical evidence to support the assumption that families and households were typically, and necessarily, large and complex in the past because of their unique social and economic functions. For example, whatever we may presume about the relative inability of nineteenth-century parents to limit the size of their families even if they had desired to do so, contemporary commentators constantly sang the praises of large families as the source of all economic security and social improvement. The labour value of many children was as good as money in the bank. Thus 'a numerous issue ... are considered a blessing and a source of wealth, instead of bringing with them, as in the old country, an increase of care.'[2] But the wealth which potentially might flow from the labour of many hands is neither the only, nor perhaps the most important, reason for assuming that nineteenth-century households were large and complex. In its report, the Canadian Royal Commission on Dominion-Provincial Relations (1940) argued that one of the principal causes of the severe social dislocation which accompanied the Great Depression of the 1930s was the inability of the individual to fall back on the social security once afforded by the nineteenth-century farm household, a 'mutual welfare association'[3] whose functions had not been adequately replaced by public institutions. If the mid-Victorian rural household was indeed a home for the aged, the infirm, and the incapacitated, a refuge for the unemployed and the orphaned, a close economic unit of family and relatives joined in a common enterprise of self-help, the size and structure of these 'virtuous and mutually attached households'[4] necessarily must have reflected this unique, now redundant social function.

On the other hand, there is an equally important body of theory and evidence to support the argument that the size and structure of families and households in past time were not constant even within particular societies; and that significant variations not only from time to time but in point of time can be traced to the influence of factors, internal as well as external, as subtle and complex as those which explain our own preference for small families and simple households. For example, several scholars have argued, convincingly, that the relative availability of cheap or free land, differential levels of education among adult populations, social rank, ethnicity, and the ability of parents to make a rational choice between having more children or attaining a better standard of living for themselves and relatively few children all account for significant variations in fertility, and hence family size, in rural mid-Victorian North America.[5] Similarly, there exists compelling evidence that in the past household size and structure also varied from one age, or vocational or economic group to another within particular communities, and that permanent, common alterations to the boundaries of their households not only took place through time, but represent the effects of fundamental, profound, long-term social change.[6] It has also been argued that the simple family household — parents and children living together alone — has been the preferred domestic arrangement in most western societies for a very long time; and that the large households and complex domestic structures of received history are at worst figments of romantic historical imaginations, at best aberrations produced by unique cultural circumstances.[7] Whatever the case, it is certain that family and household were the lowest common denominators of social and economic organization in pre-industrial societies and that knowledge of their forms and functions is essential for understanding both the nature of individual experience in those societies as well as the structure of society itself.

There is little consolation in early Canadian census records for the historian seeking precision in determining the size and structure of households. The rural returns were prepared by underpaid, badly informed, and often poorly educated enumerators,[8] whereas urban householders completed their own returns. Consequently, in the rural districts one household is not easily distinguished from another (except in the 1871 returns on which households were numbered in order of visitation); and the relationships among inmates of households were never articulated. Thus, similar surnames are all that distinguish the conjugal family unit from everyone else in the household. Some residents — servants, farm servants, apprentices — often can be identified by their designated functions within the household; and in many instances it is perfectly apparent, though only implicit, that certain residents were in fact related to the head of household. It would be unwise to presume too much given the lack of explicit evidence; hence the broad categories of 'extras' used here: servants, non-domestic employees, and non-family children (ie, those most likely to function as 'hired help' in the household); relatives, boarders, and visitors (those with no apparent function); and secondary conjugal family units. All these 'extras' were present from time to time in the households of this rural community. Whether there were decided patterns of household composition and size remains to be seen.

As Table 17 indicates, in every decade the majority of Peel's households were simple family households, parents and children residing together without the aid of servants or other 'hired help,' without relatives, boarders, or visitors, in single family dwellings. Moreover, that characteristic became the standard as time passed. By 1870 nearly three-quarters of Peel's households were of the simplest variety, compared with only half the households a decade earlier. This pronounced contraction of household structures represents the disappearance from many households of hired help in particular, but as well of that class of extras designated here as 'relatives, boarders, or visitors', many of whom, in any case, may very well have been hired help not identified as such by the enumerator. The declining representation of these extras in the households of Peel during the 1860s coincides with two other developments. First, in the same decade there was a sharp reduction (5%) in the proportion of unskilled labourers in the work force represented by male heads of family at a time of general rigidity in the occupational structure of the community (see Table 40 below). Second, in the same decade there was a notable increase in the proportion of young, single men and women aged 16-25 residing in their parents' households. This 23% increase in the ratio of still-dependent children to householders above the age of 50 (155/100 in 1851, 167/100 in 1861, and 190/100 in 1871) together with the contraction, within households and the community, of the unskilled labour force suggests that a prolonged period of dependence, and therefore of servitude, in their parents' households for at least some of the young men and women in the community had the effect of reducing the demand for hired labour. This tendency toward a prolonged state of dependence affected the children of both farm

TABLE 17

Household size and structure, Peel County

	1851	1861	1871
(a) Mean household size	6.2	6.2	5.7
(b) Median Household size	5.9	6.0	5.4
(c) Percentage of simple family households	56.4	53.1	72.6
(d) Percentage of conjugal family units			
+ (1) relatives, boarders, or visitors	12.5	13.2	9.6
+ (2) servants, employees, other children	21.9	21.7	12.4
+ (3) relatives, boarders, or visitors *and* servants, employees, other children	4.6	6.7	2.3
+ (4) second conjugal family unit *and* relatives, boarders, or visitors	3.1	3.6	2.7
+ (5) second conjugal family unit *and* relatives, boarders, or visitors *and* servants, employees, or other children	1.5	1.7	0.4
(e) Percentage of all households with 'extras'	43.6	46.9	27.4
(f) Mean no. of relatives/boarders/visitors			
(1) per 100 households	46	55	28
(2) per 100 households with 'extras'	204	217	186
(g) Mean no. of servants/employees/other children			
(1) per 100 households	48	51	20
(2) per 100 households with 'extras'	171	170	135
(h) Mean no. of all 'extras'			
(1) per 100 households	112	127	62
(2) per 100 households with 'extras'	261	272	203

TABLE 18

Distribution of families with still-dependent children at home (mother aged 50 or older)*

	1851	1861	1871
Farm families (%)	72.7	72.5	77.1
Non-farm families (%)	59.6	53.2	60.0
All families (%)	68.5	66.6	71.1

* The table summarizes the results of three cross-tabulations in which the significance of all χ^2's is 0.01.

and non-farm households (Table 18); but to the extent that it was especially pronounced among farm children, this development suggests that the land and inheritance crisis of the late 1850s and 1860s did bring about a change in both household and family structure, and in individual experience. As Michael Katz has shown, even in the 1850s young adults in an urban environment (Hamilton) had begun to experience a stage of 'semi-autonomy' between school-leaving and the independence of married life, a stage during which they worked and lived outside their parents' household, usually in a surrogate family setting as boarders or as employees of the householders with whom they lived.[9] Thirty miles away, in Peel County, the 1860s clearly produced a significant decrease in either the necessity, or the opportunity, for young people to live and work outside the

TABLE 19

Distribution of persistent householders by frequency of presence of extras in households 1851-71

	Never had (%)	Ever had (%)	Had once (%)	Had twice (%)	Had always (%)
All extras	27.4	72.6	36.2	29.6	6.8
All hired help	41.4	58.6	39.0	16.2	3.2
Relatives/boarders/visitors	58.8	41.2	31.3	9.0	3.4

Adding horizontally, 'ever had' + 'never had' = 100%; 'once' + 'twice' + 'always' = 'ever had'.

parental household and still remain in the community, as households increasingly reverted to simple family units sheltering parents and, for a lengthening stage of their lives, some dependent children.

However, this evolving pattern of household structures obscures the fact that at one time or another in the life cycles of most families, their households were commonly augmented by non-family residents. This phenomenon can be illuminated best with reference to the most persistent group of householders in the community, those enumerated on each of the three successive mid-century census returns. Because they were persistent they were more likely than their transient neighbours to have had servants, relatives, boarders, or other extras in their households (see Table 23 and Chapter 5, below). What is of interest, nevertheless, is the relative frequency with which non-family residents were present in their households over a twenty-year period, and the identity of these extras. As Table 19 indicates, only one in fourteen of these households *always* contained additional residents. But almost three in four (73%) housed extras at least once in the twenty years between 1851 and 1871, and in more than one in four households (29.6%) they were present on two occasions. In short, the vast majority of Peel's households commonly housed additional non-family dependents at some time during the cycle of family life, as many, on the average, as two or three (see Table 20) at a time. Moreover, it is clear that their presence was related, above all else, to the economic functions of the household. In 70% of the households which contained extras only once, the additional residents fall into the category of 'hired help' (Table 20). Similarly, both in households with 'extras' on two occasions and in those in which additional residents were always present, hired labour was the most common adjunct of the conjugal family unit. Relatives, boarders, and visitors were considerably less common in these households (though more numerous when they were present), and more likely to have appeared only once during the cycle of family life.

At first glance, then, the evidence seems contrary. At any given point in time the vast majority of households contained the elementary biological family — husband, wife, and children; but most households contained additional, non-family residents at least once in their history. In fact, the longitudinal analysis reveals the frequency with which these rural families required additional

TABLE 20

Distribution of types of extras in persistent households with extras by frequency of presence of extras

	Had extras		
	Once	Twice	Always
Had hired help (%)			
(a) never	30	10	3
(b) once	70	41	22
(c) twice		49	25
(d) always			50
Total	100.0	100.0	100.0
Had relatives/boarders/visitors (%)			
(a) never	70	30	19
(b) once	30	46	41
(c) twice		24	28
(d) always			12
Total	100.0	100.0	100.0

TABLE 21

Percentage distribution of households with extras by type of extras and age cohort of heads of household

Age of head of household	Type of extras				
	Relatives boarders, visitors	Servants other helpers	Relatives, etc., servants, etc.	Second family	All households
In 1851					
15-34	43	37	49	35	40
35-49	34	35	27	28	33
50-64	17	20	19	20	19
65+	6	8	5	17	8
Total	100.0	100.0	100.0	100.0	100.0
In 1861					
15-34	34	31	36	21	32
35-49	35	34	40	23	34
50-64	24	24	18	27	24
65+	7	10	7	28	10
Total	100.0	100.0	100.0	100.0	100.0
In 1871					
15-34	41	23	44	32	32
35-49	29	34	26	21	30
50-64	21	28	23	22	25
65+	8	14	7	24	13
Total	100.0	100.0	100.0	100.0	100.0

Significance of $\chi^2 = 0.01$ for 1851, 1861, 1871.

labour or provided social security for relatives, while cross-sectional analysis illustrates the timing of the appearance of extras in these households and serves to distinguish between the characteristics of those households with, and those without, additional residents. Table 21 therefore summarizes for three successive cross-sections the distribution of households with extras in relation to the identity of the extras and the age cohort of householders. As it indicates, within the context of a community dominated by simple family households, at each cross-section the households of the youngest generation of householders (aged 15-35) were invariably overrepresented among those homes which sheltered relatives, boarders, and visitors. Similarly, the households of the oldest generation in the community (householders over age 65) were always disproportionately visible among those households containing two or more conjugal family units. This suggests that widows and widowers in particular, but perhaps bachelor uncles and spinster aunts as well, were taken into the homes of the younger generations of families. If both aged parents were living, however, the family of one of their children — a son or son-in-law, perhaps the eventual inheritor of the estate — might share the older couple's household. Interestingly, in 1861, just after the economic débâcle of 1857-60, one in every six households of men over age 65 housed two or more families, double the proportion in 1851. Evidently in times of great distress the family farm did provide succour for at least some of its progeny; but in a much more general sense its principal function, beyond sustaining the family, was to provide social security for the aged and partnerless.

All of this begs the equally important question of household size. It is clear from Table 17 that these rural households were quite large. In 1851 and 1861 half the households in the community contained more than 6 people (see *median* size), and in 1871 households were only marginally smaller in spite of the considerable contraction, in terms of the relative presence of extras, that took place in the 1860s. The difficulty is that variations in household size are necessarily highly correlated with family size. The households of parents most of whose living children are still at home obviously will tend to be larger, on the average, than households containing incomplete or fragmented families. Thus, it is important to distinguish between variations in household size which are merely the products of the relative numbers of children at home and variations, in spite of family size, attributable to other factors in order to understand whether family size alone is an adequate explanation of the tendency for some households to be larger or smaller than others. Tables 22 and 23 accomplish this by presenting, comparatively, variations in household size in 1852, 1861, 1871 (1) when family size is a contributing factor (unadjusted category means) and (2) when family size is held constant, and when each of the other 'predictors' is controlled for, so that variations in household size can be attributed to the most powerful predictors. Table 22 summarizes the results of the analysis by describing which categories of predictors were most significant (an F score significant at the 99% [0.01]

TABLE 22

Sources of variation in mean household size by selected variable 1852-71 (summary statistics)

	1852			1861			1871		
	F sig. at	Eta	Beta	F sig. at	Eta	Beta	F sig. at	Eta	Beta
Main predictors									
Age cohort of wife	0.001	0.35	0.05	0.001	0.34	0.05	0.007	0.42	0.02
Householder's occupa- tional category	0.001	0.21	0.12	0.001	0.28	0.11	0.001	0.23	0.07
Householder's ethnicity	0.21	0.10	0.04	0.060	0.11	0.04	0.260	0.16	0.02
Property ownership	0.44	0.14	0.01	0.002	0.19	0.03	0.02	0.09	0.02
Mobility	0.032	0.11	0.02	0.209	0.13	0.01	0.001	0.25	0.02
Covariates									
No of children at home	0.001			0.001			0.001		
Overall F	0.01			0.001			0.001		
Multiple r	0.87			0.85			0.94		
R_2	0.75			0.73			0.88		

TABLE 23

Actual and predicted mean responses by category, household size 1852-71

	1851	1861	1871
Mean household size	6.4	6.5	5.9
Wife's Age			
15-34	5.8 (6.5)	5.9 (6.5)	5.1 (5.9)
35-49	7.7 (6.2)	7.8 (6.3)	7.5 (5.9)
50-64	5.9 (6.4)	6.1 (6.9)	5.7 (5.9)
65+	6.4 (6.8)	5.4 (7.0)	4.8 (6.2)
Householder's occupational classification			
agriculture	6.7 (6.4)	7.0 (6.6)	6.4 (6.0)
skilled labour	6.2 (6.7)	6.1 (6.7)	5.8 (5.8)
unskilled	5.5 (6.1)	5.2 (5.9)	5.5 (5.7)
commerce	6.3 (7.2)	6.8 (7.3)	5.5 (6.2)
professional	6.2 (6.5)	5.8 (6.4)	5.1 (5.8)
other	4.5 (5.2)	4.4 (5.7)	3.8 (5.2)
Property owner or	6.9 (6.4)	7.0 (6.6)	6.1 (6.0)
tenant	6.1 (6.4)	5.9 (6.4)	5.6 (5.9)
Persister or	6.9 (6.5)	7.0 (6.5)	6.9 (6.0)
transient	6.1 (6.3)	6.2 (6.4)	4.5 (5.9)
Householder's ethnicity			
native-born Anglican	6.0 (6.6)	5.8 (6.8)	5.3 (6.0)
native-born Catholic	5.5 (6.1)	6.4 (7.1)	6.0 (6.1)
native-born Methodist	5.9 (6.5)	6.3 (6.7)	5.5 (5.9)
native-born Presbyterian	5.5 (6.4)	6.1 (6.6)	5.5 (5.9)
foreign-born Anglican	6.3 (6.4)	6.5 (6.4)	6.1 (5.9)
foreign-born Catholic	6.5 (6.3)	5.9 (6.3)	5.5 (5.9)
foreign-born Methodist	6.8 (6.5)	6.8 (6.5)	6.8 (6.1)
foreign-born Presbyterian	6.4 (6.3)	6.9 (6.5)	5.0 (5.8)

level of confidence) in explaining variation in household size, and by ranking (partial beta co-efficients) the predictors in order of importance after the effects of the predictors on each other have been considered. Table 23 then provides the actual and (in parentheses) the adjusted category means which describe, respectively, the real and the probable variations in household size associated with particular individual characteristics (see Appendix 2).

In every decade, household size in Peel County varied with the head of household's occupation and his wife's age. In 1861 his economic status, that is whether he owned or rented land, was an additional source of variation which was still quite important a decade later when social stability — the fact of having been a permanent resident of the community for at least ten years — became an equally significant predictor of relative household size. The degree of absolute variation within these categories is revealed in the unbracketed columns in Table 60. At each cross-section, however, households potentially containing completed families (wives aged 35-59) were invariably the largest, as expected; and in any event the behaviour of the covariate (number of children at home) clearly obscures the real distinctions between the households of the labourer and the farmer, between the landowner's and the tenant's domestic establishments, between the households of the persister and of the transient; hence the need to abandon the unadjusted category means and the measure of their association (eta) with the dependent variable and to turn to a more exacting estimate of the sources of variation in household size among the families of Peel. This is the function of the adjusted category means and of the beta coefficients through which the predictors can be assigned an order of priority which reflects the relative importance of each category of predictors after the effects of all the other predictors and covariates have been taken into account. They indicate that in each of the cross-sections the occupation of the head of household in fact holds the key to an explanation of variation in household size among these families, although by 1871 the relative power of occupational classification to sustain this distinction was much diminished, no doubt because of the general contraction of household size and structure in Peel in the 1860s. Nevertheless, the households of merchants and to a lesser extent of skilled artisans and of farmers were likely to be larger than the households of other occupational groups when differences in family size, which are in turn a function of differences in stages of the life cycle of families, are minimized. Perhaps for quite different reasons the merchant, the farmer, and the skilled craftsman each maintained domestic establishments housing a greater assortment of people than the essentially simple family households of the professional, the unskilled labourer, and the 'gentleman.' But with the single exception of the tendency on the part of merchants and skilled artisans in the 1850s to maintain hired help rather than relatives, boarders, and visitors, there is no evidence that the composition of their households, or those of farmers, was necessarily related to occupational *function*. A much more appealing possibility is that household size was one of several attributes of social rank and success which distinguished some men from others, and that farmers, commercial capitalists, and highly skilled craftsmen were more likely to possess those attributes of a particular class than other men (see Chapter 5 below).

We will return to this important question in the next chapter. In the meantime, it will suffice to conclude that households, with or without children, were indeed large in mid-Victorian Peel County; but most of them were also of the simplest variety, parents and children living together, and working together, not only a 'mutual welfare association' but also a 'chain of affection'[10] whose links were forged from the hard metal of shared industry, reciprocal obligations, and the anticipation of mutual rewards. By the 1860s, however, the social and economic obligations of parents to their children in return for the younger generation's contribution to the economy of the family farm had produced a crisis of considerable proportions. Land for the next generation had become scarce and exorbitantly expensive. The wholesale adoption of a preferential system of inheritance victimized the very individuals it was meant to serve by enforcing the prolonged dependence of some young adults on their parents and burdening them with debt when they did acquire their patrimonies, by divesting many more young men of their interest in the family's real property and hence of their stake in the community, and by imposing on daughters and wives settlements which had the appearance, and perhaps the effect, of 'domestic calamity.' The problem was one of too many people competing for too few resources at a time when the wellsprings of the farm economy, land, markets, and cereal grain production capacity, were beginning to dry up. Short-term adjustments to these new circumstances could not resolve their long-term effects on the quality of rural life. Ultimately, maintaining, let alone improving, the farm family's standard of living meant, among other things, reducing future demands on its precious resources. That trend was already under way in Peel County by 1870.

Family size, as it is revealed in nineteenth-century documents, depends entirely on the way one chooses to define it. In one sense, the Haight's family of six children was not very different in size from the families of rural Peel County two or even four decades later. Women who had just completed their families (mothers aged 35-49) appear, in each decade, to have had about five children living at home, and the typical conjugal family unit consisted of approximately seven people (see Table 24). This figure obscures, however, the actual numbers of children raised by parents in rural Peel County because census enumerators were concerned only with the co-resident group and asked no questions about the history of child mortality in the family or about children who were not at home on enumeration day. Aggregating the census returns of Peel's persistent families in order to identify the largest number of family children ever resident in these households yields a different figure. The maximum average number of children ever resident at one time in the households of parents with surviving children was between six and seven. In short, the size of the conjugal family unit varied with the coming and going of children from time to time and, clearly, with particular stages in the cycle of family life. But most children, like Canniff Haight, would have grown up in the company of five or six brothers and sisters. This, however, is quite a different matter from the question of how many children actually resulted from a marriage, again because analysing family size cross-sectionally or even by comparative stages of family completion isolates only those children actually at home on a particular day. By reconstructing individual families as accurately as possible, another picture emerges. Among the cohort of women, from persistent families, aged 20-4 in 1850 who began bearing children in the late 1840s and who had completed their families by 1871, the average number of different children recorded on three census returns was 7.8. Within the group there were some important variations. Wives of foreign-born husbands tended to bear more children (9) during their childbearing cycle than the wives of second or third generation Canadian men (6.8); and wives whose husbands did not own land appear to have conceived more children (9) than the wives of men who owned land (7.5). In short, apparent family size, completed

TABLE 24

Family size, Peel County 1851-71

	1851	1861	1871
(a) Average no of children, all families	3.4	3.3	3.4
(b) Average no of children in completed families (mother aged 35-50)	5.2	5.1	5.2
(c) Average no. of children ever enumerated in completed permanent families ($N = 474$)		6.2	
(d) Average no of children born to women aged 20-25 in 1851 (persistent families) ($N = 161$)		7.8	
(e) Average no. of children resulting from all marriages (persistent families) ($N = 474$)		5.6	

family size, and total marital fertility represent three quite distinct measures of familial populations. Only the latter, marital fertility, is sufficiently sensitive to reveal the effects of social, economic, and demographic change, if any, on the natural propensity of women in a society without the benefit of artificial contraceptive devices to bear children at regular intervals of 30 months, more or less, from marriage to menopause.[11]

The basic measure of fertility employed here is a child/woman ratio, the number of children not yet 10 years of age per 1,000 *married* women in a given age cohort. Among other things, it is predicted on the assumption that marriage and conception were synonymous, that is, that conception normally only took place within marriage.[12] This may be an enormous leap of faith since almost nothing is known about the sexual mores of nineteenth-century Canadians.[13] In Peel County during these two decades several cases of infanticide were reported — 'the corpse of a male infant was discovered in a necessary at Brampton,'[14] and in a nearby township a servant girl was arrested for giving birth in a field and leaving the infant to die.[15] One unfortunate young man, intent upon an assignation with a farmer's daughter, found himself in a barn where he was confronted by her brother, dressed in woman's clothing, and several of his friends who promptly tarred and feathered the unfortunate Lothario.[16] Incidents such as these, as well as the substantial numbers of women over 60 who claimed, on the census, to be the mothers of the infant children in their households, all suggest that much work remains to be done on the question of extramarital fertility and illegitimacy if we are ever to comprehend total fertility among the historical populations of Canada. Meanwhile, this discussion necessarily must be limited to marital fertility and its variations.

In Peel County between 1851 and 1871 a substantial decline in fertility occurred among married women in the 15-19 and 20-4 age cohorts. The extent of this reduction in marital fertility is described in Table 25. The child/woman ratio for married women aged 15-19 declined, in two decades, by almost 70%, and for the next cohort by more than 25%. Since employing children not yet 10 rather

TABLE 25

Marital fertility: children not yet 10 per 1,000 married women by age cohort and decade

	Age of wife					
	15-19	20-4	25-9	30-4	35-9	40-4
1851 (N = 2,246)	1,463	1,762	2,403	3,189	3,185	2,527
1861 (N = 1,995)	500	1,493	2,356	3,222	3,200	2,429
1871 (N = 2,475)	452	1,302	2,333	3,292	3,124	2,562
Absolute change 1851-71	−1,011	−460	−70	+103	−61	+34
% change 1851-71	−69	−26	−3	+3	−2	+1.4
% change women 15-24 =	−46%					

than children not yet 5 as the numerator for this ratio tends to exaggerate the substance of this decrease among 15-19 year olds, the decline of fertility among the broader age cohort 15-24 is also presented — 46%. In either case, however, the magnitude of this decline in marital fertility, its timing, and the identity of the women who experienced it are all crucial. As for the timing of this historical event, the fact that it took place first in the 1850s seems to be unmistakable evidence that this decided shift in the patterns of fertility among the youngest group of married women in the community was related to those other events — social, economic, and demographic, internal as well as external to the community — associated with this decade of crisis. What is of equal, if not more significance is that this alteration in marital fertility persisted for at least another decade. It was not, in short, a temporary response to a fleeting crisis. Whether the new pattern became the normal pattern for the rest of the century remains uncertain; but given the fact that marital fertility among all women aged 15-44 declined, in Ontario, by nearly 40% between 1850 and 1890, it is more than likely that the events of the 1850s started marital fertility in Peel on a continuing downward slide.

If this trend was particularly manifest among the youngest cohort of married women in the community, those aged 15-24 years, it did not affect them equally. As Table 26 illustrates, the fertility of farm women in each of the two age cohorts 15-19 and 20-4 decreased more sharply than did the fertility of the entire female population of those cohorts; and even among married women age 25-9, the fertility of farm women declined substantially, particularly between 1860 and 1870 (13%), while fertility across the entire cohort remained virtually unchanged. That this transition in patterns of marital fertility was especially pronounced among young farm wives in each age cohort and extended even to farm women in their late twenties must be taken as incontrovertible evidence that the land, inheritance, and demographic crises which arose within the farming community in the late 1850s, and the general economic instability of the period, had a decided, far reaching effect on the very foundation of life in this society. The

TABLE 26

Marital fertility: children under 10 years of age per 1,000 married women by age cohort of wife 1851-71

	Wife 15-19 years			Wife 20-4 years			Wife 25-9 years		
	1851	1861	1871	1851	1861	1871	1851	1861	1871
All wives	1,462	500	452	1,762	1,494	1,302	2,402	2,356	2,333
Farm wives	1,585	533	385	1,879	1,405	1,124	2,492	2,558	2,222
% decline: all wives		−69.1			−26.1			− 2.9	
% decline: farm wives		−75.7			−40.2			−10.9	

farm family, beseiged on all sides by changes which threatened its traditional expectations, underwent an equally profound parallel change in the form of a permanent alteration in its customary patterns of reproduction. It would take time before the effects of this transition, begun on the eve of Confederation, had a visible effect on the demography of the community. But, for example, between 1861 and 1891 the birth rate for the county fell from roughly 40 births per thousand of population per annum to less than 30 as these rural families adjusted to the new realities of the society and economy of post-Confederation Ontario.

How was this transition accomplished? In the modern era, individual control over fertility is increasingly commonplace. Many, though not all, women may decide when, and how often, they wish to conceive a child, and they have access to both information and birth control devices to assist them in family planning. It is not so certain a fact that mid-Victorian Canadian women had access to either. There is some evidence that by the last quarter of the century the rhythm method, coitus interruptus, and prolonged nursing were popularly understood to be more or less effective natural safeguards against conception. But the widespread availability at the end of the century of patent medicines whose promise was self-induced abortion suggests that either the available wisdom or the technique of family limitation (probably both) were badly interpreted.[17] In any event, although there is titillating evidence that at least some women in this society were clearly able to limit the size of their families through some medium of birth control invoked in their mid-thirties (see Table 31 below), the fact that the mid-century decline in fertility in this community took place exclusively among the youngest group of married women suggests that they shared some other common characteristic which accounts for their collective reproductive behaviour.

The gossipy accounts of early travellers in Upper Canada were riddled with information of dubious authenticity about life in the colony, but the frequency with which they mentioned the very young age at which most women married suggests that they were conscious of a visible distinction between English and Canadian marriage patterns. As one of them remarked in 1835, Canada 'bids fair to give the go-bye to Calcutta ... as a marriage market' for young English émigrées.[18] Even as late as the 1850s, commentators alluded to the imbalanced sex ratios, especially in the backwoods of Canada, which were responsible for the 'present uncomfortable state of forced celibacy' among young men and which made every marriageable girl a coveted prize.[19] Less than two decades later, however, it was possible for Nicholas Flood Davin, in his reminiscences, to treat early marriage as an anachronistic curiosity from a remote past.[20] By the end of the century, C.S. Clark, in his study *Of Toronto the Good*, was prepared to argue that the incidence of marriage, especially among the middle classes, had declined to the point where the employment of unmarried women had become

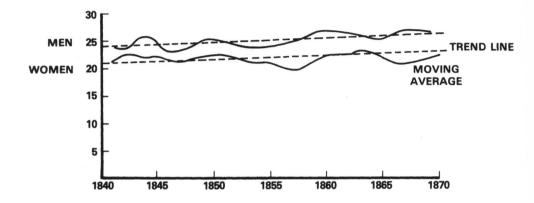

4 Trend line and three-year moving averages for age at marriage, men and women under 35, 1840-70

one of the city's principal social problems.[21] In sum, if literary accounts are at all reliable, one of the major demographic changes which took place in Ontario during the nineteenth century was a reversal in the patterns of age at marriage and in the frequency of marriages from one generation to the next as society advanced from a more to a less primitive state, from an essentially rural backwoods to an urban industrial environment. Any significant contraction of the age at which young women marry produces a disproportionately large reduction in total marital fertility,[22] and consequently a significant reduction in completed family size. Whether this relationship was the cause and effect of Ontario's declining birth rate in the latter half of the nineteenth century still requires extensive investigation. But it is certain that the age-specific decline in marital fertility among the young women of mid-Victorian Peel County was the product of delayed first conceptions resulting from later ages at marriage.

Figure 4 graphically illustrates the behaviour of two measures of age at marriage from a time series analysis of age at marriage for men and women under age 35, for three decades. The straight line represents the long-term trend while the fluctuating line describes annual variations in age at marriage averaged across three consecutive years to dampen annual fluctuations. As Figure 4 indicates, over these three decades the long term trend of ages at first marriage among young women in the community was upward, contracting more than two years in the period under study. More important, after a gradual downhill slide during the prosperous years before 1856, with the onset of hard times and the land crisis in Peel the average age at which young women married shot upwards,

TABLE 27

Distribution of married rural women by age cohort and number of
living children 1851-71

	1851	1861	1871
(a) Women 15-24 (N)	(607)	(397)	(407)
% with *no* children	28.8	31.2	34.2
% with *one* child only	10.2	15.9	24.6
% with *more than one child*	60.9	52.2	41.1
(b) Women 25-9 (N)	(454)	(515)	(602)
% with *no* children	22.3	18.4	21.1
% with *one* child only	5.9	5.8	7.5
% with *more than one child*	71.7	75.7	71.4

from 20 to 23, in just five years. The moving average dipped briefly in the late 1860s, but then resumed its upward climb as the decade drew to a close. It is this sharp reversal in age at marriage after 1856 which evidently accounts for the simultaneous reversal in the patterns of marital fertility among the youngest age cohort of married women in the community.[23] The effects of this change in marriage patterns are illustrated in Table 27. By 1871, the proportion of married women in the 15-24 age cohort with more than one child had declined by one-third since 1850, while the proportion with only one child by age 24 had doubled. Put another way, in 1851 three out of five married women aged 15-24 had been married long enough to have borne at least two children. Twenty years later, nearly three in five in a similar age cohort had only been married long enough to conceive one child, and of this latter group (240 women) only 40% had actually given birth to their first child when the 1871 census was taken. The mid-century decline in fertility, then, was the result of the delay which these women experienced in the timing of their first conception as the result of relatively later ages at marriage. Delayed marriages, in turn, were one more by-product of the forces set loose by the mid-century social, economic, and demographic crises.

Before individual control over fertility was considered to be either possible or desirable, societal controls and natural controls nevertheless could have a significant effect on patterns of fertility. In this case, the same forces which promoted the prolonged dependence of young men and women within their parents' households after 1860 similarly delayed family formation. Young adults, especially young men, unable to secure their economic independence by acquiring land, a skill, or capital with which to launch a business enterprise, consequently were unable to secure their social independence from their parents by marrying, setting up their own households, and starting a family. More serious, from the vantage point of young women of marriageable age, was the impact which the land, economic, and inheritance crises had on the relative opportunities to marry.

TABLE 28

Number of males per 1,000 females by age cohorts 1850-70

Age	1851	1861	1871
10-15	1,090	1,081	913
16-20	1,102	957	984
21-30	1,216	1,160	1,072

Sources: *Census of the Canadas, 1851-2*, Vol. i, Table 3; *Census of the Canadas, 1860-1*, Vol. i, Table 6; *Census of Canada, 1870-1*, Vol. ii, Table 7

Table 28 describes sex ratios in Peel County during these two decades. Between 1850 and 1870 the number of males per 1,000 females in each of the age cohorts 10-15, 16-20, and 21-30 declined by 16%, 11% and 12% respectively. The declining population of young men between 15 and 30 in particular undoubtedly reflects higher levels of out-migration in consequence of the land and inheritance crisis and, as well, reduced opportunities even for unskilled labour in the community. The resultant imbalance in sex ratios together with lengthened dependence for those young men who remained in the community conspired to reduce opportunities for marriage and to delay the formation of new families by the generation of young people entering upon man- and womanhood on the eve of Confederation. Social and economic constraints on marriage, family formation, and fertility, emanating from within the community, were the final answer to the demographic crisis within the traditional farm family.

Collectively, the changes which were wrought in these rural households in the two middle decades of the nineteenth century constitute a transformation of major proportions. Household structures contracted, some children began to experience a prolonged stage of dependence on their parents in turn creating a visible change in family structures, the age at which young men and women were permitted (or were able) to marry and start new families increased, marital fertility decreased, and, last but not least, the population of the county itself declined by a little over 4%. All of these historical 'events' describe a community in transition, a community, though it was only 50 years old, no longer young, one in which it had become necessary to constrain, especially among its younger generation of men and women, traditional expectations and the customary rhythms of life. The transformation took place quickly, but it was not brought about by revolutionary methods. It was brought about by very ordinary people responding to, better still trying to accommodate, the forces promoting change by adapting traditional strategies to the needs of the moment.

Within this climate of change, life went on in mid-Victorian Peel County. Children were born, went through childhood, were educated, took up a vocation, and married; parents raised families, lost partners, found new ones, at length rested from their labours, and finally departed this life with high hopes for their children's future. The record of their individual encounters with these commonplace

events is no less a biographical record than the 'lives and times' of those historical characters whose nobility or notoriety of word, deed, or spirit make them
objects of intellectual curiosity. The difference between them is that in the latter
case character appears to conspire with events to modify the course of history. In
the former, individual experience conforms to 'events,' to the material regulari-
ties of life as they are in time and place, changing when it is necessary to change,
staying the same when it is necessary not to change. Thus, the lives and times of
ordinary people must be written in terms of shared encounters with, and collective responses to, change and continuity in a world of familiar experience,
because in the end it is the commonality, rather than the uniqueness, of individual experience under these circumstances which makes an unremarkable life and
its times one.

Few enough ordinary men and women in nineteenth-century Ontario
thought that their 'voyage through life' was sufficiently remarkable, or typical,
to set down the facts of their experience, however briefly. One who did was John
Brown, a farmer in Caledon Township. He was born in Paisley, Scotland, in
1806. His parents were itinerant weavers, and by the time he started to use the
loom at the age of 10 John Brown had already lived in three different mill towns.
He had acquired a little education as a child, but he was struck by the difference
between his own childhood experience and that of Caledon's children in 1870.
Even the poorest of them were educated 'free of charge.' He, on the other hand,
had been working steadily, doing a man's job, for thirteen years when he left Scotland for America in 1829 at the age of 23. Evidently, the Brown family pooled its
resources to send John 'with a light purse and a heavy heart' to reconnoitre
the new world. His route lay from Greenock to New York, then 'up the
country ... [where] I worked at a great many kinds of labour, and afterwards
came to Canada.' In Toronto, where he again found work, John Brown also met
his future wife, a 'fair daughter of Eve' and a native of Howwood, Scotland, a village in which Brown had once lived. The newly married couple then moved to
Caledon Township in 1831 where they settled on a 100-acre Clergy Reserve and
took up farming. They also started a family which increased, ultimately, to six
sons and five daughters. As well, the Browns raised three orphans. Reflecting
upon his life in his sixty-fifth year, John Brown thought that his personal history
ought to 'cheer up the poor man who is industrious.' Without the help of a 'fat
uncle or aunt,' Brown had amassed a 'modest sum of property.' He took particular
pride in his threshing machine which had cost $350 and earned his son $7 a day and
board at harvest time, and in a 'Yankee invention' — a knitting machine which
made a pair of stockings in half an hour. These new contraptions, together with
his other implements, livestock, orchards, vineyard, and wheatfields scarcely
amounted to a 'Peabody Fortune,' but John Brown was content with his life and
his lot.[24]

Brown's life fell into four distinct stages. His childhood came to an abrupt
halt at least by the age of 10 when he entered the adult world of work. Yet he was

not an adult, remaining his parents' dependent, living in their household until his mid-twenties. When he did leave home, finally, to emigrate to America, the bonds of dependence were not entirely severed in so far as he emigrated as his family's agent. And it is apparent that he spent another two years not only working as other men's servant, but probably sharing their roofs as well. In short, real independence commenced for John Brown only with his marriage at age 25 and his pioneering venture into Caledon's wilderness. This stage of life brought with it geographical and occupational stability, as well as the responsibilities of parenthood, in this case the raising of fourteen children. What seems remarkable is not the size of this family (although it was considerably larger than average) but the duration of the Browns' parental responsibilities. At the age of 64, when most modern parents might confidently expect to be free of those obligations, John Brown still had six children at home, two minors, three unmarried daughters in their twenties or early thirties, and one older son. If the two youngest children also stayed home until their mid-twenties, John Brown, by age 75, would then have spent 50 of his 56 years of adult life (he died at 81) surrounded by his dependents. Put another way, Brown and his wife, Janet, who outlived him, probably spent only the first year and the last five years of their half-century marriage in their own company.

Childhood, youth, parenthood, and, very briefly, 'old age' were the four seasons of John Brown's life. Each had its demands, its expectations, its own rhythms dictated by the circumstances of time, place, and social condition. None conformed in duration or expectation to the stages of life through which we customarily pass. It remains to be seen whether most of John and Janet Brown's peers shared their experiences; and, more importantly, whether their children and grandchildren repeated them.

It is certain that John Brown's babies, with the exception of his youngest son who was born in 1855 and his last daughter born in 1858, had childhood experiences not unlike their father's. They did not, to be sure, become factory hands at ten years of age; but for them as for the majority of their peers in pre-confederation rural Upper Canada, childhood represented merely a brief interlude between infancy and entry into the world of daily labour while they were still very young. Moreover, it is equally certain that even during this period they were being trained to enter the adult's world of work, training which did not necessarily involve formal education. As Susanna Moodie explained, 'children are riches in this country' where labour was both expensive and in short supply.[25] Thus, although formal schooling normally occurred between the ages of 7 and 14, it was unlikely that rural children would 'be left at school beyond the age of ten or twelve,' if they were sent at all.[26] Nevertheless, by mid-century educational reforms designed to equate childhood with an extended period of formal education were already in the wind. Essentially urban and middle class in its orientation and philosophy,[27] this reform movement's objectives were to allay the propensity toward social disorder in Upper Canadian life, and to elevate the moral, intellectual, and economic development of the province, by creating an educational environment from which the young would emerge better disciplined to advance the interests of a no longer primitive society than their parents had been.[28] The visible agent of this movement was Egerton Ryerson, the province's first Chief Superintendent of Common Schools. His first victory was the Common Schools Act of 1846, which created a system of common schools throughout the province. His final achievement was the Comprehensive School Act of 1871, which made elementary education in Ontario free and compulsory.

The experience of children in rural Peel County, 1850-70, reflects the tensions between the traditional and the 'progressive' view of childhood. In July 1859, the Toronto Gore Township Council unanimously rejected the principle of free, tax-supported education and instructed its clerk to have the council's views, the views of 'the majority of the ratepayers of this community,' published in the Toronto *Globe*.[29] This open hostility to a general levy in support of schools clearly illustrates the extent to which the formal education of children was assumed to be a matter of parental discretion in this society. The facts of school attendance in Peel throughout this period, as described in Table 29, support this conclusion, and illustrate the pace of change under the auspices of the school promoters. In 1851, fewer than 45% of the county's school age children attended school at some time during that year. Their attendance was undoubtedly sporadic at best, that is, seasonal; and it would be misleading to assume that the minority who sometimes attended school were any better educated than the majority who did not since school attendance, before the 1890s, was so erratic. But in so far as school attendance differentiates the childhood experience of some children from the experience of others, it is evident that formal education outside the home was not yet a common attribute of childhood here. In this respect, children in Peel were no different than their peers in nearby Hamilton where only 40% of school aged children attended school in 1851.[30] Within the community, however, there were significant variations in attendance ratios from family to family related to two categorical predictors, father's occupation and township of residence, and to a covarying factor, family size.

The largest families always sent a greater proportion of their school aged children to school than did small families. Whether this resulted from a more equitable division of labour within larger families, or from the family's ability to educate its youngest members while older children worked, is not entirely clear. It may also be that parents with the largest families felt obliged to provide an education for those children who could not confidently expect to have their futures secured by their parents. Whatever the case, family size continued throughout the period, even when elementary education became compulsory in law, to determine how many children in fact would be sent to school. So did township of residence. In spite of the dramatic general increase in school attendance in the 1850s

TABLE 29

Comparative number of children in school per 100 school age children, Peel County 1850-70

	1850	1860	1870
Grand mean	44.6	59.6	73.7
Father's occupation			
Farmer	46.7	63.5	75.5
Manufacture of textiles	18.5	50.0	70.1
Manufacture of apparel	35.2	51.0	75.1
Manufacture of wood products	58.4	58.9	68.3
Manufacture of metal products	100.0	78.5	100.0
Manufacture of food products	32.7	76.7	63.7
Manufacture of Misc. articles	33.4		73.6
Construction	41.0	58.9	78.3
Labourer	34.5	58.1	74.5
Commerce	37.6	58.1	74.5
Transportation	49.5	53.6	77.3
Domestic servt	33.4	68.4	62.6
Professional	84.4	27.8	68.9
Education/govt	72.1	73.0	73.5
Father's place of birth			
England	51.0	58.9	74.7
Ireland	42.9	58.7	69.3
Scotland	36.9	61.8	78.1
USA	38.6	67.8	74.5
Upper Canada	33.4	60.6	78.7
Father's religious affiliation			
Church of England	42.8	57.1	72.0
Roman Catholic	44.0	52.6	67.3
Methodist	50.1	64.5	76.2
Dissenting Presb.	50.1	59.5	74.5
Church of Scotland	64.6	66.8	71.0
Family's township of residence			
Albion	42.2	58.4	69.9
Caledon	19.4	53.8	67.3
Chinguacousy	51.0	64.2	76.1
Toronto	55.6	64.2	76.1
Toronto Gore	54.7	62.4	86.4
Significance of family size (covariate)	0.001	0.001	0.001
Significance of each variable (F)			
Occupation	0.001	0.001	0.086
Place of Birth	0.361	0.789	0.028
Religion	0.198	0.055	0.347
Township of res.	0.001	0.002	0.001
R^2	0.156	0.065	0.057
Multiple R	0.395	0.255	0.239

and again in the 1860s, the most remote, last settled, least developed townships — Albion and Caledon — always lagged behind the other three in the proportion of children attending school, although the rate of educational improvements in these townships (because they had the farthest to go) was all the more spectacular. One further reason for the extremely low ratios in Caledon Township in particular is suggested by the marginal significance of religious affiliation as a discriminating factor in 1861. Peel's Roman Catholic population consisted primarily of highland Scots concentrated in Caledon. Given the politics of education in the 1840s and 1850s, politics which militated against the expansion of the infant separate school system,[31] the unwillingness of Roman Catholic parents to send their children to non-sectarian common schools also restrained school enrolments.

Finally, in both decades how the head of household earned hs living was a principal determinant of who went to school. At one extreme professional men, educators, and highly skilled artisans demonstrated the greatest propensity to educate their children, as might be expected of men who had reason to equate formal instruction with either social position or the requirements of skilled trades. At the other end of the scale, tailors, weavers, farm hands, domestic servants, carpenters, and, surprisingly, small businessmen were least inclined to send their children to school in 1850. A decade later, these pronounced differences between the attitudes of the educated and the skilled on one hand and the unskilled on the other still obtained. By 1870 they had substantially disappeared, and indeed the decennial increase, between 1860 and 1870, in the numbers of children sent to school reflects the conversion of unskilled parents to the idea of educating more of their children even before the element of compulsion was introduced in 1871. Still, providing more education for more children was a long way from the principle of keeping all of them in school 200 days a year for eight years. Less than half of the school aged children in Peel in 1870 attended school for more than half the school year. For the majority childhood was still associated with work (Table 30).

Local superintendents were quick to defend their school boards' diligent pursuit of universality in the face of parental 'indifference' and 'carelessness,'[32] and there may have been some substance to their criticism. In mid-Victorian Upper Canada it was assumed that there was no stigma attached to functional illiteracy. Samuel Strickland commented on the election, in a municipality near Peterborough, of two councillors 'one of whom could neither read nor write, whilst the other could write his name, but could not read it after it was written.'[33] Similarly, more than 15% of the men of property whose wills were proved by the Peel County Surrogate Court between 1867 and 1878 could neither read nor write,[34] and few of those who could read had books listed among their inventoried possessions. '[Books] without leisure are practically valueless,' as one farmer's son explained.[35]

TABLE 30

Summary statistics on education, Peel County 1850-70

	1851	1861	1871
Number of common schools	73	75	79
Number of teachers	–	76	–
Number of free schools	–	40	–
Boys as percentage of children at school	59	58	54
Girls as percentage of children at school	41	42	46
Percentage of children at school less than half the year	–	58	58

Sources: Province of Canada, Legislative Assembly, *Journals*, Vol. xi, 1852-3, Appendix jj and Vol. xix, 1861, Sessional Paper 17; Ontario Legislature, *Sessional Papers*, 1871-2, Appendix 3

In spite of parental indifference to the more subliminal arguments for educating their children, there were nevertheless practical reasons for sending children to school, however briefly, by 1870. What seems to be of particular significance is the fact that in Peel, at least, this change of attitude coincided with the land, agricultural, and demographic crises of the 1860s. The disappearance of cheap land nearby, the tendency to concentrate the family's land in the hands of one or two offspring, the prospect of increased competition for employment in some vocation other than farming and in some other place — the city, for example — were all strong arguments in favour of providing more children with at least a modicum of formal education. It is also clear that parents increasingly identified the benefits of a formal education for their children as one of the anticipated rewards of the improving farmer or small capitalist; hence, for example, the growing tendency throughout these two decades to educate girls (Table 30), a matter in which rural families lagged considerably behind their city cousins.[36]

If childhood became associated during these two decades with more formal schooling than preceding generations would have considered to be either necessary or desirable, it nevertheless remained a staging ground for the responsibilities of adulthood in a workaday world. Boys of 15 and 16 were already 'inuring themselves of the hardest manual labour in support of their parents,' work which they had begun to do as seven or eight year olds.[37] Similarly, girls became accustomed early in life to 'perform most cheerfully what would be the duties of a female servant in England,'[38] and by puberty had already served a full domestic apprenticeship. Thus, if not sooner, then certainly by the time they had completed whatever elementary education they were fortunate enough to get, most of these children left the world of childhood far behind them and entered the next phase of their lives. It was a state of semi-dependence in which they worked as adults with adults but remained the charges of their parents or some other master. No single women under the age of 25 and less than two dozen men of the same age were reported to be living alone, or in the company of other young single people, on the 1851, 1861, or 1871 censuses of rural Peel County. How long this stage of dependence lasted, then, was largely dictated by how soon 'youths' and 'maidens' (neither the term 'adolescence' nor its distinctive connotations were recognized before the 1880s)[39] married and began their own households. In the meantime, the vast majority of twelve-year-olds, boys and girls, could look forward to a decade or more of essentially indentured labour.

The long apprenticeship normally took place within their parents' household and involved a direct contribution of manual labour to the family's economy. It was not unusual even for minor children to be placed, as servants, in some other household where their labour contributed small cash incomes to the economy of the family, while their absence represented one less body to be fed and clothed. John Brown's servant in 1871, Daniel Fletcher, was a mere lad of twelve. Throughout these two decades, in fact, one in every twenty rural households in Peel was home to at least one minor who was not a member or relative of the resident family. Moreover, there is evidence that placing minor children with surrogate parents was related not only to the general economic interests of some families, but in particular to their situation in times of stress. Thus, the number of minors farmed out in 1861 represented a dramatic increase (455) over the number in 1851 (240); but by 1871 their number was only 20% greater than it had been two decades earlier. More commonly, older children found employment as servants in neighbouring households. In 1851 and in 1861, two in every seven enumerated households employed a domestic servant (a term which appears to have been used to describe both male and female helpers still in this semi-dependent state, and then reserved for female domestics who had advanced into spinsterhood). Ten years later, the number of households with domestic help had declined to one in twenty-five. It is unlikely that prolonged schooling reduced the pool of youthful labour available. The vast majority of these servants were between the ages of 16 and 26 (in Chinguacousy in 1861 their mean age was 22), well past the age of formal instruction. It seems more probable that the declining availability of land and a rigid occupational structure (see Table 46) conspired in the 1860s to force large numbers of youths to remain dependent on their parents for an extended period of time, and forced many more to emigrate. Thus, in 1851, 65% of the families where the wife was between 50 and 55 years of age still had 'children' over the age of 16 at home. By 1871, four-fifths of the wives in the same age category had dependent older children living in their households (Table 32(d)). Clearly, more of the first-born children of these women remained in the family household longer than the oldest sons and daughters of women who had completed their families at mid-century. Shrinking opportunity, and especially the requirement that some children remain dependent upon their parents if they hoped to inherit land, had the effect over time of prolonging the stage of 'youth,' and delaying the entry into man- and womanhood, of those young people who aspired to remain in the community. For the rest, the open road was the way to autonomy, independence, and a new life in some other place. Young men and women eager to be independent may have found the changing economic circumstances of their times oppressive. But one parent, writing about his children in an earlier age under similar conditions, remarked that the absence of the excessive democracy which 'ruined and contaminated' American families in which 'subordination is trampled upon in its own house' by children who wanted their independence too soon was one of the eternal virtues of the Canadian family.[40]

The age of independence for most young people was the age at which they married and started their own families and households. It has already been noted that the timing of this watershed was not only different for men and women, but varied over time as land became scarcer and employment opportunities fewer (Chapter 3). Thus, for men and women alike age at marriage advanced, on the average, two or three years between 1840 and 1870, prolonging their state of semi-dependence, which was only partially mitigated by the prospect of a similarly prolonged period of formal education. In any event, the timing of marriage and, subsequently, family formation represented a vital, indeed the most vital, decision in the lives of young men and women. Given our ability to decide how many children we will have, the timing of their arrival, and, consequently, the nature of our own adult life cycles, we can scarcely appreciate the importance of the age at which people married in the past. A hundred years ago, and less, age at marriage was the single most important determinant of family size and, hence, of the structure and culture of the family as parents passed from youth through middle age to old age and death. Their experience from first to last can be described simply as variations on a single theme — parenthood. This interminable domesticity may appear, in retrospect, to have been the worst sort of social entrapment. But it must also be remembered that, in these families, form and function were so closely related that John Brown may have counted it an economic blessing, rather than a social inconvenience, to have been the parent of still dependent minor children at an age when modern parents have surrendered those responsibilities. In short, the elementary form of the family, parents and children sharing the same roof, endured almost for the entire span of a marriage and in so doing permitted the family to sustain its essential social and economic functions over the longest possible period of time. Only when those functions became irrelevant, or no longer tenable, did family structure and, more importantly, the determinants of family structure — age at marriage and fertility within marriage — change.

Commencing with the formation of their new family women faced, in the first instance, a prolonged period of childbearing. For those women just beginning this phase of their lives in the late 1840s and early 1850s, the average number of years between first conception and last birth was slightly more than 18, from their twenty-first year until their thirty-ninth year. Later ages at marriage gradually shortened this period by two or three years for the next generation of women, those starting their families in the seventies; and as well there is evidence

TABLE 31

Summary data for marital fertility of women under 24 years starting families in
Peel County 1848-52*

(a) Distribution of cohort by completed family size (percentages)

No children	2-4	5-7	8 or more	Median
13.3	7.7	33.3	45.6	7.1

(b) Childbearing cycle

Mean age first birth, all women	21.1 years
Mean age last birth, all women	38.5 years
Mean age first birth, native-born women	20.5 years
Mean age last birth, native-born women	35.7 years
Mean age first birth, foreign-born women	21.5 years
Mean age last birth, foreign-born women	39.4 years

(c) Distribution of cohort by age at last live birth (percentages)

Under 35	35-7	38-40	40-4
18.5	16.1	23.4	41.9

*Data are derived from family reconstitutions of 161 permanent families in which wives
were aged 20-4 in 1851 and lived to complete their families.

to suggest that, within limits, some forms of artificial constraint on the duration of the childbearing cycle were practised. For example, native-born women tended to bear their last child almost four years earlier than immigrant wives (Table 31), a feat they could not have accomplished without making a deliberate attempt, however crude, to limit the size of their families. Still, the years between family formation and last birth remained a long and taxing ordeal which made young wives 'old women at the age of thirty' as babies appeared, on the average, every thirty months.[41] Consequently the estimated annual live birth rate in the community, 38 per thousand of population in 1860 for example, was nearly double the rate for Ontario a hundred years later, just as the completed families of these women (median = 7) were more than three times the size of modern Canadian families. On the other hand, the childbearing experience of these wives was not very different from that of their American counterparts of the previous century[42] or, for that matter, rural Russian peasant women at the end of the nineteenth century.[43] Age at marriage, health, the onset of menopause, and early death were the only real checks, in this perfectly natural regime, on what Frances Stewart called the 'everlasting nursing business.'[44]

It has been estimated that a Canadian woman reaching the age of 20 in 1871 could expect to live for another 47.3 years.[45] By that standard, a woman starting her family in this community in 1851 could expect to bear children for nearly 40% of her remaining lifespan. She could expect to be in the company of small children (under 10) for more than 60% of that time, to be the mother of still

TABLE 32

Phases of motherhood among Peel County women 1850-70

(a) Percentage of married women bearing children, by age cohort and census year

	15-19	20-4	25-9	30-4	35-9	40-4
1850	32	50	44	45	36	22
1860	46	52	46	42	38	23
1870	53	61	64	61	45	33

(b) Percentage of married women with children under 10, by age cohort and census year

	20-4	25-9	30-4	35-9	40-4	45-9	50-4
1850	79	87	92	89	85	73	43
1860	81	88	91	89	81	68	33
1870	77	86	94	92	85	77	39

(c) Percentage of married women with children 10-16 by age cohort and census year

	30-4	35-9	40-4	45-9	50-4	55-9	60-4
1850	41	74	78	78	61	63	23
1860	37	71	79	76	65	49	17
1870	41	71	80	85	72	51	16

(d) Percentage of married women with children over 16, by age cohort and census year

	35-9	40-4	45-9	50-4	55-9	60-4	65-9	70-4
1850	26	55	73	65	83	75	70	32
1860	26	53	71	74	78	63	54	32
1870	20	56	76	80	82	70	62	40

dependent children (under 16) for 75% of it, and, in the end, never to be wholly free from the obligations of motherhood. Table 32 reveals the successive watersheds of motherhood through which the women of Peel County passed on their voyage through life. The first included childbearing and the rearing of small children and lasted, for the majority of women, from family formation until their late forties (Table 32). Since old age was assumed to begin at 50,[46] by the standards of the time, caring for younger children consumed both youth and middle age. In the meantime, first-born children had matured — some had already left home — and the last arrival might be reared as much by eldest daughters as by the mother herself; hence the enduring pity of popular writers like Susanna Moodie and Julia McNair Wright for these surrogate mothers for whom motherhood began long before they formed their own families.[47] How long these older children remained at home depended, again, on age at marriage if they were females or age of economic independence if they were males. In either case, it is clear that the vast majority of wives in the community were surrounded by still dependent children past their sixty-fifth year. Until their late fifties most had children under the age of sixteen at home and might expect to have older children with them for yet another decade. In fact, in each of the census years 1851, 1861, and 1871 at least 35% of the married women aged 65-9 had more than two older unmarried children still at home. From first birth, then, until all of her children were either independent or of an age to be independent represented, for the typical married woman in this community, a span of at least 45 years. Briefly, between the ages of 45 and 54, she might be surrounded by most of her surviving children; but even before the last-born left home the first-born might already be a grandparent.

'There seems to be no limit to their families,' remarked one gallant who marvelled at the fecundity of Canadian women compared to what he assumed to be the American woman's preference for fewer children.[48] It was scarcely a matter of choice. Janet Brown's daughtes would produce fewer children than their mother had because they married eight or ten yars later than their mother; and even Janet Brown's contemporaries had surmised that prolonged breast-feeding might delay conception.[49] But beyond delayed marriage, continence within marriage, and physiological constraints, natural fertility and its social consequences remained unchanged throughout the nineteenth century; and successive generations of rural women repeated their grandmothers' and mothers' experience of marriage and its seemingly endless procession of children.[50]

One in every five women who married and started a family in the 1850s did not survive this childbearing cycle.[51] Another one of the five was widowed while still the mother of young, dependent children.[52] In other words, only 60% of the women who embarked on marriage and motherhood survived, with their original partners, to enjoy the fruits of their labours — a mature family and, however briefly, the pleasure of each other's company. For those women who outlived their partners, widowhood, as we have already seen, was a calamity the consequences of which clearly troubled even the stoutest hearts. In 1871, 175 of every 1,000 of the ever-married women in Peel were widows. Only 42% of them were mistresses of their own households, although even this represented a significant change from 1861 when nearly 65% of the county's widows were enumerated as dependents of the heads of the households in which they lived. The quality of these women's lives clearly depended on the nature of the contractual arrangements which deceased partners had made with their heirs, and on the strength of sentimental attachments within the family. Few would have suffered the fate of one unfortunate grandmother in Toronto Township who was reported to have died 'like a hog up in the garret' through the indifference of her family.[53] Nevertheless, the predominance of poor and destitute widows among those who relied on the charity of township councils for their survival suggests that widows were the least secure group in the community. Contemporary observers recognized the problem; but they invariably concluded that charity properly ought to begin at home. Thus, Mrs Wright advised her readers, it was no 'great evil,' but rather an opportunity for daughters to develop 'new graces,' when mother 'left her home ... clad in the weeds of widowhood, to dwell among her children, till health and strength left her.'[54]

It is tempting to conclude that the life cycle of these rural women consisted simply of stages of relative dependence, first on their fathers during the years of domestic apprenticeship, then on their husbands during marriage, and finally on their own children at the end of life. It is an even greater temptation to infer that the prolonged subordination was at best undignified, at worst exploitative, and in either case neither particularly enlightened nor modern. But as one historian of the family has suggested, it is equally wrong to ascribe the nineteenth-century rural woman's domesticity to the dictates of an archaic culture as it is to equate it with the 'housewifery' practised by modern women.[55] What these women did in their roles and functions as wives, mothers, and mistresses of their households was quite inseparable, in terms of the economy of the farm family, from the equally specialized functions of other members of the family whose well-being was determined by its collective productivity. Domesticity and motherhood were not preoccupations. They were occupations on which the survival of the family depended in a world made more secure by the strength of its dependent relationships. That is not to say that the subordination of women, in law and in fact, to the 'sterner sex' was not one of life's enduring realities in the nineteenth century. But the fact of subordination was partially, if not wholly, mitigated by environment which cast women in a central role in the farm family's struggle to improve, and endure.

The life cycles of the men of this community cannot readily be hived off into successive stages of domesticity and fatherhood. Yet domesticity, if we understand it to mean home work in support of the household, and fatherhood were the principal themes in the lives of these men from family formation until retirement or death. The vast majority of them were farmers whose place of work was the family homestead, and they laboured at their vocation surrounded and aided principally by their wives and children, occasionally by relatives and servants. Even non-farmers conducted their business or carried on their trades from their places of residence, a setting in which the economic and domestic functions of husbands, wives, or children — different in kind and degree, but not intent — were indistinguishable. The success of familial enterprise depended on the cohesiveness of the domestic group, over a very long period of time, and the commitment of its mutual labour to the common objectives of the family. The life cycles of male householders in the community represent one measure of the duration of that bond of mutual social and economic dependence.

By the standards of the time, John Brown married relatively late in his 'youth.' Men marrying before 1840 in the community were commonly wed by their twenty-fourth year. The fact that Brown had to lease a Clergy Reserve in remote Caledon Township at a time when he could have purchased a partly improved farm for a relatively modest outlay of capital suggests that economic circumstances militated against earlier marriage and independence. Still, John Brown began married life in 1830 as a farmer, albeit a tenant. Thirty years later, his generation, more than three-quarters of whom were farmers, still worked their land. Their sons and grandsons, however, increasingly faced the prospect not only of a prolonged period of celibate dependence, but even after marriage of an interval of several years before they would have land of their own. Table 33 illustrates the extent to which, in the 1850s and 1860s, farming was underrepresented and unskilled day or seasonal labour overrepresented among the vocations of young married men. The average age of farm purchasers in the community 1850-70, about 34, is further evidence of the extent to which marriage and independence were not necessarily synonymous with security; Chapter 5 will describe the degree of geographical and vocational mobility among youthful householders whose young and small families were apparently no hindrance to their peripatetic search for stability, or its fleeting image, in this or some other community.

In effect, men who were not fairly well established by the time they were 35-40 were not likely to make their fortunes and find security here. This plateau coincided with another, the stage at which the great majority of them would no longer labour alone or with the help only of their wives and hired servants. As Table 34 indicates, for at least thirty years, from the householder's fortieth through his seventieth year, most parents could anticipate the rewards which flowed from a large and industrious family. For twenty of those years, fathers were surrounded by sons old enough to work (aged 10-16), that is, old enough to be taught their fathers' skills in preparation for the day when they would bear a man's share of the burden of the family economy. Indeed, for the last quarter of their appointed three score and ten years, fathers worked increasingly in the company of their mature children whose numbers, even among the families of men already advanced in years (aged 60-70), were astonishingly high (Table 34(c)). It is difficult to imagine a society of households in which aged parents not only continue to share the same roof with still dependent children, but share as well common goals, a common domestic economy, and common labour. This was clearly the case among the rural householders of Peel in which the basic structure of the family, that is, parents and children living together, remained unchanged for most, if not all, of the parents' adult lives — allowing, of course, for the inevitable coming and going of some children from time to time. And while the family's structure survived, so too did its ability to sustain its essential function.

TABLE 33

Comparative distribution of age groups by occupational categories 1851-71 (figures are percentages)

	Farmer			Manufacturing			Construction			Unskilled			Commerce			Transportation			Professional		
	1851	1861	1871	1851	1861	1871	1851	1861	1871	1851	1861	1871	1851	1861	1871	1851	1861	1871	1851	1861	1871
All male heads of families	64	61	59	9	8	7	4	4	4	14	17	15	3	3	5	4	3	4	2	2	2
15-34 years	53	53	57	12	9	7	7	5	4	17	22	15	4	4	7	7	4	5	1	2	3
35-49 years	62	59	57	10	9	8	3	4	5	17	17	16	3	4	6	3	3	4	2	2	1
50-65 years	78	71	63	5	6	7	2	3	4	8	12	15	2	2	2	2	2	2	2	2	1
+65 years	84	72	65	3	3	3	1	2	2	5	10	10	0	0	1	0	0	3	3	2	1
Variation is significant at 0.01 or better	yes	yes	no	yes	no	no	no	no	no	yes	yes	no	no	no	yes	yes	no	no	no	no	yes

TABLE 34

Phases of fatherhood among Peel County Men 1850-70

(a) Percentage of households with no children aged 10-16, by age of father

	35-9	40-4	45-9	50-4	55-9	60-4	65-9	70-4
1851	57	36	28	26	35	46	54	75
1861	63	37	25	25	32	46	75	85
1871	59	27	24	21	32	46	75	79

(b) Percentage of households with no children over age 16, by age of father

	40-4	45-9	50-4	55-9	60-4	65-9	70-4	75-9
1851	74	48	31	35	26	26	39	36
1861	75	47	39	33	31	34	48	42
1871	67	39	30	31	26	36	35	45

(c) Percentage of households of men 60-70, by number of mature children at home

No. of children over 16	1851	1861	1871
none	26	32	28
1	21	19	18
2-4	49	40	48
5 or more	4	9	6

It was an axiom which men knew well, and acted upon when structure and function were threatened. In contrast to their own expectations that their widows would not remarry and that a fatherless household nevertheless would endure, as widowers they obeyed the dictum that 'marriage out in the bush is the first duty of life.'[56] Among the permanent male householders of Peel under age 35 in 1852, 20% lost their wives to early death in the next eighteen years. Ninety per cent of these widowers remarried and, moreover, married women who were, on average, nearly a decade younger than the wives they replaced. Among the permanent male householders in the next cohort, that is, aged 35-49 in 1851, again, 20% became widowers in the succeeding two decades. Of these, less than three quarters (12) remarried, of whom only three — the three whose wives died before completing their families — married women young enough to start a second family. It is impossible to know with certainty how many men experienced two or more partnerships: but it is clear enough that among men, family completion was as urgent a priority as family formation.

For that reason, three-fifths of the fathers in the community were over 55 before they ceased to be the parents of very young children. This fact inevitably leads to speculation about the meaning and nature of old age in a society which commonly supposed that men and women were already old at fifty. Among other things, whatever the problems of aging in the nineteenth century might have been for most men and women they could not have involved the prospect of a sudden reversal of customary roles and functions once they had achieved a certain age. Given the structure and function of the farm family, obligations remained the same for sixty-year-old husbands and wives as for forty-year-old parents, and indeed were compounded by the pressing necessity to promote the security of their remaining dependents while time and health permitted. Charlotte Clarkson's observation that her aging parents got the 'rareups' once in a while and that their children's insecurity was the principal source of this agitation underlines the point.[57] It may be useful, in the final analysis, simply to borrow the terminology of the provincial superintendent of education in these matters. In his annual estimates submitted to the legislature he included an item for the support of 'superannuated and worn out' teachers. In this little world of the family, few men planned for superannuation. Most simply wore out.

John Brown's voyage through life was typical of his generation and class, just as his wife's life experience was common to her peers. The lives of their children, and more particularly their grandchildren, if they remained in Peel County, would reflect the beginnings of a transition in the expectations and experience of life in the county. The trend toward institutional rather than familial responsibility for educating children and the tendency to equate childhood with a longer period of formal instruction were well under way by 1870. Delayed marriages for both men and women and, consequently, extended stages of youthful dependence, lower marital fertility, and smaller families were forerunners at midcentury of a much greater, permanent transition that would take place thirty years later. These were significant developments; but in broadest outline, life from the cradle to the grave remained for both sexes very much the same throughout the nineteenth century. It could not have been otherwise while the family and its time-tested strategies for survival remained the essential instrument of social and economic security.

5 The Promise of Canadian Life

One of those strategies, perhaps the most common and, therefore, the most important, was the perpetual motion of these nineteenth-century families. Wherever the historian of nineteenth-century North American society looks he finds evidence of internal migration, seasonally, annually, decennially, on an astonishingly massive scale. For example, in a typical rural community in Michigan less than 15% of the proprietors of land in 1830 still owned property in the community thirty years later. Similarly, in Trempleau County, Wisconsin, fewer than 40% of the farmers enumerated in one mid-century census return persisted until the next decennial 'numbering of the people.' Neighbouring Iowa experienced, as did Kansas, equally high decennial rates of emigration among its farm families. Nor was this phenomenon limited to rural populations. Boston, Philadelphia, and, much closer to Peel County, the city of Hamilton also lost from 40% to 60% of their adult male population through outmigration in any decade and gained an equal or larger number of new residents.[1] Peel County was no exception. Sixty per cent of the adult (male and female) heads of families enumerated in the 1851-2 census of Peel left before 1861. In the next decade only a third of the heads of families present in 1861 persisted until the enumeration of 1871. In all nearly 10,000 different families were counted on the 1851, 1861, and 1871 census returns for Peel: after generous correction for mortality and underenumeration it is safe to conclude that less than 10% of them were perennial residents of the community. Seventy per cent appeared on only one return, one-fifth on two enumerations.

Put another way, the population of Peel County in 1861 can be viewed, at the most elementary level of analysis, in terms of two distinct groups of families. One group, about 25% of the families present in 1861, had roots deeply set in the soil of their respective townships. They represented the county's past and its future. The second group, three-quarters of the population in 1861, represented present realities. For them, Peel was simply one of a succession of way stations along the road from someplace to somewhere. That, at least, is what this place was to them from the historian's perspective. How *they* perceived their purpose in migrating to and subsequently abandoning Peel after one, five, or a dozen years' residence is quite another matter, one which has much to do with the promise of life in mid-Victorian Canada West, social betterment. They came to Peel in search of vocational and social mobility defined in terms of occupying land, acquiring property, and emulating the material success of Peel's most established farmers. Few enough achieved their goal, at least in part because these migrants failed to comprehend the fundamental irony of Canadian life. They were taught to equate moving on with moving up. Yet the race was invariably won by those who stayed put.

Like most of the adult population of mid-Victorian Peel, John Brown was an emigrant from the British Isles. He could recall vividly how, in Scotland, he had stood *'hat in hand*, half begging for work ... at the warehouse doors of some upstart manufacturer, with his thread-bare black coat, and possibly not having one dollar to call his own,' always at the mercy of some 'stuck-up foreman' intent on finding fault with the cloth Brown had woven. Leaving this 'house of bondage' for the backwoods of Canada, he argued, had secured for him the 'rights of men' — independence, security, respectability, and social betterment — which were unattainable by the weavers who continued to 'yoke the loom at Kilbarchan.' Brown did not profess to be rich by British standards. He could not vie with Lord Bute or the Duke of Westminster (two of Britain's wealthiest landowners) in terms of the income he derived from his little estate in Caledon. But he professed to be the equal of any of the 'London nobs' in respect to the independence he derived from his land. Canada, in Brown's opinion, was a 'good poor man's country,' just the place for 'working men ... [who] ... know their rights as men' and who desired to follow his example of social improvement.[2]

In nearby Albion Township, not far from John Brown's farm, John Colley in 1871 worked 300 acres and raised purebred livestock with the assistance of a family of Irish farm servants. Colley had been a farm labourer himself in southern England during the years when rural labourers openly rebelled in defence of their traditional way of life which had been threatened, in the 1820s and 1830s, by the introduction of new farming techniques, by reductions in farm wages and employment, and by the imposition of legal restrictions on their mobility in search of agricultural employment.[3] Colley left England in 1834, arrived in Upper Canada with £1 in his pocket, and worked for ten years at a variety of menial jobs — cellar digger, woodchopper, farm servant — until he had saved enough money to put a down payment on a mill which he eventually 'parlayed' into an estate worth, by his own estimate, $20,000. His religion, Colley said, was and 'always had been, work' and he thought that his own rise from humble beginnings to a state of affluence was evidence enough that in Ontario individual betterment was simply the product of right attitudes.[4]

James Reid sold his farm in Toronto Gore Township and retired to his native Scotland in the 1860s after more than four decades in Canada West. Reid gloated over the fact that, having left Britain in abject poverty when his laird drove him off the bit of land he had farmed, he was returning to Scotland with enough money to purchase a substantial estate and retire comfortably leaving four sons and a daughter in Ontario, each with an improved farm.[5] His friends in Scotland, he was fond of reminding them, had been 'living on the husks and selling the kernel' while their neighbours who had emigrated to America had enjoyed prosperity unknown in Scotland since 'the time of Buonaparte's wars.' 'I am truly soory [sic] so few of you leaves [sic] home,' Reid wrote to his brother in Ayrshire in 1847, 'you might soon have a farm as well as me.'[6]

These 'success' stories from Peel County contain all the elements common to the published pioneer reminiscences, emigration tracts, and traveller's accounts which constitute one of the richest veins of Ontario's literary history. They deal, among other things, with the motivation of emigrants who left the British Isles, 'an act of severe duty,' according to Susanna Moodie,[7] but nevertheless a necessary response, for some classes at least, to the adverse conditions of life in post-Napoleonic Britain. Between 1830 and 1870, it has been estimated, nearly one-third of Britain's population lived in 'painful poverty' and half of these were in fact destitute.[8] The debasement of formerly skilled or semi-skilled trades by technological change and the growth of the unskilled labour force created chronic underemployment in England's industrial towns and cities, which became the forcing houses of the nation where the skilled and the unskilled scrambled to survive in a wage-dependent world of social and economic insecurity. Among the labouring classes, men like John Brown, perhaps 15% might have anticipated social betterment depending on the value which the economy placed on certain skills.[9] In the countryside, the effect of the enclosure movement of the late eighteenth century was to concentrate nearly three-fifths of England's rural land in the hands of 4,000 great landholders and another 25% in the estates of the yeomanry.[10] Consequently, the small landowner had virtually disappeared in mid-Victorian Britain. Less than one-fifth of its 300,000 farmers were owner-occupiers.[11] They provided work by the day and wages subsidized from parish poor rates for a million and a half agricultural labourers condemned, through massive underemployment in an underdeveloped rural economy, to a 'brute subsistence level' of existence.[12] It was an existence which they shared with Scottish crofters like James Reid, with Ireland's burgeoning peasant population who eked out a primitive existence on less than an acre of land per family, and her million and a half impoverished non-farm labourers.[13] They became the lowest, cheapest, and most ubiquitous drays harnessed to English industry, and then the denizens of the cholera-infested timber ships which dumped their human ballast on the shores of North America in the 1830s.

All this is familiar ground, which nevertheless bears repetition because it was precisely this social landscape of which men like Colley, Reid, and Brown had first-hand experience. That is not to say that every Irish, Scots, or English emigrant to Upper Canada had experienced a close encounter with the material condition of England's working poor, Scotland's impoverished crofters and artisans, or Ireland's starving peasantry. Many emigrants were small capitalists, skilled artisans, or men of property who left Britain unscathed by the forces of change. But it is clear that they shared a common motivation. They represented Britain's 'uneasy classes'[14] who were prepared 'to do violence to all of those traditional affections, loyalties and attachments upon which the mid-Victorian ... set peculiar binding value,'[15] in order to escape either the threat or the reality of economic and social adversity. Consequently, they couched their autobiographies and advice to intending emigrants in phrases familiar to 'the poor ... struggling against becoming poorer,' to the labourers destined to be 'born and [to] die in their own parishes,' to those 'afraid of the workhouse' and of 'rent ... rates, tithes and taxes,' and to men simply fearful that their children would suffer even if they had not.[16]

Given the material circumstances which they hoped to evade through emigration, Upper Canada's immigrant population in their private and public correspondence necessarily measured success in terms of the social distance which separated them from their British cousins. 'Place the honest and industrious peasant in Canada, and, no matter how ignorant he may be ... he will in a short time better his situation in life, and most likely become the possessor of a freehold ... and consequently a cleverer and a more enlightened person, than he was before in his hopeless servitude.'[17] The right to work, to accumulate capital which might be converted to land, to profit from both the productive capabilities and the speculative potential of cheap and abundant land, and, in the end, to achieve economic independence, social respectability, and perhaps even cultural refinement 'in contrast to a whole life of labour and poverty'[18] represented not only the promise of Canadian life but the plain facts of the Canadian experience of emigrants like Brown, Colley, Reid, the Moodies, the Stricklands, and a hundred other publicists. They were the proof that in Canada where the virtues of industry, thrift, domesticity, and temperance were uncompromised by arbitrary restraints on the making of livings the British emigrant had 'taken upon himself a new existence.'[19]

As valuable and as perceptive as these personal observations may be, they tell us very little about the rate or the process of social betterment in nineteenth-century Canadian society. Colley, Brown, and Reid are cases in point. How typical was their experience? How many of their neighbours in Peel shared their characteristics? After half a century of social and economic development, how far had the people of this rural society progressed from the material circumstances of a crude, pioneer existence toward the emigrant's ideal of improvement measured in terms of the promise of Canadian life? What yardsticks of social improvement or, conversely, of the lack of improvement or of the inability to achieve a 'new existence' will best reveal the processes of social betterment and the relative condition of the least and the most improved elements in society? Finally, to what extent did the pursuit of an ideal condition the attitudes and the behaviour of a society steeped in its promise?

Historians, geographers, sociologists, and economists have employed several indicators of the social distance between groups of individuals in past time. For example, in Peel County at mid-century inequality in property ownership was ostensibly the line of demarcation between improved and unimproved families just as it was in the Canadian city.[20] In Peel less than half of the county's householders were freeholders in 1850 and in 1860. By 1870 slightly more than two-thirds were freeholders. But in every decade property ownership was strongly associated only with farmers whose historical level of ownership, about 70%, was fairly constant from 1850 onwards. Among non-farming householders the proportion of freeholders was much lower, less than 30% in 1850 and 1860 climbing to about 50% in 1870. In short, Peel replicated the situation in mid-Victorian rural Britain, where access to land was the great divide between the yeomanry and those below them in social and economic status, just as the amount of land owned or occupied distinguished the most aggressive from the least secure freeholders (see Table 37 below, and Chapter 3).[21] Similarly, in the United States of America in the middle of the nineteenth century, approximately two-fifths of the adult (free) male population were property owners, a statistic that remained constant from 1850 until 1870. The conclusion of the most recent investigation of American society is that, within the context of a society in which 'the have-nots substantially outnumbered the haves,' the young and the foreign-born were least likely to have been numbered among the haves.[22] In short, whatever other indices of social betterment are to be employed, the ownership of property is one of the most suitable measures of economic and social distinction if our purpose is both to understand degrees of improvement among the people of Peel and to compare their situation, historically, with other societies in which real property was, apparently, the lowest common denominator of betterment, permanence, and social standing.

It was not, however, the only recognizable attribute of social betterment. The quality of individual existence was also reflected in, and symbolized by, living conditions, another important indicator of social mobility. The man who successfully progressed from the pioneer's usual accommodations, a pole shanty, mud hovel, or log cabin, to a frame, stone, or brick house constructed by a skilled craftsman had demonstrably outdistanced his poorer neighbour who continued to inhabit accommodations to which he had long since consigned his livestock or poultry.[23] By the same token, the manor was far more likely than the shanty to house an assortment of relatives, visitors, lodgers, orphaned children, and resident hired help in addition to the householder's family. Household structure, in effect, has been shown to have been a surrogate for social status in other nineteenth-century societies in which a large domestic establishment was commonly associated with social improvement.[24] Within this context, the employment and maintenance of domestic servants in particular appears to have been an essential line of demarcation between the lower and the middle classes in mid-Victorian Britain and in Upper Canada.[25] Upper Canadians were dismayed by the shocking independence of their household servants;[26] but in Canada as in England the complexities of master-servant relationships (servants are not 'admitted to our tables, or placed on an equality with us, excepting at "bees" ')[27] appeared to elevate the employer of domestics above the farmer who ate with his field hands and shared their labour.

These four basic measurements of social betterment — property ownership, improved housing, household structure, and the employment of domestic servants — do not exhaust the list of variables which might be potentially useful in an analysis of relative degrees of improvement. They do represent, however, the most appropriate indicators for mid-Victorian Peel. Few assessment rolls survive for the period, although it is tantalizing to speculate about their contents on the basis of published aggregates of assessed wealth. In 1867, when only incomes of $400 or more were calculated into total assessed value, in each of Peel's five townships the assessed value of real property accounted for more than 90% (average 93%) of total assessed value, and average taxable income per individual assessment was $3.[28] In short, it is clear that only a handful of Peel's householders had cash incomes beyond what could be earned by a railway 'navvy' fully employed at the going rate of $1 a day. But these data also tend to reinforce an overall impression of a society in which real property represented real wealth. Neverthless, there were men who styled themselves 'gentleman,' 'esquire,' and 'squire' as symbols of social standing derived from secure incomes, a practice which left contemporary observers unconvinced of their real worth.[29] Indeed, the editor of the Streetsville *Weekly Review* found the misappropriation of styles of gentility so confusing that he begged his readers who indulged in this 'worse than childish' preoccupation to cease and desist.[30] Suffice it to say that Peel County data will not support the correlation of real and presumed affluence, confirming Mr Barnhart's assumption that the unemployed, the retired, and the mischievous were as likely to appropriate these airs as those who truly conformed to their connotations.

Table 35 provides the relative proportions of the families of Peel County who, in 1861, possessed none, some, or all of the four attributes of social betterment described above. Two immediate generalizations arise out of this distribution.

TABLE 35

Distribution of Peel County families by number and type of attributes of social betterment 1861

Four attributes	($N = 136 = 3.7\%$)	One attribute	($N = 1264 = 34.6\%$)
		property	(491)
Three attributes	($N = 486 = 13.2\%$)	Housing	(456)
P—IH—HHS	(291)	HH structure	(277)
P—IH—S	(52)	Servant(s)	(40)
P—HHS—S	(60)		
IH—HHS—S	(77)		
Two attributes	($N = 1,064 = 29.2\%$)	No attributes	($N = 701 = 19.2\%$)
P—IH	(345)		
P—HHS	(281)		
P—S	(53)		
IH—HHS	(300)		
IH—S	(39)		
HHS—S	(46)		

Legend: P, proprietor; IH, improved housing; HHS, resident 'Extras'; S, Domestic servants

The first, and perhaps most important, is that roughly one-fifth of the family units possessed no attributes of material improvement and may be said to have been, for whatever reason, demonstrably disadvantaged in relation to all other socio-economic groups in the county. It is interesting to note in passing, moreover, that one hundred years later approximately the same proportion of the Canadian population lived at or below the poverty level.[31] The second obvious point about Table 33 is that fewer than one in twenty families possessed all the attributes of betterment employed here and, like their vastly poorer neighbours at the other end of the scale, would have been immediately recognizable to even the most casual observer. Yet Table 35 raises more questions than it answers because the remaining categories shed no light on the real distinctions, if there were any at all, among those families who possessed one or more of these symbols of improvement. Therefore, Table 36 sets out the actual distribution of attributes of betterment within each category of improvement and reports the results of a test designed to rank order these attributes according to their relative power in explaining the differences among families with one or more signs of improvement.

As Table 36 indicates, among the least improved (but nevertheless improving) families in Peel in 1861 (those with just one attribute of social betterment) the ownership of property and living in improved accommodations were, more or less equally, the most common visible signs of improvement. Fewer than one in twenty-five employed servants to the exclusion of all other vestiges of improvement, while about one in five maintained complex domestic households. At the other end of the scale it was precisely household complexity which seems to have distinguished the most improved families from those below them on the ladder

TABLE 36

Distribution of attributes of improvement by number of acquired attributes, and test of association

(a) Percentage distribution and correlation of attributes of improvement by number of attributes acquired by 1861* (coefficient of correlation, r, in parentheses)

	No. of attributes				
	0	1	2	3	4
Property owner*	–	38.8 (–0.34)	63.8 (0.09)	84.0 (0.23)	100.0
With improved Housing	–	36.0 (–0.38)	64.8 (0.10)	87.7 (0.27)	100.0
With resident 'Extras'	–	21.9 (–0.49)	58.9 (0.13)	89.3 (0.35)	100.0
With domestic servants	–	3.2 (–0.32)	12.9 (–0.08)	38.9 (0.26)	100.0

(b) Strength of association (r) between individual attributes of improvement and total number of attributes acquired by 1861

	1-4 attributes	1-3 attributes
'Extras' in household	0.53	0.51
Employs domestics	0.53	0.36
Improved housing	0.42	0.39
Owns property	0.38	0.34

*In both computations the dependent variable is dichotomous and interval.
Note: all coefficients are significant at 0.01.

of improvement. This is nicely borne out by Table 36(b), which reports the magnitude of the correlation (r) between the total number of attributes possessed and the fact of having any particular indicator of betterment. Among all of Peel's families with one or more of the four indices of improvement, household complexity measured equally in terms of employing domestic servants and maintaining non-domestic 'extras' distinguishes the most from the least improved households. Among still improving families (those with 1 to 3 attributes of improvement) the presence of extras alone segregates those further along the road of improvement from families just commencing the journey. Conversely, in both instances property ownership appears to have been the lowest common denominator of improvement, perhaps even the prior condition on which the accumulation of other material attributes of betterment depended.

To test these impressions we can ask what the chances were of having some or all of these symbols of social improvement given the acquisition of any particular one of them. Table 37 considers this relationship. The presence of domestic servants in households greatly increased the probability that families would exhibit all of the other attributes of betterment and that, in any event, they would not have fewer than two of the remaining three indicators of improvement. In

TABLE 37

Relative importance of individual material attributes as predictors of degrees of social improvement 1861

	If one had:				
	Property	Extras	Housing	Servants	
Chances (%) of having:					
(a) all other attributes =	9	9	9	20	5% = 4
(b) two other attributes =	27	30	28	32	16% = 3
(c) one other attribute =	42	44	42	25	36% = 2
(d) no other attribute =	22	16	21	18	43% = 1*

*Compared with the proportion of the improving population who had this many attributes

short, no other indicator serves so well to distinguish the most from the least improved of the improving families as the social structures of their respective households. This seems not only to confirm contemporary wisdom but suggests as well that in this corner of rural Canada West, as in other Victorian societies, the presence in households of those who worked 'below stairs' was indeed a crucial hallmark of material comfort. On the other hand the presence of non-domestic resident extras in the household was scarcely more likely than either property ownership or improved housing to distinguish among families with two or three, though not all, of the four indicators of improvement. However, the fact of having a complex, rather than a simple, household was associated with a greater degree of improvement than were property ownership and improved accommodations. Property ownership served best to identify improving families with just one attribute of social betterment. Table 38 puts these generalizations into somewhat bolder relief by assessing the probability of householders possessing specific attributes of improvement when each indicator is considered, in turn, as the principal determinant of what other attributes he might have acquired. Again, household structure seems to be a much better measure of how far a family had progressed than any of the other indicators. Property ownership and housing contribute less to the explanation of variations in the proportion of householders possessing particular attributes of material improvement than does either the employment of servants or the presence of extras.

In sum, such evidence as is available suggests that, in terms of the material condition of the families of rural Peel, property ownership, by itself, merely represented the potential for social betterment. Domestic servants and, to a lesser extent, complex domestic establishments were testimonials to the fact of improvement. Improved housing, albeit a visible manifestation of apparent prosperity, did not necessarily distinguish the most from the least 'comfortable' classes. All this seems to be a matter of common sense and consistent with the assumption of progressive stages of improvement among the families of Peel,

TABLE 38

Probability (%) of possessing various attributes of improvement given the possession of a particular attribute

	If one had:				
	Property	Extras	Servants	Housing	
Chances (%) of having:					
property		51.0	58.0	58.0	47.0
extras	44.0		61.0	46.0	40.0
servants	17.0	21.0		17.0	14.0
housing	48.0	54.0	54.0		47.0*

Order of importance (beta) of individual attributes as determinants of probability of having a specific attribute†

	Probability of having:			
	Property	Extras	Servants	Improved housing
Is explained by	servants	servants	extras	extras
other attributes in	0.09	0.17	0.17	0.12
this order of	extras	housing	housing	servants
importance	0.07	0.12	0.08	0.09
	(housing)	property	property	(property)
	0.01	0.07	0.08	0.01
R^2	0.02	0.05	0.05	0.03

* Compared with the actual proportion of the improving population with any attribute
† Predictors in parentheses are not significant factors in the explanation of variation.

stages of improvement associated first with the making of livings from the land or in some non-farm vocation, with the relative labour requirements of improving and improved families, with the disposition of surplus income from that labour, and, finally, with standards of living (or perhaps social status) associated with relative degrees of success in these matters. Thus, what is ultimately important here is not which, or how many, of these indicators of material improvement particular families acquired, but rather how far they had progressed and what factors regulated both the potential for betterment and the rate of improvement among the families of Peel County.

Toward this end it seems necessary, using the results of this preliminary analysis as a guide to the identification of appropriate stages of improvement, to refine further the categories of betterment which appear to have segregated the families of Peel into several distinct cohorts. The improvement cohorts I have created are clearly arguable if only because, in attempting to group together families at similar stages of improvement (or disimprovement as the case may be), I have been rather arbitrary in applying the criteria which define apparent similarities and dissimilarities in the material condition of families. For example, families with all four attributes of betterment must be classified as the most improved cohort. But they cannot be easily separated from those other families who owned property, lived in improved accommodations, and maintained *either* domestic servants *or* non-domestic resident extras. The census returns reveal little enough about the function of resident extras, although the correlations in Table 38 suggest that the distinction between servants and non-domestic extras was important. On balance, however, it seems prudent to allow this distinction to remain blurred and to conclude that about one in eight (13%) of the families of Peel in 1861 were 'improved.'

A second group of families can be characterized as having (a) property *and* improved housing, but no other attribute of betterment; *or* (b) either property or improved housing, though not both, and at least one other indicator of material improvement; *or* (c) much-improved housing, but no other sign of improvement. Among the families in cohort (b) the most common additional attribute was the presence in their households of resident extras. In any event, what is important here is the identification of a group of clearly improving families who enjoyed more or less common material circumstances although the sources of their improvement were diverse. For some, betterment was associated with property ownership. An equally large number of families who were not freeholders, perhaps because their domestic economies were not dependent on property ownership, nevertheless shared the other attributes of improving freeholders. They may have been substantial tenant farmers whose lifestyle was in fact preferable to that of the small freeholder's family crammed into a log cabin with their hired help and servants. Whatever the case may be, it seems useful to envisage the existence of two subgroups of these improving families: (1) improving freeholders who constituted 20% of Peel's householders in 1861, and (2) improving tenants who represented 25% of the 1861 householders. (It seems necessary to include among the 'improving tenants' families with improved housing but without other attributes of improvement. This is because it is possible to envisage equally prosperous tenant farmers and skilled artisans who did not own property but who enjoyed the amenities associated with their relatively higher standards of living.)

Finally, it is possible to consign the remaining families to a single group whose common characteristic was that they had not passed beyond the pioneer stage of existence. The group includes those with no material advantages as well as those with only one, excluding families with improved housing but including freeholders. This conclusion is clearly contentious, but in a mature community which had, in 1861, one of the most highly developed wheat economies in the most developed region of Canada West, families who retained all the characteristics of 'the backwoods life,' whether tenants or freeholders, cannot be equated with those who have moved beyond the primitive amenities of a pioneer society. In short, after all is said and done one must resort to the historian's usual stock-in-trade, subjective judgments; hence the size and composition of this last group of families, those in the pioneer stage comprising 41% of the families of Peel in 1861.

Assuming that these four groups of families represent degrees of betterment that would have had some meaning in mid-Victorian rural Canada West, it is important to ask who populated each of these ranks of improvement? Among other things, if these stages of improvement are even remotely plausible approximations of historical reality they should serve to identify distinct socio-economic groups within the community, groups whose vocational, demographic, or perhaps even cultural characteristics explain their comparative rate of social improvement. Table 39 accomplishes this by comparing the propensity of specific vocational, ethnic, religious, and demographic cohorts to belong to one or another of the four categories of improvement with the tendency of the total population toward that category. It is important to note first, however, that the variables used to explain the membership of each level of betterment are not equally important (see test of significance in which an F of 0.01 indicates a significant explanatory variable). Age is useful only in explaining who the most improved householders were. Vocational classification plays a significant role in explaining membership in each of the ranks. Place of birth and religious affiliation distinguish only the least and the most improved householders. Moreover, with the exception of the 'improving tenant' category, the combined power of all the variables in accounting for variation in the membership of any group is relatively weak (R^2). This suggests that either the categories have not been drawn sharply enough or, preferably, that this rural society was much more fluid than its urban counterparts. This is a theme to which I shall return in due course.

Vocation, religious affiliation, and place of birth, in that order, identify those householders most and least likely to have led a backwoods existence in 1861. Among these variables, vocation was the most important factor, and a cursory review of the mean (%) representation in the pioneer level by vocational classification reveals that the source of this variation is the considerable overrepresentation of the least skilled householders in this group. Unskilled labourers, householders with no definite occupations, and John Brown's friends in the cloth industry — weavers, dyers, carders, and woolpickers — were the least improved vocational groups in this community. Clearly this has something to do with the rewards associated with their labour compared, for example, with those for the next highest level of skills, tailors (apparel), artisans who produced luxury goods, brewers and butchers (foodstuffs), chairmakers, and carpenters. But the least improved families might also include farm families who were more or less equally represented at this level of improvement. Whether we should interpret these farming, unskilled, and semi-skilled householders as a class of 'rural poor' is open to question. But as the data for religious affiliation and place of birth suggest, the most recent immigrants, Irish Catholics, and Ulstermen were also considerably overrepresented among the least improved families. As

TABLE 39

What individual characteristics differentiate among householders with different levels of betterment?

	Pioneer stage	Improving tenant	Improving freeholder	Improved
Percentage of all families	40	24	22	14
Percentage by vocational category				
farmers	39	14	29	18
Manufacturers				
textiles	49	41	3	7
apparel	28	53	12	9
wood products	26	72	1	0
metal wares	28	58	0	13
foodstuffs	22	48	8	22
luxury goods	0	97	1	2
misc. goods	21	56	1	20
construction	27	56	9	8
labour	58	29	0	4
commerce	6	61	17	16
transportation	29	55	9	7
domestic service	98	2	0	0
professional	25	59	11	5
education/govt	31	44	14	11
not given	50	28	5	17
Percentage by age cohort				
15-34	43	25	21	11
35-49	40	24	23	13
50-64	39	23	21	17
65+	33	21	26	20
Percentage by ethnic group				
English-born	34	30	21	17
Irish	45	20	23	11
Scots	42	21	21	12
American	34	34	20	14
Upper Canadian	35	26	22	18
Other BNA province	44	42	26	0
Percentage by religious affiliation				
Church of England	41	24	22	13
Roman Catholic	51	25	17	8
Wesleyan Methodist	34	24	24	18
Episc. Methodist	31	28	22	19
United Presbyterian	43	20	23	14
Free Kirk of Scotland	34	24	25	17
Baptist	39	26	20	14
Congregationalist	31	41	19	9
Church of Scotland	50	21	20	8

Test of significance for independent variables (F statistic) and beta ranks (in parentheses)

	F	F	F	F
Age cohort	not sig. (0.05)	not sig. (0.03)	not sig. (0.04)	0.01 (0.08)
Vocation	0.01 (0.23)	0.01 (0.38)	0.01 (0.24)	0.01 (0.17)
Place of birth	0.01 (0.10)	not sig. (0.06)	not sig. (0.02)	0.01 (0.09)
Religion	0.01 (0.12)	not sig. (0.06)	not sig. (0.02)	0.01 (0.11)
R^2	0.095	0.161	0.067	0.067
Multiple R	0.308	0.402	0.260	0.260

the last wave of emigrants to be absorbed into the local economy the apparent quality of their lives, and perhaps even their poverty, is hardly remarkable.

At the other end of the scale of betterment, all the variables contribute, in some way, to an explanation of membership in the group. With the exception of vocation, however, these variables convey a single impression. Men and women above the age of 50 were much more likely to have acquired all of the attributes of improvement than young or middle-aged people. In short, then as now, time was on the side of social mobility. With the passage of each year from family formation until retirement gradual improvements in material condition, if not inevitable, were at least foreseeable. This conclusion is reinforced by the behaviour of the ethnicity and religious affiliation variables which suggest that the earliest wave of emigrants (the English Protestants) and second- or third-generation Canadians were the most improved elements in society. It is nevertheless certain that improvement was dependent on other attributes, principally vocation. As we shall see, what a man called himself, or what he did for a living, explains very little about his goals and aspirations. It is true, nevertheless, that a man's chosen method of making a living is a fairly reliable, perhaps the most historically reliable, time-specific indicator of his status.[32] In mid-Victorian Peel farmers, country merchants, millers (manufacturers of foodstuffs), a few implement manufacturers, and even some of the self-styled squirearchy were most likely to have acquired all the material attributes associated with a lifetime of labour.

The two middle stages of betterment are more problemmatical because they are artifacts of the research design: all that separates them is the ownership of property. Consequently, farmers are overrepresented among the improving freeholders and underrepresented among the improving tenants. Conversely, skilled artisans, professionals, small businessmen, and men engaged in the county's vital transportation industry, in short men for whom land was not essential to the making of livings, are to be found among the improving tenants. It is not unimportant, however, to hypothesize that some vocational groups in this society may have attached less significance to property ownership than to certain other comforts, good housing and servants for example. It may have been desirable for them to have had liquid capital assets if they perceived geographical mobility as their most valuable economic advantage. Nor should we ignore the fact that nearly one in three unskilled labourers and the vast majority of the semi-skilled and skilled artisans in the community possessed at least two of the attributes of social betterment in spite of the fact that they were propertyless. And with the exception of domestic servants men from every vocational category are represented, to a greater or lesser degree, in those levels of social betterment for which property ownership was a necessary prerequisite. In sum, mid-Victorian Peel County does appear to have been a much more open society than, for example, urban Hamilton, whose structural rigidity condemned more than half the population to social and economic immobility.[33]

TABLE 40

Distribution of heads of family by vocational category (percentages)

	1851	1861	1871
Agriculture	64	59	62
Manufacturing of textiles	2.0	1.5	1.4
Manufacturing of apparel	3.8	3.2	2.3
Manufacturing of wood products	1.9	1.8	1.7
Manufacturing of food products	1.0	1.2	1.0
Manufacturing of metal products	0.1	0.4	0.1
Manufacturing of luxury goods	0.0	0.0	0.0
Manufacturing of miscellaneous products	0.3	0.1	0.2
Construction	3.5	3.1	3.3
Unskilled labour	11.4	15.3	10.3
Commerce	2.9	3.3	3.6
Transportation	2.6	2.8	3.1
Domestic service	0.2	0.1	0.9
Professional	0.8	0.9	1.0
Government/education	1.2	0.7	0.8
Others	4.6	5.8	7.9

Social mobility clearly was possible for the families and individuals who migrated to Peel in the middle of the nineteenth century. It was, however, a very slow process with unequal effects.

Economic opportunity in mid-century Peel took two forms, essentially, farming and the provision of goods and services to the farming population. There were not, however, unlimited opportunities for the making of livings here even in the mid-fifties when Peel's population was expanding. Table 40 shows the decennial distribution of male householders among the various functional categories of vocations. With the single exception of unskilled labourers, demand for whom varied from decade to decade and, no doubt, from season to season, the percentage of the independent male population in any vocational category remained remarkably constant from one decade to the next. In other words, there were real limits to the ability of this local economy to absorb population, limits fixed not only by the availability of land but as well by the relative constancy of demand for particular goods and services. Even the percentage of householders engaged in farming remained fairly constant although the distribution of land among them changed significantly just as the proportion of owner-occupiers among both the farm and non-farm population changed, for the better, in the two decades after 1850. All of this argues strongly for the conclusion that non-farm employment opportunities had less to do with the expansion of trade and the numbers of persons required to provide goods and services in the rural areas than with the displacement or replacement of population. In short, outmigration accounted for most employment opportunities encountered by immigrants. It is true that some outmoded occupations occasionally disappeared from the county (potter and basketweaver for example) and that new

TABLE 41

Changes in occupational rank among householders, Peel County 1850-70

(a) Rate of change in occupational rank among persistent householders 1850-70

	1852-60	1860-70	Total
Changed rank (%)	22.8	12.2	19.8
No change (%)	77.2	87.8	80.2
N	(1,262)	(1,445)	(2,707)
$\chi^2 = 13.4976$ DF $= 1$ Sig. $= 0.01$			

(b) Direction of occupational and geographical mobility among farm and non-farm householders 1850-70

	1851 pop'n			1861 pop'n		
	Farm	Non-farm	All	Farm	Non-farm	All
Persisted next 10 years as farmers	48.1	6.3	29.3	36.2	5.8	21.4
(N)	(924)	(97)		(862)	(131)	
Persisted as non-farmers (%)	5.2	11.8	8.2	3.4	14.5	8.8
(N)	(100)	(184)		(80)	(328)	
Emigrated (%)	46.7	81.9	62.5	60.4	79.7	69.8
(N)	(897)	(1,278)		(1,438)	(1,800)	
Total (%)	100.0	100.0	100.0	100.0	100.0	100.0
(N)	(1,921)	(1,559)		(2,380)	(2,259)	
		$\chi^2 = 732.043$, DF $= 2$, Sig. $= 0.01$		$\chi^2 = 726.986$, DF $= 2$, Sig. $= 0.01$		

tastes or technology provided opportunities for people with skills formerly unrepresented in Peel, for example marble workers (in the tombstone business, one assumes) and melodeon makers. But the typical migrant to mid-century Peel, if he did not have capital or access to credit with which to purchase land, had to adapt his skills to the exigencies of a labour market created primarily by the movement of skilled artisans, businessmen, and labourers out of the community on a fairly regular basis.

Within this context, however, it was demonstrably possible for individuals to improve their status, at least in terms of vocational preferences, once they had identified an opportunity to make a living, however humble, in Peel. For example, one-fifth of the male householders who were residents of Peel in both 1851 and 1861 not only changed occupations at least once during the decade, but underwent as well a categorical change in vocational status (see Table 41). In the next decade, there was both a real decrease in vocational mobility across ranks and a relative decline, of significant magnitude, in the proportion of the population who changed their occupational status for better or worse. Hard times, land scarcity, and urban development undoubtedly go far in describing the conditions which tended to lock people in place, vocationally, in the 1860s; hence, too, the much increased drop-out rate among farmers in this decade. One thing is certain. Those whose vocational status changed in either decade showed a single-minded preference for farming. Thirty-five per cent (97/281) of the non-farm householders who persisted from 1851 to 1861 became farmers during that decade; and by 1870 28% (131/459) of the non-farming 1861-71 persisters had taken up farming. The traffic going the other way was not nearly so heavy. Fewer than 10% of the farmers resident in the county in 1851-61 or 1861-71 abandoned agriculture for some other vocation (Table 41(b)).

If one in three non-farming 1851-61 persisters moved into farming, another one in five (averaged across the non-farm ranks) moved from one non-farm vocation to another, sometimes for the better, sometimes for worse. These 'second choices' appear to be more predictable (Table 42). Manufacturers of durable goods reverted to the status of skilled wage labourers or unskilled labour if fortune fled. The merchant ceased to be the vendor and became the producer of goods. The skilled artisan might hope to become the owner of a mercantile or small manufacturing establishment — an employer of labour and capital — or he might equally join the ranks of the unskilled who aspired, in turn, to acquire a skill, to own a small business, or to acquire land. These processes were still at work in the 1860s although some men, professionals and skilled artisans in particular, had become less mobile than others. One possibility is that the explosive growth of Brampton after 1860 and the concentration of commercial, political, legal, and manufacturing activity there actually improved conditions for those professionals and artisans who stayed in place providing goods and services to their local rural clientele.

But farming and the attributes of farmers — land, equity, tangible evidence of social security — were irresistible to all who could rent or buy land in what had become a farmer's, rather than a speculator's, frontier. As Table 43 indicates, one of the principal changes that took place in Peel in the 1850s was the transition from an economy in which the largest landholders were not farmers to one in which large holdings were significantly associated only with the occupation of farming. This is consistent with the expansionist movement documented in Chapter 1 and with the effects of the wheat boom which focused attention on the land's productive, rather than its speculative potential. In either case, farming, rather than landholding per se, became a primary objective of vocational mobility; but in the long run, as we shall see, owning rather than merely occupying farm land was the ultimate goal of the putative farmer. Gaining access to sufficient land, through either rental or purchase, to pursue farming as a calling and not merely as a sideline carried on in conjunction with some other

TABLE 42

Direction of occupational mobility among persistent householders, Peel County

(a) 1851-61

	1852 status					
	Farmer	Manu-facturer	Pro-fessional	Merchant	Skilled artisan	Unskilled
1860 status						
farmer	91.3	28.3	27.6	27.3	26.1	39.5
manufacturer	1.1	47.2	–	–	6.3	1.2
professional	–	1.9	65.6	–	–	–
merchant	1.2	5.7	5.6	52.3	7.2	7.0
skilled artisan	1.1	9.4	–	13.6	57.7	8.1
unskilled	2.1	7.5	2.1	4.5	2.7	41.0
no occup.	–	–		2.3	–	–
$N = 1,262$						

(b) 1861-71

	1861 status					
	Farmer	Manu-facturer	Pro-fessional	Merchant	Skilled artisan	Unskilled
1871						
farmer	91.5	23.6	3.8	27.3	15.7	41.1
manufacturer	1.4	59.7	–	3.0	2.1	1.7
professional	.1	–	76.9	3.0	–	–
merchant	1.7	4.2	3.8	53.0	5.0	3.9
skilled artisan	1.4	5.6	7.7	7.6	72.1	5.0
unskilled	3.5	6.9	–	3.0	5.0	48.3
no occup.	.3	–	7.7	3.0	–	–
$N = 1,445$						

vocation clearly required capital in an era of escalating competition for land. Above all it required endurance in a community in which both the vocation of farming and its principal asset, land, were in the hands of a generation of aging pioneers. Patience, persistence, waiting for an opportunity, and in the meantime adapting one's skills to the opportunities of the moment, that was the way to move up. For those men who would not, or could not, wait or, perhaps, who had no interest in farming the community offered short-term employment and business opportunities in a wide variety of trades and professions. Moreover, the facility with which men not only changed jobs as readily as they changed hats, but leaped from low to high profile work and vice versa — teachers becoming labourers, carpenters entering commerce, merchants turning to bricklaying — suggests that 'jack-of-all-trades' indeed had found the road to full employment here, there, wherever the search for security took him and the other 9,000 householders who passed through, but did not stay, in Peel County between

TABLE 43

Correlation (*r*) of selected variables with amount of land owned or occupied, Peel County 1850-70

	1851-2	1860-1	1870-1
Occupation			
farmer	no	yes (+)	yes (+)
mfct. textiles	no	yes (−)	no
mfct. apparel	no	yes (−)	yes (−)
mfct. wood products	no	no	no
mfct. metal products	no	no	no
mfct. food products	no	no	no
mfct. luxury goods	no	no	no
misc. manufacturing	no	no	no
construction	no	yes (−)	yes (−)
labour	no	yes (−)	yes (−)
commerce	yes (+)	no	no
transportation	no	yes (−)	yes (−)
domestic service	no	no	no
public service	no	no	no
education/govt	no	no	no
professional	yes (+)	no	no
others	no	no	no
Place of birth			
England	no	no	no
Ireland	no	no	yes (−)
Scotland	yes (+)	no	yes (+)
USA	no	yes (+)	yes (+)
Upper Canada	no	no	no
Age	yes (+)	yes (+)	yes (+)
Persistence		yes (+)	yes (+)

1850 and 1870. They did not stay for a variety of reasons, some of them imponderable, others tantalizing to speculate about but unfathomable using local data, a few comprehensible in terms of the historical circumstances of rural life in mid-Victorian Ontario.

Successful Upper Canadians explained their achievements not only in terms of right attitudes — thrift, industry, sobriety, and domesticity — married to the abundant resources of the Canadian backwoods, but in terms of a fundamental distinction between old and new world mentalities. One of the most important lessons they claimed to have learned from their Canadian experience was that the man who became 'too local in his ideas,' like the parish-bound Briton, ran the risk of social entrapment, of being locked into the forms and structures of established societies which had been the essential source of social inequality in the old world.[34] In North America 'local country no longer exists'; men's sense of place, as one essayist argued, had given way to the concept of unlimited social and economic space in which they could pursue their common cause of social betterment.[35] This 'frontier' theme ran through contemporary explanations of the peripatetic behaviour of Canadians long before the American geographer Frederick Jackson Turner raised it to the level of metahistory in the 1890s. The 'waves of population which perpetually flow westward' finding new opportunities in each successive community were touted, in the 1850s, as examples of the unlimited potential in Upper Canada for social improvement.[36] A resident of Simcoe County complained in the 1860s that 'the too prevalent notion that all an immigrant has to do, is to hurry on to the west as fast as possible' was the cause of underdevelopment in her county.[37] Twenty years later another writer elevated both the rate and direction of geographical mobility in Canada to the status of the 'law of the movement of population.' 'The older settlements in the east send forth their emigrants who settle upon and cultivate the virgin soil of the west ... and room is made in the old settlements for those who leave the still older and more crowded countries of Europe.'[38]

It is impossible to judge the extent to which this frontier mentality informed the behaviour of those thousands of families and individuals who passed through Peel in each decade. Discovering where they had been and where they were going would help to solve the riddle. Did they perpetually move from more to less developed areas? Did they, in the process, improve themselves? It is a monumental and practically impossible task to follow them from place to place. All that can be discovered about these migrants with certainty is their behaviour in this place where, as the foregoing analysis attempted to demonstrate, a restrictive climate of economic opportunity but one nevertheless conducive to vocational and social mobility had created, in 1860, a predominantly improved or improving society in which longevity, land and/or capital, and the vocation of farming distinguished the most from the least improved families. It remains to be seen whether there was any relationship between the propensity of some families to put down roots and of others to stop only briefly here, and the apparent processes and facts of social betterment in mid-Victorian Peel.

First, however, it is important to review the primary facts of geographical mobility in mid-nineteenth-century Peel which are set forth in Tables 44 and 45. The principal outlines of population movement through Peel in 1850-70 as described in the introduction to this chapter are set forth in Table 44. What may be added at this point is a further reflection that the proportion of families present at any cross-section who had resided in the community for at least ten years was remarkably constant throughout the period (about 40%), and that, given the aggregate decline in the rural population in the 1860s, the most persistent families would have constituted a larger proportion of the total population as time passed. These are important facts because they anticipate a future in which rural depopulation and fairly constant levels of persistence might have produced a society with the appearance of being as stable as memory and tradition would have it.

TABLE 44

Summary data for mobility of Peel population 1851-71

(a) Emigration

	1851	1861
Percentage of householders who persisted next 10 years	38.7	31.1
Percentage who emigrated (corrected for death)	61.3	68.9

(b) Immigration

	1851-2*	1861	1871	1880†
Percentage who persisted from previous record	68.5	38.7	40.3	39.8
Percentage of Immigrants	31.5	61.3	59.7	60.2

* previous record was 1850 Directory of Peel County
† householders who appeared on the 1879-80 Assessment Rolls of Albion, Caledon, Chinguacousy, and Toronto Gore townships
Note: the linkage procedure employed here to define persistence and transience (see note 39) includes manual correction for mortality.

TABLE 45

Transience and persistence among Peel householders 1849-61

(a) Percentage of 1852 householders listed in 1850 directory and 1852 census	36.35
(b) Percentage of 1852 householders listed in 1850 directory and 1852, 1861 census	28.86
(c) Percentage of 1852 householders listed in 1852 and 1861 census	9.15
(d) Percentage of 1852 householders listed in 1852 census only	25.62
	100.00
(e) Percentage of all 1852 householders there in 1849	65.2
(f) Percentage of all 1852 householders immigrants 1850-51	34.8
(g) Percentage of all immigrant householders 1850-1 who failed to persist to census of 1861	73.7
(h) Percentage of all other 1852 householders who emigrated before 1861	36.4

How unstable that society was at mid-century is best illustrated by Table 45, which, although annual data are not avaiable for Peel, provides a starting point for some interesting speculations.[39]

One-third of the householders — cohort (f) — enumerated in the 1852 'numbering of the people' of Peel were recent arrivals, so recent that they were not listed in the comprehensive directory of the county issued in 1850 and probably compiled in 1849. Of these 1,064 most recent immigrants nearly three-quarters (g) did not stay long enough (8½ years) to be counted on the next census. Assuming a perfectly equal distribution, they arrived at the rate of 425 families per year and left at the rate of 90 per year. But these emigrants were joined by 1,112 emigrants from the other cohorts — (a) and (d) in Table 45 — whose members did not persist until 1861. Again assuming an equal distribution, these migrants left at the rate of 130 per year over the next 8½ years. Meanwhile, between 1853 and 1861 approximately 2,000 new families arrived in Peel (Table 44(b)). Together, the three groups would have represented a migration rate of 500-600 families per annum, more than 5,000 in the period between the census of 1852 and the census of 1860-1. The theoretical net gain in this case, 205 families per year, 1,743 families between 1852 and 1861, overrepresents the actual increase in the number of families by 584. This may be the result of the extraordinary rate of immigration in 1850 and 1851 on the heels of the latest wave of European immigration into Upper Canada. It may also reflect problems of underenumeration in the 1851 census. In any case, the example serves the purpose of demonstrating the possibility that, at a minimum, the decennial rate of transience must have been nearly double the number of families ever present in the community.

What explains this perpetual motion or, conversely, the stability of the persistent minority whose 'roots' were entrenched in the soil of these five townships? Several explanations must be canvassed, not least of all the real or apparent potential for social improvement here. Both less and more complex considerations may enter into an explanation of this phenomenon: relative economic opportunity in the form of land or employment, cultural factors, and demographic patterns must all be considered potential sources of social insta-bility in mid-Victorian Peel County. Moreover, it is especially important to consider these factors in relation to the timing of the decision on the part of householders to stay put or to leave their townships of residence, however imprecise our sense of their timing may be, if we are to understand the reasons for the persistence of some families and the mobility of others. Consequently, Tables 46 and 47 compare the relative power of several factors to explain the choice of persistence or outmigration during the 1860s by the families who were resident in Peel in 1861 and who fall into one of two possible categories: (1) migrated into the country *after* the *1852* census was taken, were enumerated on the 1861 census, and *either* stayed in Peel until the next census (1871) was taken *or* left Peel before 1871; or (2) were residents of Peel in 1852 *and* in 1861 and subsequently *either* stayed until 1871 *or* left before the next census was taken. In short, Table 46 deals with the experience of those who, in 1861, were the most recent immigrants, Table 47 with the experience of those who, in 1861, were the country's most persistent families; and both tables seek to explain their sub-sequent behaviour from the vantage point of their relative condition in 1861.

Using the 'correlation ratio' Eta it is possible to compare the relative ability of degrees of social improvement, the life cycle, property ownership, and voca-tional rank to explain variation in the rates of persistence among the families of

Peel. Among the most recent immigrants (Table 46), as the weak correlation ratios suggest, everything and nothing equally explains persistence and mobility. The proportionate distribution of stayers and movers is, in each case, nevertheless of some interest. Persisters were considerably overrepresented among recent arrivals who had acquired land by 1861 (Table 46(b)), just as they were among immigrants who had been able to take up farming (Table 46(d)). Conversely, outmigrants were disproportionately represented among tenants and the families of unskilled householders and those with no particular vocation. This is scarcely surprising in the light of evidence presented earlier in connection with the factors promoting or hindering vocational mobility and social betterment. Consequently, neither is it surprising that among the most recent arrivals the subsequent persisters are overrepresented among those families who in 1861 had acquired all of the attributes of improvement or who were at least improving freeholders (Table 46(a)).

All the variation in the choice among recent arrivals of moving or staying after 1861 which can be accounted for by age cohort is associated with the experience of the oldest householders. Since the available evidence tends toward the view that mobility was principally a characteristic of the young while old age was associated with permanence, it seems remarkable that two-fifths of Peel's householders over the age of 65 [total 65+ cohort in Tables 46(b) and 47(b)] were still 'on the road' in their late fifties and early sixties (when they migrated to Peel County). But the next move of the 85% who do not appear to have lived out their lives in Peel is at best a matter for speculation. Perhaps it was truly upward! All that is certain is that neither they nor their spouses were householders in 1871. Consequently, it seems advisable to control for the effects of this group in order to arrive at an approximation of 'normal' patterns of mobility and persistence among the other, younger, families. When this is done, age ceases to be a significant factor in explaining mobility among both the most recent arrivals and those families who had resided in the county for at least ten years before 1861. Thus, again among a series of relatively weak predictors, occupation provides the best explanation of the decision of two in five of the most persistent families in 1861 to remain in Peel for the next decade. Perpetual residents are overrepresented among those engaged in farming in 1861 while 1852-61 persisters who subsequently migrated represent more or less equal proportions of the other vocational categories, except for men in the construction trades and those with no definite occupation. The higher rates of mobility among the latter group after 1861 may have been a function, however, of relative age. The somewhat greater tendency for men in the construction industry to persist could reflect the ongoing building boom in Brampton and the effects of continued railroad construction in the county.

Nevertheless, occupation is scarcely a better indicator of persistence than degrees of social betterment, land ownership, or cultural identity. Predictably,

TABLE 46

Factors promoting mobility and persistence among the most recent arrivals in Peel County 1861

(a) Distribution of stayers and movers by stages of social betterment (percentages)

	At 'Pioneer stage' in 1861	Improving tenant 1861	Improving freeholder	Improved	All
Arrived after 1852, left before 1871	75	76	61	60	71
Arrived after 1852, stayed until 1871	25	24	39	40	29

Eta = 0.143 χ^2 = 51.75   DF = 3   Sig. = 0.001 (N = 2,531)

(b) Distribution of stayers and movers by age cohort in 1861 (percentages)

	15-34	35-49	50-64	65+	All
Arrived after 1852, left before 1871	67	69	72	89	70
Arrived after 1852, stayed until 1871	33	31	29	11	30

Eta = 0.109 χ^2 = 27.635   DF = 3   Sig. = 0.001 (N = 2,335)

(c) Distribution of stayers and movers by land ownership (percentages)

	Tenant in 1861	Freeholder in 1861	All
Arrived after 1852, left before 1871	78	62	71
Arrived after 1852, stayed until 1871	22	38	29

Eta/phi = 0.173 χ^2 = 75.026   DF = 1   Sig. = 0.001 (N = 2,351)

(d) Distribution of movers and stayers by vocational category 1861 (percentages)

	Agric.	Sec. mfct.	Unskilled labour	Con-struction	Transport. & comm.	Profess.	Others
Arrived after 1852, left before 1871	65	74	79	78	77	74	85
Arrived after 1852, stayed until 1871	35	26	21	22	23	26	15

Eta = 0.149   (N = 2,495)

Note: for the purposes of Tables 46 and 47 the dependent variable has been computed as a dichotomy of the order O/1.

TABLE 47

Factors promoting mobility and persistence among the most persistent householders in Peel 1861

(a) Distribution of stayers and movers by stages of social betterment (percentages)

	At pioneer stage 1862	Improving tenant	Improving freeholder	Improved	All
Present in 1852 and 1861 but not in 1871	64	64	56	52	60
Present 1852-71	36	36	44	48	40
Eta = 0.104 χ^2 = 12.193 DF = 3 Sig. = 0.006 (N = 1,120)					

(b) Distribution of stayers and movers by age cohort in 1861 (percentages)

	15-34	35-49	50-64	65+	All
Present in 1852 and 1861 but not in 1871	54	57	53	81	59
Present 1852-71	46	43	47	19	41
Eta = 0.200 χ^2 = 43.825 DF = 3 Sig. = 0.001 (N = 1,094)					

(c) Distribution of stayers and movers by land ownership (percentages)

	Tenant in 1861	Freeholder in 1861	All
Present in 1852 and 1861 but not in 1871	66	56	60
Present 1852-71	34	44	40
Eta/phi = 0.104 (N = 1,120)			

(d) Distribution of stayers and movers by cultural identity (percentages)

	Foreign-born Roman Catholic	Foreign born Protestant	Native Protestant	All
Present in 1852 and 1861 but not in 1871	75	60	48	60
Present 1852-71	25	40	52	40
Eta = 0.125 χ^2 = 17.434 DF = 2 Sig. = 0.001 (N = 1,120)				

(e) Distribution of stayers and movers by vocational category 1861 (percentages)

	Agric.	Sec. mfct.	Un-skilled labour	Con-struction	Trans-port. & comm.	Pro-fess.	Others
Present in 1851 and 1861 but not 1871	57	71	70	63	68	70	76
Present in 1851, 1861, and 1871	43	29	30	37	32	30	24
Eta = 0.121 (N = 1,112)							

among the persistent minority in 1861 disproportionate numbers of landed proprietors, improving freeholders, and improved families chose to remain in the county. This seems to reinforce the argument that for recent arrivals and earlier cohorts of settlers alike it was the realization of the promise — social, economic, and psychological — inherent in the soil and its successful cultivation which promoted longer term attachments to place among families and individuals in whom, apparently, a sense of place was not very well developed. Table 48 provides some valuable additional perspectives on this relationship. Freeholders who occupied more than 150 acres in 1861 (Table 48(a)) were more likely to have acquired all the attributes of social improvement than freeholders with less land, further evidence that farm size and the potential for betterment were more closely related, irrespective of which factor was the cause and which the consequence of improvement, than contemporary observers like Samuel Phillips Day were willing to concede. This also suggests that the farm expansion movement of the 1850s in Peel, whatever other reasons may be advanced for it, was also either a strategy on the part of improving farmers calculated to increase productivity and surplus capital to support a higher standard of living, or the reinvestment of surplus capital by improved farmers in this essential source of their social security.

In either case, the effect was the same. Freeholders who occupied the largest farms in the county (100 acres or more) had significantly higher rates of persistence than families with small farms. Given the mobility of smallholders, and even of freeholders with fairly substantial farms, the impermanence of the tenant class is hardly remarkable. Unless they were fortunate enough to have leased a large, improved farm, the opportunity to improve their material condition cannot have been very great. Even among freeholders improvement was, apparently, an exasperatingly slow process. As Table 48(c) suggests, persistence, the very trait that the majority of Peel's families did not espouse, and improvement were bedfellows. Families who, in 1861, had been freeholders for at least fifteen years were more likely to have passed beyond the circumstances of pioneer life than those who arrived after 1845. In short, time was on the side of improvement; but that was small consolation to men ready, and willing, to hurry on to some new locale in the hope of circumventing the social processes evidently at work here.

Among those processes, finally, cultural intimidation, implicit or overt, appears to have been one of the causes of outmigration among some elements of Peel's population. Foreign-born Roman Catholics, Scots and Irish alike, were the least likely of Peel's principal cultural groups to put down roots in this county (Table 47(d)), in which the number of native-born Roman Catholic householders was too small to be statistically significant. This is not a surprising discovery. The 1850s witnessed the widespread and rapid proliferation of the Orange Order in Canada West. Among the counties of south-central Ontario,

TABLE 48

Mobility and improvement among freeholders by farm size and date of purchase 1861

(a) Degrees of social betterment among property owners by acreage occupied 1861 (percentages)

	1-25	26-50	51-99	100-50	151-249	250+	All
Pioneer stage	25	41	31	31	16	16	29
Improving	45	43	52	46	38	37	44
Improved	30	15	18	23	46	47	27
							100

$\chi^2 = 95.299$ DF = 10 Sig. = 0.01

(b) Geographical mobility among property owners by acreage occupied in 1861 (percentages)

	1-25	26-50	51-99	100-50	151-249	250+	All
1861 owners resident 1850-70	18	25	25	32	38	45	31
1861 owners who did not persist to 1871	83	75	75	68	62	55	69
							100

$\chi^2 = 26.781$ DF = 5 Sig. = 0.01

(c) Degrees of social betterment among 1861 property owners by date of purchase (percentages)

	Before 1840	1840-5	1846-9	1850-5	1856-60	Total
Still at 'pioneer stage'	18	21	33	25	32	25
Above 'pioneer stage'	82	79	67	75	68	75

$\chi^2 = 15.03$ DF = 5 Sig. = 0.01

Peel had one of the highest concentrations of Orange lodges, visible testimony to John Brown's candid admonition that all were welcome in Peel save the 'Pope, bishops ... [and] Fenians.'[40] As in the rest of Canada West, in Peel County the nativist reaction to the threat of social instability posed by the famine migrations of the late 1840s ironically added to demographic instability by making it doubly difficult for the most recent wave of migrants to become an integral part of rural or urban society.

All these factors, collectively considered, help to explain mobility and persistence in Peel County. No single factor, however, was a more important determinant than any other of the propensity of some families to develop an attachment to this place, and of others to depart after a brief, or in some cases a fairly prolonged, stay. It seems necessary to conclude, then, that the decision either to move on or to stay in Peel, a dilemma confronted perhaps perennially by these families, was the product of very complex considerations. These included not only questions of economic opportunity, material condition, and

social security, past, present, and future, but still more fundamental considerations such as the prospect of a peaceful existence free from social strife and
cultural confrontation. And beyond these 'public' factors undoubtedly lay
private motives which remain hidden to the historian. The ultimate irony, in
any event, is that social improvement, even a very modest start in that
direction, was a consequence of persistence in this place where access to land
and its rewards was principally a question of time. Few enough of the families
who ever lived in mid-Victorian Peel County, however, were willing time-
servers. Nor should we expect them to have exhibited infinite patience in these
matters. Unlimited social space in the rest of the continent made the restricted
confines of Peel's five townships, in spite of the advantages offered by a society
rapidly maturing under the tutelage of the metropolis, too narrow a compass
for their ambitions.

There is no better way to illustrate the endless variations on this theme of
transience and persistence than to cite examples of the perambulations of
some of the people who stopped, however briefly, in Peel County. William
Thomas, for example, was an Irish emigrant who left Belfast in 1856 at the age
of 23. He made his way first to Collingwood, on Georgian Bay, where he
found employment as a school-teacher in this new, bustling railroad terminus
and port. Subsequently he surfaced in Albion Township, as a storekeeper in
Bolton. His last move was to Toronto, where he worked as a housepainter,
then as a builder, and at last established himself as a building contractor.[41]
Similarly, Noah Barnhart, born and educated in Upper Canada, worked in the
United States before returning to Port Credit in the 1840s, where he was a
miller, merchant, and grain dealer. With the decline of Peel's wheat economy
Barnhart moved to Collingwood, then Meaford, again dealing in grain,
eventually retiring to Toronto in 1867.[42] Charles Fuller's career was more
diversified and peripatetic. He was educated in Prince Edward County,
attended the Normal School in Toronto, taught in Michigan, was a coal
merchant in Belleville, a grain dealer in Aylmer, and a private banker in
Streetsville, Toronto Township, before retiring to Toronto.[43] The only truly
remarkable fact about Fuller's vocational history, or Barnhart's or Thomas's,
however, is that their route to full employment can be documented from a single
source because they finally persisted long enough in one place to be included in a
biographical dictionary of its citizens.

If Charles Fuller, Noah Barnhart, and William Thomas were representative
of Peel's non-farming transient population, James Shaw, Thomas Cole, and
William Taylor typify the county's farming population. Cole was born in Peel
in 1825, inherited his father's farm, married into one of the Gore's most
prominent farm families, the Blands, and passed his farm on to his son when
he retired in 1889. James Shaw inherited 100 acres of his father's farm, one of
the oldest in the Gore, in 1860, worked it until 1871, then sold it and invested

the capital in Toronto real estate. Taylor, a tenant farmer in Chinguacousy, weathered the storms of the sixties; but as soon as the vacant lands of the west were secured for the new Dominion of Canada, Taylor packed his family and his possessions in a wagon and headed for Owen Sound, secured passage on a steamer for the Lakehead, then trekked overland to start a new life as a farmer in the province of Manitoba.[44] In short, although farming promoted stability, and roots deeply set in the farming community encouraged continuity and permanence, neither was a certain guarantee of persistent attachment to this society. Nearly half (47%) of the farmers resident in Peel in 1851 were not there a decade later. Even with ample correction for mortality, it is certain that more than 40% of them had emigrated, many undoubtedly squeezed out by their improving neighbours, others bought out by new men, farmers and non-farmers alike, with the capital to acquire their rapidly appreciating land. The profits from these transactions would buy as much, or more, land in the 'Queen's Bush' or in the American mid-west. Indeed, abandoning improved farms for the rigours of a less civilized existence appeared to contemporaries to be a habitual trait of a class of professional pioneers. As one writer explained, 'the qualities which constitute fitness for enduring the hardship and privation of roughing it in the bush, are not in every instance associated with those which give stability and success in a more advanced state of society.'[45]

It is more certain that some of this motion was the direct result of the depression and the first of the crop failures which struck the province at the end of the decade. In a series of letters to their brother, Henry, who had emigrated to Minnesota, George, Lorenda, and Charlotte Clarkson described the situation in one part of Toronto Township. One neighbour and his family 'have gone bag and baggage,' simply abandoning their farm. Another had managed to keep his farm, but his creditors had taken everything else, leaving him 'picked as bare as a bird's ass.' Their own brother, William, a Port Credit storekeeper, had been jailed for debt; and George was contemplating following Henry to Minnesota if he could not rent a farm in Peel for a third of the yearly crop rather than cash. Better still, with the prospect of striking it rich in the gold-fields of California there was talk of a large party forming to meet Henry at Pike's Peak in the summer of 1859.[46] By the middle of the next decade, farmers and their families were in full flight from Peel County. Three-fifths of the farm families who had appeared on the 1860-1 census left the community before 1870. Amid the ravages of crop failures, indebtedness, plummetting land prices, lost markets, and, withal, concern for the social security and cultural integrity of the 'hardy and industrious family' whose plight engendered so much debate in the provincial legislature,[47] migration may have appeared as the lesser of several evils. As James Reid reported them, conditions in Peel were anything but favourable in 1862. 'The rot was very bad ... Markets very low Business of all kinds dull ... Land about one third lower since the [American Civil] war commenced ...'[48] The worst of the crop failures and the bottoming out of wheat prices were yet to come.

The exodus from Peel continued, unabated, for the remainder of the nineteenth century. For example, when the Dominion Lands Act of 1872 effectively opened the new province of Manitoba to agricultural settlement one of the new arrivals from Ontario was William Taylor from Chinguacousy Township. He arrived in August 1874 and filed on a 160-acre homestead with a pre-emption on 160 additional acres, three times as much land as he had rented in Peel County. What surprised and delighted Taylor was the discovery that his nearest neighbours — Noah Chant, George Lipsett, Josiah Hunter, and James Anderson — were Peel County men too. Chant was 59, Lipsett 50, Anderson in his forties. Only Hunter was under 35. All had growing or completed families. Anderson and Taylor had been tenant farmers in Peel, but Chant, Hunter, and Lipsett each had been proprietors of substantial farms. They had all been wheat farmers in the 1850s and 1860s but by 1870 they had converted to forage and field crops, oats, peas, barley, and hay.[49] In Manitoba they grew wheat and were convinced that in spite of the lack of adequate transportation facilities they were better off growing wheat and selling it at 75¢ a bushel in Winnipeg than they would have been had they stayed in Ontario where the costs of production ate up their profits.[50] Taylor and his friends wanted no part of Ontario, and they despised the youngsters from Ontario who 'left their hearts with their mothers' and emigrated to Manitoba expecting rural life there to be an imitation of life in Ontario.

It was not. Taylor, Chant, and the others had succeeded in turning back the clock to the days of cheap land and wheat mining, of generous man/land ratios, of labour- rather than capital-intensive agriculture. They may have had other motives as well. As late as 1879 the American consul at Sarnia reported to his superiors in Washington that the Canadian farmers who were streaming across the border were all men whose farms 'of one hundred acres were at one time sufficient to yield a comfortable living for [themselves] and family ... [They are now] surrounded by grown up sons for whom [they feel] it incumbent upon [themselves] to provide ... and proceed to Michigan, or some other western state or territory ... to buy land sufficient for [themselves] and [their] boys.'[51] It was the same impulse that had propelled David Long toward Albion Township half a century before.

The motives which guided families toward or away from mid-Victorian Peel County are far more complex than a simple analysis of their relative prosperity will reveal. And we must assume that the large numbers of migrants who were attached to Peel came there for reasons just as complex as those which account for the identity of the outmigrants described above. Whatever their motives, it seems likely that the circumstances of material improvement in each place they came to must have been much the same as the conditions of

life in the places they had just left, places, in short, more or less like Peel
County. There, the distance between the most and the least improved families
was measured in terms of property and time. The 60 couples who drank
'champaign' and waltzed until two at the annual Plank Road Ball, the 120
farmers who sat down to Henry Rutledge's outdoor supper held yearly in
connection with the county ploughing match,[52] and the officers of the seven
battalions of Peel County Militia,[53] whatever their respective characteristics,
would have shared three common traits. They owned land. They farmed it.
And they stayed on it through thick and thin, adapting when necessary to the
forces of change which required adaptation, continuing as before when it was
necessary not to change. These families, and the other permanent residents of
Peel, were islands of continuity in a sea of change. Its tides consisted of waves
of people who measured improvement in terms of distance rather than time.
They were people in a hurry. But, as Robert Louis Stevenson would have said,
they must also have been people for whom 'it was better to travel hopefully
than to arrive.'

6 *The Urban Frontier*

By 1870 the farmers' frontier had shifted north and west to the fertile riparian soil of southern Manitoba. But in Ontario there was yet another 'frontier,' the urban frontier, whose potential was created and unleashed by the railway age. After 1850, in the agrarian hinterlands of Kingston, Toronto, Hamilton, and a dozen lesser lake ports new towns sprang to life and dormant hamlets were revivified equally by the hope as by the reality of the coming of the railroad. Many were ruined by the financial burden of the new technology. Others saw their hopes dashed by its false promises. But some of these new places flourished, even to the point where they could gloat over their success and pretend to have replaced, in ambition and progress, the older cities whose clients they nevertheless remained and whose characteristics they nevertheless shared.

One such place was Brampton, in Peel County. In 1851 Peel contained no incorporated places. Its principal hamlets, Brampton, Streetsville, and Port Credit, counted among them fewer than 2,000 inhabitants associated with the primary functions of each place, the grain trade in Brampton, fishing and shipping in Port Credit, and the cloth industry in Streetsville. Twenty years later Streetsville and Port Credit were still hamlets, in fact, declining villages. But Brampton had become an urban centre with all the trappings of mid-Victorian urbanism: the railway, proto-industrialization, vigorous commercial development, high rates of transience, and a rigid, indeed restrictive, social structure. And Brampton's 2,000 inhabitants were urban people, but not merely because they were smugly imperious toward their rural neighbours.[1] After less than a dozen years of separate development the two populations had quite distinct demographic characteristics which set them worlds apart.

Brampton's spectacular rise began in 1854 when the village council acceded to a request from the Grand Trunk Railway Company to rearrange the village's streets to accommodate the railroad's proposed right of way and station facilities.[2] Two years later the municipality sat astride the road's main line which spanned Ontario linking Montreal to the American mid-west. The village's population almost tripled in the next five years as opportunists of every stripe tested its possibilities. William Mahaffy, for example, was a recent Irish emigrant. A carriage maker by trade, Mahaffy arrived in Brampton in 1856, set up a carriage works, and by 1870 had become one of the town's wealthiest men. Briefly, Wesley Todd was one of them too. After forging drafts on the Bank of Montreal using the names of local citizens this 'merchant' skipped town with $84,000 in 1861. He spent the last seven years of the decade in Kingston Penitentiary.[3] In contrast, the Englishman George Tye and his newspaper, the *Times*, seem to have embodied perfectly Brampton's place in the scheme of things. Judging from the few issues that survive, Tye eschewed the local gossip which dominated the Streetsville *Weekly Review*. The *Times*' news came from the pages of the Toronto, New York, and London newspapers, just as its advertising copy rapidly linked Tye's subscribers to metropolitan purveyors of taste and technology. In 1856, local (ie, Peel County) advertisers accounted for 80% of the commercial advertising in Brampton's newspapers. The largest external sources of copy were Toronto merchants whose advertisements were no more numerous (18% of the total) than those of the merchants in Peel's outlying hamlets — Edmonton, Cheltenham, Streetsville, and others. Six years later the Brampton papers were no longer sources of information about the availability of goods and services in the surrounding countryside. Brampton advertisers accounted for half of the advertising copy in local newspapers in 1862. Of the remaining 50%, three-fifths represented Toronto establishments. Third place was shared by Orangeville, Brampton's immediate rival twenty miles to the north, and New York City. The fourth largest group of advertisers were British mercantile establishments.[4] Together, the newspaper, the railroad, and a generation of enterprising middlemen had altered irrevocably, in less than a decade, the historical patterns of trade, commerce, and communications in the region.

Forwarding the region's produce, especially to the new grain market created in Toronto by the railroad network, and distributing the consumer goods that arrived by rail from the metropolis were Brampton's principal functions. One pioneer recalled seeing a 'procession of teams nearly a mile in length start out from Brampton loaded with goods destined for ... Caledon, Amaranth, Mono, Mulmur and Melancthon [townships].'[5] By 1871, 15% of the town's employed male heads of family were engaged in some aspect of the transportation industry (Table 49). But Brampton's role was by no means limited to this function. The town's economy had a vigorous commercial sector of which the purveyors of food and of luxury goods to the carriage trade were, as we shall see, the most successful element. Similarly, although Brampton could scarcely be described as a factory town, the Haggert Brothers' agricultural implement factory alone employed about 140 men while two cabinet factories, two carriage works, and two sash and door mills provided employment for a wide variety of skilled tradesmen. Finally, Brampton's designation in 1865 as the county seat added a

TABLE 49

Distribution of male heads of family by occupational classification, Brampton 1861, 1871 (%)

	1861	1871
Unskilled labour	17	14
Skilled trades and crafts	22	20
Transportation	9	15
Construction	17	15
Commerce	17	16
Professions	6	7
Education/gov't/pub. service	4	6
Agriculture	7	6
Industrialists	1	1

new dimension to the town's ascendancy as court, gaol, registry, and administrative offices were visibly enshrined in new architectural monuments to Brampton's importance.

By 1875 the town's whirlwind growth had come to an end. Its population in 1880 was only slightly greater than it had been in 1870. For a decade and a half, however, Brampton was a classical, if at times anomalous, model of secondary urban development in south-central Ontario between 1850 and 1880. It was anomalous because (as the geographer Jacob Spelt has argued) most of the secondary urban development spawned by railroad construction and the diffusion of capital and technology along these new lines of communication during the period took place on the agrarian frontier, in the newest areas of settlement. There, freedom from the competition of older, larger towns and the presence of an improving, expanding client population in need of goods and services produced centres of localized manufacturing, retail trade, and essential services. Brampton, at the heart of an older settled area in the shadow of Toronto, ought not to have sprung to life with the speed and intensity which characterized its development.[6] Another geographer, James Gilmour, has explained this first anomaly by relating it to a second. Unlike other new towns of the period whose economic growth took the form of secondary manufacturing and tertiary (retail and service) functions developing in consort with increased employment in their regions' primary manufacturing sectors, Brampton developed as a centre of tertiary-sector employment in spite of a significant decline, in Peel, of primary manufacturing in the 1860s and of secondary manufacturing in the 1870s. In effect, Brampton appears to have been the exception to the rule that secondary urban development in Southern Ontario was promoted by the interdependence of all three areas of manufacturing activity, each reinforcing and stimulating growth in the others by creating a favourable climate for investment.[7]

Brampton is exceptional in this respect, however, only if the historian interprets the facts of Peel's demographic history in the 1860s as evidence of economic stagnation or decline rather than as a necessary adjustment which had the

TABLE 50

Occupations new to Brampton's economy 1862-71

Services	Transportation	Retail
Veterinarian	Conductor	Clothier
Boarding-school mistress	Engineer	Gunsmith
Auctioneer	Fireman	Cordwainer
Bank agent	Railwayman	Milliner
Agent	Roadmaster	Photographer
Bookkeeper	Switchman	Marble dealer
	Trackman	Weaver
Public servants	Carter	Hardware merchant
Constable	Driver	
Coroner	Hosteler	*Unskilled*
County Treasurer		Warehouseman
Deputy clerk	*Manufacturing*	Gardener
Judge	Boiler maker	Watchman
Sheriff	Tanner	Foundry worker
Gaoler	Pump maker	House painter
Turnkey	Potash maker	
Court clerk		
Wholesale		
Cattle dealer		
Leather dealer		

plausible effect of improving standards of living among Peel's farm population. In preserving a favourable family/land ratio, indeed promoting a return to more favourable ratios than had existed for over a decade, and thereby maintaining production values, demographic stasis may have been the engine of continued economic improvement in the rural areas, improvement which in turn promoted the growth of a local centre of retail trade and service industries. The validity of this line of reasoning is substantiated, at least in part, by even the most cursory examination of the new occupations which appeared in the town in the 1860s. Of the 45 occupations which were new to the artisanal, retail, industrial, and professional sectors of the local economy in 1870 (ie, they did not appear on the 1861 census), 73% were in the service and retail sectors and, of these, most would have been associated in the minds of Victorian Canadians with the tastes of increasingly sophisticated consumers (Table 50). The cordwainer made expensive shoes and slippers from fine leathers for people who had occasion to wear something other than workboots or the shoemaker's roughly sewn products. The veterinarian and the boarding school mistress offered services to a clientele who, a mere two decades earlier, took pride in neither the quality of their livestock nor the quality of their daughters' education. The clothier and the milliner catered to tastes no longer satisfied with, or confined to, homespun. Moreover, the extent to which the availability of any or all of these goods and services was dependent on corresponding developments in other areas of the local economy can also be seen from the list of new occupations which appeared in Brampton in the 1860s. The presence, for the first time, of a tanner, a cattle dealer, an auctioneer, and a bank agent all testify to the growing importance in the region of agricultural production other than cereal grains — Brampton's original raison d'être. Both commerce and agriculture, finally, were dependent on the growth of the transportation sector which was Peel's link to foreign and domestic markets and, through the labour of carters, drivers, teamsters, conveyors, and hostelers, the axle grease of an efficient local distribution network.

For all these reasons, Brampton's growth, although remarkable in its swiftness, was not exceptional in terms of the economic and demographic developments which took place in its immediate hinterland in the 1850s and 1860s. It was exceptional, perhaps, to the extent that the town flourished in the everlengthening shadow of Toronto. The proximity of the metropolis may account for the town's rather specialized functions. Toronto's rapidly developing manufacturing sector undoubtedly defined the limits of the growth of secondary manufacturing in its hinterland, limits which Brampton's optimum nineteenth-century size and its restricted functions accurately reflected. Within the context of the limitations imposed by the nearness of Toronto, Brampton was nevertheless a satellite metropolis in its own right, dependent on and imperious toward its local hinterland. It was also a remarkably different place, measured in terms of the social processes that it embodied, from the social landscape that surrounded the town and its people.

We need look no further than the size and structure of Brampton's families to comprehend the nature of the dichotomy between rural and urban society which, even in this microcosmic context, was already sharply delineated. In 1871, average family size among all married Brampton women aged 36-49 was 3.6 children. Among those women who had ever borne a child, the average number was 4.3, at least one or two less than for the same group of married rural women. Again, however, the difficulty of identifying all family offspring from the census returns is reason enough to ask whether these averages are truly reliable, and to resort to some other measurement of comparative fertility. Table 51 therefore presents comparative age-specific marital fertility ratios for the women of Brampton and their country sisters for 1861 and 1871. The dichotomy is unmistakable, and indeed astonishingly so because every age cohort exhibits the same sharp rural/urban differential in fertility; and the differences were as great or greater between the two groups in 1861 as they were in 1871.

The implications of these numbers are of considerable importance. In the first place, these comparative ratios constitute clear evidence that the reduction in marital fertility which resulted in Brampton's comparatively smaller families was not simply a matter of later ages at marriage in the town. The

TABLE 51

Number of children not yet 10 years per 1,000 married women by age cohort, Peel County
1861, 1871

	15-19	20-4	25-9	30-4	35-9	40-4
Brampton 1861	500	904	1,857	2,434	2,489	1,592
Rural 1861	500	1,494	2,356	3,222	3,200	2,429
Brampton 1871	286	1,184	1,875	2,706	2,250	2,000
Rural 1871	542	1,302	2,333	3,292	3,200	2,429
Rural/urban difference 1861*	0	31	21	24	22	36
Rural/urban difference 1871*	37	9	20	18	30	18

* Percentage by which urban fertility ratio is lower than rural ratio

demonstrably lower fertility of the townswomen in each age cohort suggests, rather, that they were already exercising individual control over their reproductive behaviour at a time when delayed marriage, social control, was the only measurable restraint on the fertility of Peel's rural women. Moreover, those Brampton women whose comparatively small families were complete by 1870 would have commenced childbearing in the early 1850s in some other place (almost all of them migrated to Brampton after 1861). This can only mean that they had come from environments where the trend toward family limitation was much more accelerated than it was in Peel County in the 1850s and 1860s. This in turn argues strongly for the hypothesis advanced by many historical demographers that even among pre-industrial populations elements of choice predicated on taste or education and related to specific economic environments were already important determinants of local and regional variations in human fertility.[8] Finally, the magnitude of the urban/rural fertility differential is important if, as one scholar has argued, a permanent, irreversible decline has occurred when the reduction in marital fertility from one generation to another exceeds 10%.[9] By this standard, the women of Brampton achieved that permanent reduction in marital fertility at least one generation ahead of their rural counterparts among whom only the youngest age group of women had begun to experience a noticeable change in reproductive behaviour by 1861.

It is important to establish the extent to which these differences in family size and fertility patterns between Peel's rural and urban women resulted from circumstances perhaps unique to Brampton, for example the town's occupational structure or its ethnic mix, on the assumption that some consistent relationship explains the tendency among some groups of women to have particularly low levels of fertility.[10] As it happens, an analysis of variance in marital fertility among Brampton's occupational, religious, and ethnic groups in 1871 produces no measurably significant variations.[11] Women between the ages of 25 and 34 whose husbands were either unskilled or had no vocation were the only group whose fertility levels were sufficiently different from those of other women in the same cohort to appear marginally significant. And their fertility ratios were lower, by 25%, than those of the next lowest group, the wives of skilled artisans. But for all intents and purposes the propensity toward lower fertility among the women of Brampton was common to all age cohorts and to all of the women in each cohort irrespective of their social background. In the face of such evidence it is necessary to conclude that Brampton's adult population in 1871, 72% of them immigrants since 1861, were carriers of a new, whether learned or inherited, set of attitudes about family size, family limitation, and the relationship between children and improvement.

As important as these new patterns of marital fertility are, it is also true that age at marriage continued to play a significant role in determining completed family size. The average age of the 25 women who were married in Christ Church (Anglican) between 1860 and 1864 was 24.4 years. The 40 women who were wed in the United Presbyterian Church in the same time period were on the average 24.5 years old. Since both congregations represented rural as well as town adherents, however, data from their marriage registers are less informative about relative ages at marriage than the available evidence about age at first conception. As Table 52 illustrates, in 1861 and in 1871 the proportion of rural married women under the age of 25 who had conceived two or more children was significantly higher than the proportion of town women who had borne more than one child before their 25th year. What is particularly striking is the comparative behaviour of women between the ages of 25 and 29. In 1861 the rural and urban women in this cohort exhibited approximately similar patterns of conception. Ten years later, however, nearly half the Brampton wives aged 25-9 had borne only one child, while the childbearing patterns of their rural counterparts had scarcely changed at all. Later ages at marriage as well as individual control of fertility within marriage evidently contributed equally to the permanent decline of fertility in this urban setting.

If the timing of family formation, and family limitation within marriage, represented something new — the shape of the urban future — in Peel's predominantly rural society, the structure of Brampton's families provides further evidence of the rural/urban dichotomy. By 1871, as we have seen, Peel's farm families had turned their ingenuity toward the resolution of a single problem — too many children competing for too little land. One result, among others, was a prolonged period of dependence in their parent's household for at least some children of the farm, especially if they aspired to a landed patrimony. But in Brampton, as Table 53 demonstrates, the opposite situation obtained. There, in 1871, more than half of the families in which the mother had reached

TABLE 52

Distribution of rural and urban wives aged 15-29 by number of children 1861, 1871 (percentages)

	1861		1871	
	Brampton	Rural	Brampton	Rural
Cohort age 15-24				
no children	43.2	31.2	35.0	34.2
one child	31.8	15.9	37.0	24.6
two or more	25.0	52.9	28.0	41.1
Cohort age 25-9				
no children	15.0	18.4	27.4	21.1
one child	5.6	5.8	16.1	7.5
two or more	79.4	75.7	56.5	71.4

TABLE 53

Distribution of rural and urban wives of various ages by children aged 17 or older at home 1871 (percentages)

	35-9	40-4	45-9	50-4	55-9	60-4
Brampton						
none	77.1	55.7	29.6	38.5	63.6	53.3
one	18.8	26.2	25.9	26.9	18.2	20.0
two or more	4.1	18.1	44.5	34.6	17.2	26.7
Rural						
none	79.6	44.1	23.6	20.0	18.0	30.0
one	15.3	12.6	21.5	17.4	15.0	21.6
two or more	15.1	43.3	54.9	62.6	67.0	48.4

the age of 55 had no older (ie, over the age of 16) children living at home, whereas at least half of the farm families in which wives were between the ages of 45 and 65 had two or more older children at home. Two inferences, in particular, must be drawn from this comparison. The first is that the cycle of family life among the townspeople was, by 1871, already substantially different from that of the farm family. Given the later ages at marriage of the Brampton parents and the apparent tendency for urban children to leave home at an earlier age than farm children, the stage of life associated with active parenthood was considerably foreshortened, perhaps by more than a decade, for these 'modern' parents.

The second implication of the data is that, whereas the generation of farm children who reached 'adolescence' about 1860 faced a prolonged period of continued dependence on their parents, young people of the same age in the town could anticipate the prospect of increased, perhaps even complete autonomy after their sixteenth year. Since it is impossible to trace those who left, it is equally impossible to know whether young people in fact traded dependence in their own parents' households for the slightly less restrictive environment of another household, or whether they became wholly independent once they left home. In Brampton itself, however, in 1871 50% of the town's young men between the ages of 17 and 24 lived as boarders, or resident employees, in a household other than their parents'. Within this group, less than a third of those who had reached age 19 still resided in their parents' home. In short, even in this small town the experience of young men more closely approximated the lives of youths in much larger cities like Hamilton or Buffalo than the lives of the ploughboys just a few miles away.[12] Conversely, the experience of young single women in Brampton, the vast majority (70%) of whom lived in their parents' household until they married, was not very different from the experience of young farm women, except that the townswomen clearly married later. Since there were few opportunities for women's employment in Brampton, including domestic service, it would appear that remaining at home, and dependent, was preferable to migrating to a larger urban centre in search of employment.

Still, the duration of the period between school-leaving and marriage for women, or school leaving and autonomy for young men, was in any case somewhat shorter in the town than in the rural areas of the county because of the very different patterns of school attendance in Brampton. In contrast to Peel's rural parents among whom only 50% sent all their school-aged children to school in 1870, three-quarters of Brampton's parents were sending all of their children aged 7-14 to school in that year. Consequently, while less than 75% of Peel's potential rural school population attended school sometime during the year, nearly 90% of Brampton's school-age children spent at least part of the year in class. Moreover, no single variable or combination of circumstances differentiates the least from the most diligent of Brampton's parents. Three out of four school-aged children of unskilled labourers attended school, comparable to the school attendance ratio for the children of merchants. Clearly, more of the town's children, whatever their social background, attended school and for a greater part of their young lives than did children of the farm.

There are two possible explanations for these very distinct patterns. The first, and most elementary, is that town life and particularly the making of livings in a world of essentially adult labour altered the labour potential of children (a strong argument for smaller families since children no longer contributed to the economy of the family) and, consequently, the appeal, for working parents, of the school as an antidote to their children's enforced idleness. It must also have been true, in a community in which the skilled metal workers and the artisans who produced luxury goods sent more of their children to public school than did merchants, government officials, and professionals (who, to be fair, may have been able to afford private tutors), that these townspeople set greater store in the rewards of formal education than did their rural neighbours. Whether they perceived education as a necessary prerequisite for the trades and professions which their town-bred sons would one day enter, or as the new engine of individual improvement, is not clear.[13] What is certain is that for the children of

Peel County two ways of life had emerged by 1870 defined by the greater ability or willingness of some parents, 'urban' parents, to send most of their children to school and, ultimately, by the crucial differences in size and structure between Peel's rural and urban families.

The size of the family, the nature of individual experience — particularly among women and children — within the context of family life, and the nature of work were the principal characteristics then which distinguished life in Brampton from life in the town's immediate hinterland. But in other respects the two societies were similar. For example, approximately only one in three of Brampton's adult population in 1861 still lived in the town a decade later, a level of persistence comparable to that in the surrounding townships. Similarly, the contraction of household size and structure in Brampton paralleled the same development in rural Peel, although at a slightly slower rate. In 1871 two-thirds of Brampton's households contained only single family units compared to 73% of the rural households. On the other hand, in just fifteen years the structure of this urban society had become more rigid than its older counterpart ever had been.

Measuring relative degrees of affluence and status in Brampton is complicated by the lack of reliable information on incomes or assessed value for the period before 1879. However, the 1871 census return reported the number of dwellings, town building lots, and commercial structures (shops, warehouses, or factories) owned by each head of family. Using these data it is possible to describe, with great accuracy, the relative distribution of real property among the residents of the town, especially the distribution of property surplus to the immediate requirements of each family. Leaving aside the question of the actual or assessed value of different types of real estate, property ownership nevertheless may be taken as a fairly sensitive indicator of the comparative rewards from various types of employment if we begin with the assumption that home ownership was the lowest common denominator of economic achievement and social status in the town. Conversely, in a fluid, expanding, prosperous community, exercising effective control over the availability of residential, commercial, and industrial property would appear to be one of the principal sources of new fortunes.

Table 54 describes the relationship in Brampton between property ownership and vocational function. What is particularly striking (but not surprising) is that the men who provided the skills and the muscle for Brampton's most important industries — transportation, construction, and metal fabricating — as well as the unskilled were least likely to possess either a house or a building lot. Such accommodations as they could afford were provided by a small group of property owners, 13% of the householders, who owned two or more dwellings. This same minority owned most of the town's surplus building lots as well. In fact, 10% of Brampton's householders, the most affluent 10% as it turns out,

TABLE 54

Distribution of heads of family by property ownership and occupational rank, Brampton 1871

	Houses			Lots			Shops		
	None	One	Two+	None	One	Two+	None	One	Two+
Agriculture	11.1	61.1	27.8	22.2	50.0	27.8	83.3	16.7	0
Mfct. apparel	54.2	25.0	20.8	54.2	25.0	20.8	83.3	16.7	0
Mfct. wood products	50.0	50.0	0.0	50.0	41.7	8.3	8.3	8.3	8.4
Mfct. metal prod.	86.0	13.3	0.7	80.0	13.3	6.7	100.0	0	0
Mfct. food prod.	50.0	41.7	8.3	33.3	33.3	34.0	50.0	50.0	0
Mfct. luxury goods	57.1	14.3	28.6	57.1	0.0	42.9	71.4	28.6	0
Industrialist	40.0	20.0	40.0	40.0	0.0	60.0	60.0	0	40.0
Construction	60.4	32.1	7.5	60.4	32.1	7.5	90.6	9.4	0
Labour	59.2	36.7	4.1	59.2	28.6	12.2	100.0	0	0
Commerce	50.0	25.9	24.1	44.8	19.0	36.2	79.3	15.5	5.2
Transportation	62.3	30.2	7.5	64.2	18.9	17.0	84.9	7.5	7.5
Public service	44.4	44.4	11.1	22.2	44.4	33.3	100.0	0	0
Professional	52.2	34.8	13.0	43.5	26.1	30.4	82.6	17.4	0
Govt/Education	54.5	27.3	18.2	54.5	18.2	27.3	100.0	0	0
No. occup.	53.7	33.3	13.0	53.7	29.6	16.7	90.7	9.3	0
	$\chi^2 = 0.001$			$\chi^2 = 0.006$			$\chi^2 = 0.001$		
All	54.3	32.5	13.2	52.9	26.3	20.8	86.8	10.7	2.5

Note: rows add horizontally.

controlled 66% of the town's building lots in 1871 and 82% of the lots not owner-occupied. Finally, within this minority a group of ten men together owned slightly more than half of Brampton's commercial/industrial property. The distribution of residential and business property in the town, in short, was characterized by gross inequalities. At one end of the scale, half of the married male wage-earners owned no real estate. These were, predominantly, the skilled, semi-skilled, and unskilled working men employed in Brampton's major industries. At the other end of the spectrum four industrialists, three grain merchants, two retired farmers, two dozen businessmen and highly skilled craftsmen, a handful of county officials and professional men, and two very rich widows — in all less than 10% of the town's householders — owned most of Brampton's residential and commercial real estate (see Table 58). Between these two poles of affluence, the remaining one-third of Brampton's families lived in owner-occupied houses or at least had property on which to erect a home.

If vocation distinguished the wealthiest 10% of Brampton's families from the least affluent 50%, two other distinguishing characteristics were especially associated with affluence. The first was persistence in the community. Householders who had been resident in the community for at least ten years were more likely than recent immigrants to own property of any sort, and much more likely to be speculators in residential or commercial real estate (Table 55(b)). Second, although the probability of acquiring a house increased with age, the most active

TABLE 55

Distribution of heads of family by property ownership and selected variables, Brampton 1871

(a) By age cohort

	15-34	34-49	50-64	65+	All
Owns no houses	68.8	51.1	40.3	26.1	54.3
One house	24.6	32.1	40.3	56.5	32.5
Two or more	6.5	16.8	19.4	17.4	13.2
	100.0	100.0	100.0	100.0	100.0
$(\chi^2 = 0.001)$					
Owns no lots	64.5	51.1	40.3	21.7	52.9
one lot	21.7	26.3	21.0	65.2	26.3
two or more	13.8	22.6	38.7	13.0	20.8
	100.0	100.0	100.0	100.0	100.0
$(\chi^2 = 0.001)$					

(b) By persistence

	Persistent 1861-71	Immigrant	All
Owns no houses	33.0	62.8	54.3
one house	41.7	28.8	32.9
two or more	25.2	8.3	13.2
	100.0	100.0	100.0
$(\chi^2 = 0.001;$ eta $= 0.288)$			
Owns no lots	33.0	60.8	52.9
one lot	33.0	23.6	26.3
two or more	34.0	15.6	20.8
$(\chi^2 = 0.001;$ eta $= 0.249)$			
Owns no shops	78.3	90.3	86.8
one shop	17.4	8.0	10.7
Two or more	4.3	1.7	2.5
	100.0	100.0	100.0
$(\chi^2 = 0.001;$ eta $= 0.142)$			

speculators in real estate were men in their late fifties (Table 55(a)). The significance of these two facts must be interpreted in the light of what is not significant. Contrary to expectations, in Brampton there was no significant correlation between ethnicity and relative affluence, or religious affiliation and wealth, or even, in a broadly aggregated sense, between the wealth of the native-born and the recent British immigrant. Having been present at the creation of this new community was a more important determinant of economic rank than any other social characteristic. The relationship between age and relative wealth seems to underscore the importance of stability in promoting success; and in fact, as we shall see, 90% of Brampton's wealthiest and most powerful men in 1871 had been residents of the community for at least ten years, while two-fifths of them had lived in the hamlet long before the coming of the railroad. In sum, although there were clearly new opportunities for employment and even entrepreneurship on the urban frontier, the spoils from successfully exploiting that frontier, in Brampton at least, accrued to those who first understood and capitalized on its economic potential.[14]

If property ownership is an adequate surrogate index of wealth — in this case a measure of the distinction between men with sufficient surplus capital to speculate in business and real estate ventures and those, at the other extreme, who had no disposable income beyond that required to meet their daily needs — then property ownership should correlate highly with some of the other measurable attributes of economic rank and social status. One of these attributes which does bear a significant relationship to wealth is household structure; and in Brampton the relationship between affluence and household structure differed remarkably from the characteristics of rural society. In the surrounding townships, the presence of relatives, boarders, visitors, and live-in help in the household was related primarily to the cycle of family life. Within that context, the presence of employees — servants in particular — was also related to social rank. But by 1871 the contraction of rural households which took place in the preceding decade was especially reflected in the disappearance of resident employees, domestic or otherwise, from farm households. In Brampton, there was no relationship between household structure and the cycle of family life. Rather, the presence of 'extras' in these urban households was a function, apparently, of a single determinant, relative affluence. Householders whose attributes included, among others, the ownership of two or more properties invariably tended to support larger and more complex domestic establishments than their less affluent neighbours. More to the point, as Table 56 illustrates, they were far more likely to include live-in help among the residents of their households. For the public and professional men, the town's principal retail merchants and grain dealers, its leading industrialists and intellectuals, the composition of their households clearly was a symbol of status, visible testimony to their economic and social hegemony in Brampton (see Table 57).[15]

Who then, were Brampton's visible 'élite'? Assuming that persistence and the possession of two or more properties and a domestic establishment larger than the single family unit — particularly if it contained live-in help — ultimately distinguish the few from the many, twenty-nine householders, 7% of the total, met these criteria in 1871. The list (Table 58) excludes three men, a carriage manufacturer, a wagon manufacturer, and the owner of a cabinet factory, each of whom failed to meet this rather arbitrary property qualification (perhaps they had their capital tied up in their businesses) but who shared the fourth characteristic common to the twenty-five *men* in this group. From 1855 until 1870 they were, as a group, continuously overrepresented on the Brampton Town Council.

TABLE 56

Distribution of heads of household by property ownership and household structure, Brampton 1871 (percentages)

	(a) Houses			(b) Building lots			(c) Shops			
	None	One	Two+	None	One	Two+	None	One	Two+	All
(a) Household size =										
family size	71.2	67.9	47.2	72.8	67.9	51.2	69.4	60.5	10.0	67.0
Greater than										
family size	28.8	32.1	52.8	27.2	32.1	48.8	30.6	39.5	90.0	33.0
	100.0	100.0	100.0	100.0	100.0	100.0	100.0	100.0	100.0	100.0
	($\chi^2 = 0.01$; eta = 0.167)			($\chi^2 = 0.01$; eta = 0.178)			($\chi^2 = 0.01$; eta = 0.202)			
(b) Resident employees										
none	84.9	81.5	54.7	86.5	83.0	61.4	82.5	74.4	30.0	83.3
one	10.3	10.0	32.1	9.7	10.4	25.1	11.4	18.6	50.0	13.1
Two or more	3.8	8.5	13.2	3.9	8.6	13.3	6.1	7.0	20.0	8.6
	100.0	100.0	100.0	100.0	100.0	100.0	100.0	100.0	100.0	100.0
	($\chi^2 = 0.01$)			($\chi^2 = 0.001$)			($\chi^2 = 0.001$)			

TABLE 57

Distribution of heads of household by household structure and occupational rank,
Brampton 1871

	Household= family	Household greater than family	Resident Employees		
			0	1	2+
Agriculture	55.6	44.4	61.1	27.8	11.1
Mfct. apparel	75.0	25.0			
Mfct. wood products	83.3	16.7			
Mfct. metal products	86.7	13.3	81.8	13.6	4.5
Mfct. food products	58.3	41.7			
Mfct. luxury goods	57.1	42.9			
Industrialist	60.0	40.0	(included with commerce)		
Labour	75.5	24.5	90.8	5.8	3.4
Commerce	51.7	48.3	66.7	17.5	15.8
Transportation	77.4	22.6	(included with unskilled)		
Public service	55.6	44.4			
Professional	56.5	43.5	64.7	26.5	8.8
Govt/education	27.3	72.7			
No. occup.	55.6	44.4	82.7	11.5	5.8
All	67.0	33.0	80.3	13.1	8.8
	($\chi^2 = 0.001$)		(χ^2 sig. at 0.001 for collapsed ranks only)		

TABLE 58

Brampton's 'Visible élite' 1870-1

(1) *'Industrialists'*
  foundry owner†
  carriage works owner*

(2) *Skilled artisans*
  carpenter*
  bricklayer*
  cooper†

(3) *Professional and public men*
  county registrar
  doctor†
  judge†
  gaoler
  lawyer
  lawyer†
  publisher*
  publisher

(4) *Commerce*
  grain merchant†
  druggist†
  general merchant*
  chandler*
  livery stable owner*
  hotel keeper* (2)
  auctioneer†
  merchant tailor*
  shoemaker*

(5) *Unskilled labour*

  None

(6) *Others*
  widow* (2)
  gentleman† (2)

* Present before 1861   † Present before 1855

In seven out of eleven years they exercised an effective majority; and in 1869-70
their control was absolute (Table 59). Moreover, their representatives were
almost invariably men who had resided in the community since at least the early
1850s. In short, the other attribute, the most important attribute, of this class

TABLE 59

Representation of Brampton's wealthiest householders on town council 1855-70*

1855	1856	1857	1858	1859	1864
5/7	4/6	6/7	2/5	2/5	2/5

1865	1866	1867	1868	1869-70
2/5	2/5	3/5	3/4	4/4

* Information is missing for 1860-3, but presumably the figures for 1860 and 1863 are 2/5 in each case.

was the power that it exercised, through the press and local government, over employment opportunities, and over development within the town's boundaries. Power, personal and collective, was both the instrument and the reward of their hegemony in a new urban community not far removed from its agrarian origins, but far enough to have acquired many of the characteristics, especially the rigid social, economic, and political structures, of a much older urban society. Thus, the lines of demarcation between Brampton's emergent social classes were already sharply drawn within two decades of the beginning of urban development in the community. At the most elementary level those lines separated capital from labour, employer from employee, the skilled from the unskilled. But factors other than production and individual relationships to that process played an equally important role in the stratification of this society.

Not the least of these was a demographic factor — the residential stability of a very few families within a highly fluid society. To all intents and purposes Brampton was like a hotel whose resident owners built the structure, established the house rules and tariffs, and operated most of the concessions which catered to the needs of a constantly changing population of transients, some travelling first class, some economy class, but all sharing the same essential characteristic: they did not stay. Whatever value they derived from their brief sojourn in Brampton, in the end most of the benefits of their passage accrued to their permanently placed hosts.[16] For the persistent minority, as for Robert the Bruce's spider, perseverance was not merely its own reward. It was the key to success on this new frontier, just as it was in the backwoods of mid-Victorian Ontario.

The people of Brampton represented, in 1870, less than 12% of Peel County's total population. Their importance and the importance of their town in this predominantly rural society far outweighed considerations of mere numerical strength. This is not simply a matter of the rapidity with which Brampton established hegemony over its hinterland, although that, too, is of some consequence. What is significant about the town and its population is that they embodied a demonstrable departure from the forms, structures, and rhythms of life and of individual experience in the countryside. Brampton's 'urban' society was not a complete antithesis of Peel's agrarian society in 1870, nor would it ever be. By 1870 rural society had already begun to change, to move toward a new configuration of attitudes, behaviour, and structures, not least of all because Brampton, and dozens of other towns like it, vigorously pursued their mission as instruments through which the grip of conventional wisdom, tastes, attitudes, modes of production, and forms of social organization among hinterland populations was gradually loosened.[17] In Peel County, the people of Brampton could be seen to have moved farther along that path leading from a more to a less traditional world of social reality than had rural society. Their example was unquestionably important to the way in which their more conservative neighbours sought an accommodation with the forces of change prodding them along the path of transition.

7 Peel and a Wider World

The romanticized lithographs of Peel County's best farms which graced the county atlas of 1877 (see Map 5) capture better than any other source the ideal world of the mid-Victorian Upper Canadian farmer: a landscape subdued and improved by ordinary men for whom land and its material promises were the rewards of their industry. To whatever extent the realities of life in mid-nineteenth-century rural Ontario approximated this ideal, they did so, if the experience of the people of Peel County is in any way representative, as the result of the working out of a set of historical processes through which the circumstances of rural life were transformed from those of a fundamentally primitive to those of an established, improved society. In Peel County that transition came about swiftly, perhaps in less than two decades.

In 1840 Peel County was still a community of pioneers, a frontier of cheap, though not free land, much of it still vacant, the rest occupied by families whose condition was not far removed from James Reid's circumstances as he described them in the late 1820s. His cleared land and his livestock supplied his family's basic needs. Surplus production, from which he derived whatever cash income he had, consisted of some wheat and, more importantly, the timber cleared from his land, burned for potash and hauled out by sled in the winter to be sold at York.[1] By the mid-forties, however, there were visible signs of change in Peel. The proportion of improved to occupied land increased rapidly after 1842 as the appearance of a new American market for Canadian agricultural produce promoted the system of extensive cropping, especially of wheat, which became the stock-in-trade of the improving Peel County farmer. Reid, in 1849, marvelled at the transformation of his surroundings. 'Good roads ... good Houses ... great improvements going on in this place ... and we are well supplied with preaching now ... we have something to give them.'[2]

The 1850s simply produced a more dramatic variation of the events of the late forties. The coming of the railway heightened the market orientation and dependence of Peel's farmers, whose new prosperity was translated partly into

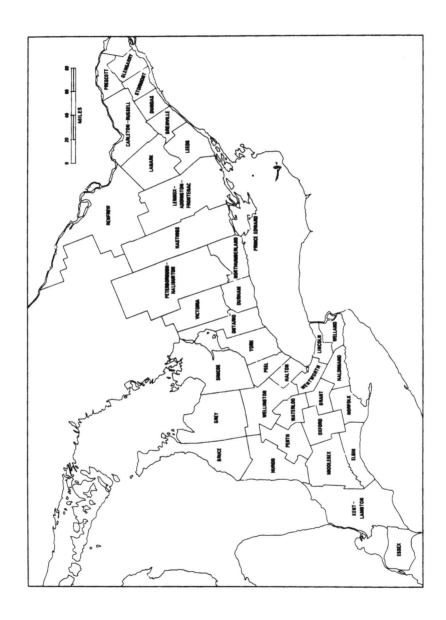

Map 5 The counties of Ontario 1871

increased creature comforts and new technology, but primarily into additional land (the average total value of implements on a Peel County farm in 1861, less than $200, was lower than the cost, $350, of a new threshing machine). As a hedge against inflation, as the agency of increased production, and as patrimonies for at least some of their sons, additional land was a good investment for these men, if it could be acquired on reasonable terms. But Peel's proximity to the Toronto and American markets, the fertility of its soil, and its excellent transportation facilities quickly attracted the attention of outsiders, as it was bound to do in the new era of prosperity and improvement. Reid noticed in 1849 that land within a twenty-mile radius of Toronto was more valuable than land only slightly further removed from the metropolis.[3] Peel lay in the next isopleth and in the mid-fifties improved transportation, migration, and farm expansion combined to drive the price of land beyond the reach of men without the capital or security to dabble in a vendor's market. Those who could risked their security on the promise of continued prosperity and improvement, a promise that remained undiminished, in spite of a major downturn in the Canadian economy, until the early sixties.

As it happened, the wheat harvest of 1861, nearly 25 million bushels, represented the most spectacular achievement of Upper Canada's wheat farmers for more than a decade to come. In the 1860s falling prices and declining export markets simply aggravated, in places like Peel County, the much more serious problem of land that would no longer grow as much wheat as before, and in some cases none at all. It nevertheless seems certain that farm expansion in the 1850s and the generally large farms of Peel County farmers in any event permitted them to sustain production values in a period of declining yields and to make the transition from specialization to mixed farming. That transition was virtually complete when better times returned with the development of an expanding domestic market for Ontario's farm products and with the revivification, after 1870, of traditional export markets.

In short, it is useful to think of Peel County's local agricultural economy in terms of three phases: a pioneer phase characterized by economic and social underdevelopment lasting from 1820 until the mid-1840s; a stage of rapid agricultural improvement, demographic growth, and, to a lesser extent, social improvement associated with a buoyant wheat economy from the mid-forties until about 1862; and, finally, a period of equally rapid economic and demographic transition which perhaps ought to be dated from the farm expansion movement of the late fifties, lasting until the early seventies when farm size, farm production, and the farm population had acquired the characteristics they would bear for the remainder of the century. These three phases in the history of this local economy should not be interpreted, however, in terms of a morphological model of growth, stagnation, and decline. Given the limited chronological parameters of this book, the successive attributes of Peel's agrarian economy represent, at best, three variations on a single theme, the time-specific effects of external factors and local circumstances which played equally vital roles in defining the nature, the duration, and the rewards of a particular type of economic activity which was pursued with unequal intensity by the people of Peel over the course of nearly four decades. If the export of staples provided the impetus for agricultural improvement and demographic growth in the county between 1845 and 1858, local circumstances, specifically intragenerational demographic pressure and the desire of established farmers to maintain a standard of living associated with intense specialization even after specialization was redundant, were responsible for the major changes which occurred in Peel in the 1860s. In effect underdevelopment, measured by declining opportunities for new men in both the farm and non-farm sectors of the rural economy after 1860, resulted, in the first instance, from the actions of the area's most established farmers in pursuit of their particular economic biases. That those biases proved untenable in the 1860s is almost beside the point in light of the consequences of their actions in the longer term when the operation of external factors again seemed to renew the historical promise of rural life in Ontario in the 1870s. In sum, the changes which took place in this local economy were neither linear nor inevitable. They had as much to do with the localized actions of men as with the operation of 'forces,' and they took place within a cultural context that remained essentially unified for half a century at least.

Nevertheless, change did take place, and those changes which occurred in the economic sphere were necessarily accompanied by transitions in the social sphere. This process of social transformation is revealed nowhere more clearly than in the much altered characteristics of Peel's families and households at the outset of the 1870s compared with their common traits two decades earlier. Among those changes which were brought about, the most elemental was the gradual attrition of the structure of rural households as the presence of 'extras' of all sorts became less and less common. Conversely, the simple family unit tended to retain its cohesiveness for a significantly longer period of time while maturing children endured a lengthening period of dependence upon their parents given the contraction of economic opportunity in the 1860s. These events, and the historical circumstances which gave rise to them, seem all the more consequential when viewed at the level of individual experience, especially in terms of the cycle of life within the farm family. Before 1860, the nature of childhood, the timing of family formation, the rates of reproduction among parents, and the relationships between parents and children reflected the attitudes of a society with a fundamentally unshakeable faith in the promise of abundance from cheap land and family labour. In 1847, at the age of 69, James Reid and his wife lived 'perfectly at [their] ease' on the rental income from their farm. One of their six living children, the daughter of their old age, was still at home. Their four sons had long since acquired farms of their own and Reid's eldest daughter was married to a farmer. These departed children had established their own households in their early twenties. The eldest, Thomas, who was 32 in 1847, was already the father of four children.[4] This pattern of early family formation and actual rates of reproduction that were close to women's natural fecundity within marriage were consistent with the economic realities of life in a developing agrarian society in which labour was a scarcer commodity than land, a society in which, as the Upper Canadian Malthus, Robert Gourlay, observed three decades earlier, 'spirited improvement require[d] many hands.'[5]

By the middle of the next decade (the 1850s), however, such improvements as labour alone would accomplish were well in hand. Further improvement, especially social betterment, had less to do with muscle than with capital and income, less to do with the economics of increased production than with satisfying the farm family's expectation of a higher standard of living from their common labour. In these circumstances, a large family presented the improving farmer with an imponderable dilemma. Whose expectations should be fulfilled, and at what cost to his own security and to the well-being of the family as a whole? The result, of course, was a significant alteration in the mechanisms for the intergenerational transmission of property and personal wealth, and therefore in the social expectations of wives and children once the brief and costly experiment in farm expansion in order to reward more children with land had failed.

These events evidently shaped the experience and conditioned the attitudes of the next generation of farm families, who were the products of significantly later (that is, delayed) ages of marriage and of somewhat revised attitudes toward children. Farm families became smaller, primarily as the result of delays in family formation but partly, as we have seen, through the determination of at least some of the women in the community, especially second- and third-generation native-born rural women, to limit arbitrarily the number of conceptions to be endured in the course of a marriage. Moreover, the extent to which this tendency toward smaller families indicates a re-evaluation of the role of children in this society appears to be reinforced by evidence from another sphere, the nature of childhood itself. The propensity of Peel's parents to send increasingly larger numbers of their school-aged children, especially girls, to school as an acceptable surrogate for the training for life which they customarily received at home suggests that a formal education was both one of the rewards of social betterment and equally one of the arguments for limiting the numbers of offspring who, in future, would contribute less to the family's common objective while continuing to anticipate the material benefits associated with improvement.

By 1860, the lowest common denominator of social improvement in Peel was property ownership. It distinguished the haves from the have-nots among the families who comprised this agrarian society, not because it was the scarcest commodity but rather because property ownership appears to have been the prerequisite for all other forms of social betterment and, in the end, the source of that most elusive of all the social attributes of mid-Victorian Canadians, attachment to place. Ironically, whether a man would acquire property and how much of it (unless he was fortunate enough to inherit it) depended, after mid-century, on his willingness to undergo a rather slow process of vocational and, if he was successful, economic mobility which in turn was dependent on persistence in this place where there was a fairly high drop-out rate, even among established farmers. Yet few of the landless migrants who passed through Peel willingly endured this time-serving. They came and left at a great rate, temporarily finding a niche vacated by some previous drop-out following the same well-worn paths to full employment and as yet unfulfilled dreams of economic security and social standing. It is this distinction between the families in motion and those for whom Peel was good country which represents the essential face of inequality in this mid-Victorian society.

By 1870 Peel County was no longer a field for 'spirited improvement' of the sort characteristic of new agrarian societies. Preserving what had already been won from the land had become as important a preoccupation as exhausting its inestimable potential had been two or three decades earlier. The transition from one set of priorities to the other was swift, indeed very nearly complete in just ten years; and it was accompanied by a complementary social transformation which conferred on the people of Peel the attributes of an agrarian society no longer young in terms of the nature of their material environment, of the rewards to be expected from it, and of the social relationships which it sustained.

These generalizations adequately summarize the characteristics of the population of mid-Victorian Peel County, Canada West, and the processes which fostered social change or promoted continuity in this society at a critical period in its history. Taken alone they convey very little about the generality or the uniqueness of the characteristics of these people in the context of a wider world of historical social experience. Peel, after all, was not an isolated world of social and economic activity. The people of Peel shared a region and a continent with a predominantly agrarian population just as they shared, in a less tangible sense, a set of fundamental preconceptions and preoccupations with other traditional societies through time. In short, how typical of similarly situated rural societies were the people of mid-nineteenth-century Peel County?

One way of assessing their characteristics is to compare them with the population of Canada West's other rural counties at mid-century. Figures 5 to 12 make this comparison graphically by locating the people of Peel and some of their time-specific characteristics along an east-west geographical axis in relation to their nearest and most remote neighbours among the province's counties. There are two ways to analyse these graphs. One is simply to observe the relationship between Peel and the other 23 counties, and another is to ask, using

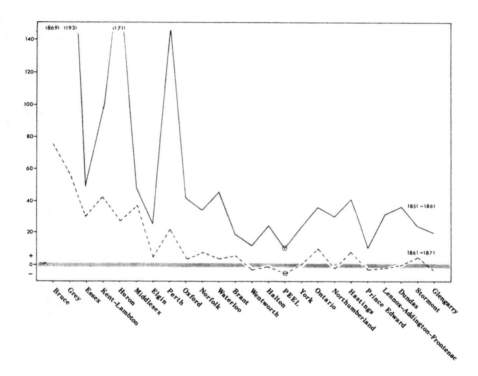

5 Population, percentage change, selected Ontario counties 1851-61, 1861-71

coefficients of correlation, whether Peel had especially unique characteristics which set it apart from the general aspect of provincial society.

In the first instance, it is clear that in a region where the major demographic and economic trends, over time, tended to flow in an east-west direction, none of Peel's demographic characteristics seems to have set it outside the mainstream of events. Indeed, if anything Peel was a model of consistency compared, for example, to the erratic behaviour of the data for some other counties, including Peel's nearest neighbours, Halton and York (see general marital fertility, Figure 7). Among the demographic indicators employed here, however, it is necessary to pay closest attention to the drift of population itself which was decidedly toward the newest areas of settlement in both the 1850s and 1860s, Huron, Perth, Grey and Bruce counties (Figure 5). The unique characteristics of these places (Table 60), smaller farms, sex ratios biased toward a preponderance of males, a lack of agricultural improvement (proportion of occupied acreage cultivated), and the absence of intergenerational land pressure (acres available

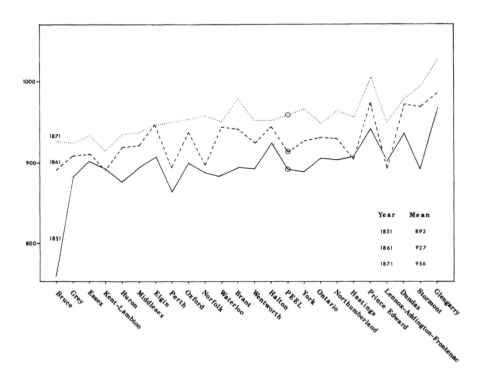

6 Females per 1,000 males, selected Ontario counties 1851-71

per man aged 15-30), are all attributes of essentially underdeveloped pioneer societies. Peel shared none of those characteristics, by mid-century, to a significant degree. On the other hand, it is clear that the lakefront counties immediately west of Toronto shared with some of the older settled counties further east the common characteristic of rural depopulation or demographic stasis by the 1860s. The reasons for this may have varied, however, from one region to another. For example, in Glengarry and Prince Edward counties population loss was preceded by the appearance of significantly higher female/male ratios and lower rates of general marital fertility than elsewhere in the province. And in each case these events were antecedents of the re-establishment of more favourable man/land ratios. In short, other areas of the province appear to have experienced, to a more pronounced extent, the same transformation that took place in Peel. On the other hand, demographic stasis in Lennox-Addington-Frontenac and in Dundas County was associated with a single unique local characteristic; farm size there, significantly smaller than in the other older

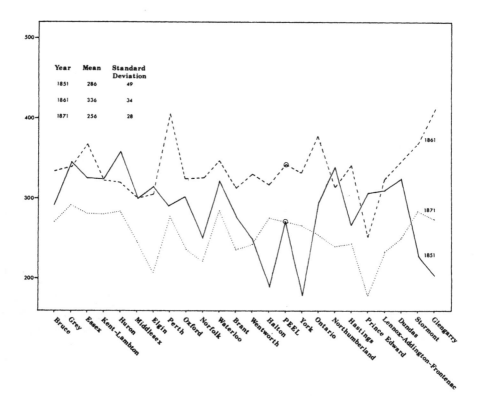

Year	Mean	Standard Deviation
1851	286	49
1861	336	34
1871	256	28

7 Number of live births (corrected for infant deaths) per 1,000 married women aged 15-49, selected Ontario counties 1851-71

townships, may indicate a tendency to subdivide older farms, a bias which had run its course by 1860 when outmigration became the only alternative for many children. This, however, is mere speculation. In Peel, where significantly higher ratios of cropped to cultivated land were the order by 1870, we already know both the cause and the consequences of that development.

In terms of agricultural practices the farmers of Peel clearly shared with their colleagues in Brant, Waterloo, Wentworth, Halton, York, and Prince Edward counties by the 1860s this propensity toward high ratios of cropped to cultivated acreage (Figure 10). By 1871 the farmers further to the west and to the east were far more specialized, as Peel had been in 1851, in terms of what their land produced (Figure 1); but the counties of Ontario which owed their original prosperity, their original impetus toward improvement, as Peel did, to the north-south exchange of staples for goods, 1845-60, still held a consistently higher proportion of land under heavy cropping in 1871 than any other region of

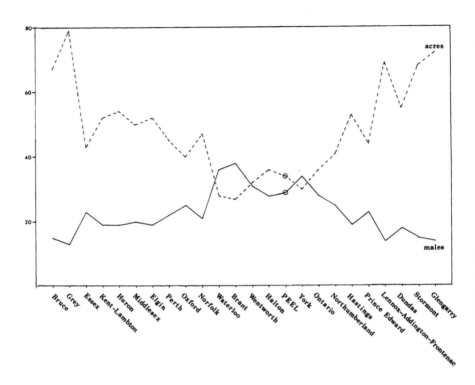

8 Ratio of males aged 15-30 per 1,000 acres of land available through mobility, mortality, and increased cultivation, selected Ontario counties

Ontario. They also happened to be the counties closest to the province's largest urban concentration. Land use, then, set the farmers of these central counties apart, just as the demographic consequences of extensive cropping were more pronounced there than in other parts of the province. The region from Waterloo County to Ontario County had disproportionately larger numbers of young male aspirants for land in 1871, and proportionately less land for them, than had either the oldest or the newest regions of settlement (Figure 8). It was also true that the area between Brant and Ontario counties, in 1871, still had the highest per acre yields of wheat in Ontario, in spite of crop diversification, further evidence that in places like Peel total production values, farm size, and standards of living were probably highly correlated.

Taken together, then, land use, intergenerational land pressure, and farm size represent a historical configuration of economic and demographic factors common to a whole region of Upper Canada at mid-century, a region of which Peel

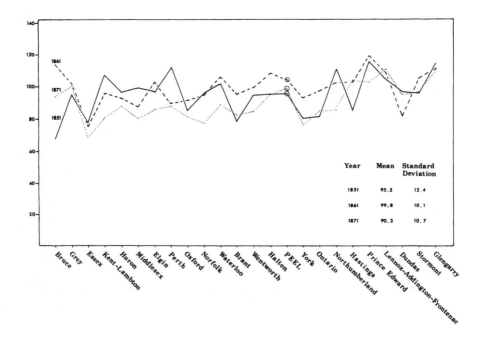

9 Average size of holding (in acres), selected Ontario counties 1851-71

was a part both geographically and in terms of a set of common factors that identify the time-specific economic and demographic characteristics of the area just before and just after the confederation of the British North American provinces. Complain as they would about the immediate causes of the crisis of confidence in Upper Canada's agrarian economy in the mid-sixties, the legislators who favoured the expansion of Ontario's agricultural frontier under the auspices of a new Dominion authority were responding, in fact, not to an immediate problem, but to a historical one, a problem that was inherent in the processes of social and economic change common to backwoods societies in transition.

   These historical processes and their consequences were peculiar neither to Peel County nor to Victorian Canada West. By the middle of the eighteenth century, when an entire continent of free land lay at their feet, the people of Massachusetts' rural villages and townships were forced to face the facts of local overpopulation — too many sons competing for too little familial land or other

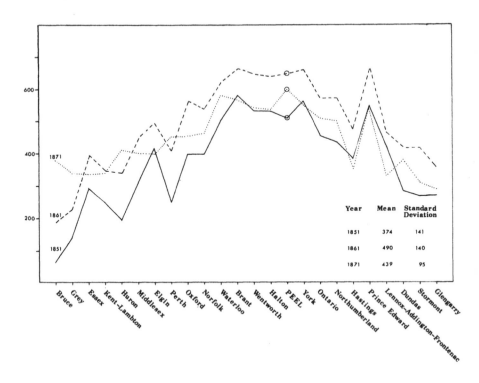

The table within the figure reads:

Year	Mean	Standard Deviation
1851	374	141
1861	490	140
1871	439	95

10 Cropped acreage per 1,000 occupied acres, selected Ontario counties 1851-71

forms of economic opportunity — and to take steps to mitigate this problem. An impartible system of inheritance, the enforced migration of new families to the region's 'frontier' in the Connecticut River valley, longer stages of dependence for children, declining birth rates, and demographic stagnation were all demonstrable consequences of the unwillingness of members of one generation to imperil their own hard-won security by sharing it equally with all of their children as the community's resources became increasingly strained.[6] Similarly, by the middle of the eighteenth century Pennsylvania's colonial farm population considered farms of less than 150 acres too small, in terms of the standards of living they provided, to be subdivided for sale or transmission through inheritance. Consequently, unless 'a young person had considerable capital or a farm to inherit he would have faced the prospect of moving to a place where land was cheaper.'[7] Here the young, the artisans, and the smallholders constituted a

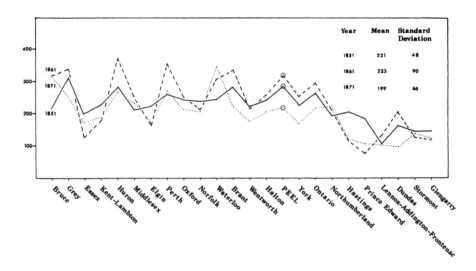

Year	Mean	Standard Deviation
1851	221	48
1861	233	90
1871	199	66

11 Acres in wheat per 1,000 occupied acres, selected Ontario counties 1851-71

population of perennial migrants who encountered in Pennsylvania's established farming communities essentially the same inequalities in property ownership and essentially the same vocational structures and levels of opportunity as the migrant who passed through Peel County a hundred years later.[8]

In the middle of the nineteenth century, but a thousand miles west of Peel County, the prairies of Iowa and Illinois were settled by the growing families of men in their thirties, a third of whom, from any settlement cohort, had already lived in two or more states of the Union or in one of the regions of British America. In any decade after 1850 only about 40% of these immigrants stayed for at least a decade, and after twenty years less than 30% of the families in any settlement cohort were still residents of the rural counties in which they had settled. The behaviour of these prairie farmers, in short, was no different from that of the population of mid-Victorian Peel. In those places, too, time-serving as a tenant farmer was often the road to property ownership in a society in which the ratio of proprietors to tenants was remarkably constant, and remarkably similar to that in eighteenth-century Pennsylvania and mid-Victorian Peel. The only significant variation in the traits of these prairie farmers was their willingness to subdivide land because they started with much larger farms (average 188 acres) than their counterparts in Peel.[9] Northward from the mid-western corn belt, the farmers of Wisconsin were equally as footloose and as likely to

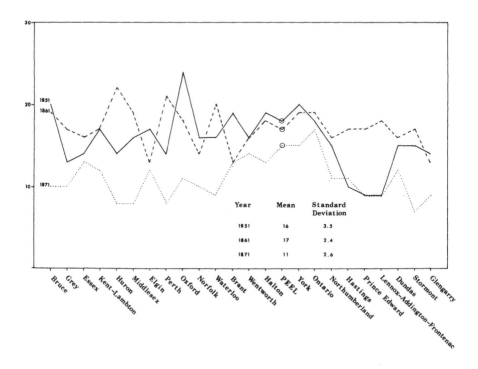

Year	Mean	Standard Deviation
1851	16	3.5
1861	17	2.4
1871	11	2.6

12 Wheat production (bu. per acre), selected Ontario counties 1851-71

equate prosperity with specialization as their cousins in Peel or in Illinois. More to the point, in Wisconsin property ownership and farm expansion were the principal rewards of persistence and essential defences against dramatic fluctuations in local productivity as the result of either soil exhaustion or shifting market preferences. Adaptability and mobility, in sum, represented the essential polarity of rural attitudes toward the changing material circumstances of life in Blooming Grove, Wisconsin, as it underwent, after 1860, a sometimes painful transition from a pioneer to an established agrarian community.[10] Indeed, among the rural population of mid-nineteenth-century America generally, the transition from the material conditions of new areas to those of old areas seems to have followed a recognizable pattern everywhere, a historical pattern sustained by the timeless equation between land, economic improvement, and social security. Whatever strategies North American rural societies developed to promote their common goal from time to time, in the end, limiting the availability of land at some point in their development and accepting the social, demographic, cultural, and emotional consequences of that restriction in order to achieve an acceptable level of material existence for the farm family and its offspring, were the most effective means of accommodating forces of change and asserting their preference for continuity.

The timing of the impetus to change and of the appearance of altered circumstances set the people of mid-Victorian Peel County, Canada West, apart from their contemporaries in rural Upper Canada and North America. But in most other respects they were not different from the people of those other agrarian societies with whom, historically and chronologically, they shared the continent. The material basis of their lives, the rewards it conferred, the exactions it demanded, and the social relationships it sustained from time to time constituted the cement of a single historical experience common to several generations of European emigrants to rural North America.[11] The role of the family was the critical bonding agent. Decisions made within the family in the light of historical experience, present realities, and future expectations, decisions made independently because the family and no other agency was responsible for its destiny, decisions taken by whole societies of families in different places and at different times but under similar circumstances and, therefore, with predictably similar effects, were the primary agents of change and continuity in individual experience.

For the mid-Victorian Canadian family, the nature, the timing, and the consequences of the decisions it made were critical. Two vital components of Victorian Canadian culture invariably hung in the balance — the cohesiveness of the family and the promise of improvement. Balancing one against the other, while striving relentlessly to sustain both, was an art practised with consummate skill and great deliberation by the farm families of nineteenth-century Upper Canada. But flexibility in the face of swiftly changing circumstances was particularly appropriate in the decade and a half before the Confederation of the British American provinces. In the social and economic, no less than in the political and constitutional spheres, these were 'critical years' in the history of Upper Canada. Between 1850 and 1870 Canada West underwent a fundamental transformation associated with rapid demographic growth, urban development, improved transportation facilities, technological change, and the introduction of new modes of production. All of these developments had their effects on the material bases of ordinary life in the cities, towns, and rural townships of the province where men, public and private, drew satisfaction from the progressive elements in this transformation, brooded over its unsettling aspects, and, in the end, adjusted their individual expectations and attitudes to accommodate present realities.

TABLE 60

Significant attributes of selected Ontario counties 1851-71 (statistic cited is Pearson's 'r' coefficient of correlation; levels of significance in parentheses)

	Pop'n growth		Sex ratio			Marital fertility			Males 15-30
	1851-61	1861-71	1851	1861	1871	1851	1861	1871	1871*
Bruce	0.958 (0.01)	0.619 (0.01)	−0.678 (0.01)						
Grey		0.425 (0.01)							
Essex									
Kent									
Huron									
Middlesex								−0.359 (0.09)	
Elgin									
Perth			−0.485 (0.01)						
Oxford									
Norfolk									
Waterloo									0.394 (0.06)
Brant									0.458 (0.03)
Wentworth									
Halton						−0.414 (0.04)			
PEEL									
York						−0.496 (0.01)			
Ontario									
Northumberland									
Hastings									
Prince Edward				0.354 (0.09)	0.378 (0.05)		−0.534 (0.01)	−0.589 (0.01)	
Lennox-Adding-ton-Frontenac									
Dundas									
Stormont									
Glengarry			0.391 (0.05)	0.437 (0.07)	0.582 (0.01)	−0.354 (0.09)	0.484 (0.02)		

* Per 1,000 free acres

No. acres free per man 15-30	Farm size			Cultivated/occupied acreage			Wheat/cultivated acreage		
	1851	1861	1871	1851	1861	1871	1851	1861	1871
0.436 (0.03)	−0.475 (0.02)			−0.470 (0.02)	−0.461 (0.02)		0.390 (0.06)		
				−0.353 (0.09)	−0.399 (0.05)				
		−0.502 (0.01)	−0.425 (0.04)						
									0.473 (0.02)
									0.398 (0.05)
−0.358 (0.09)									
						0.353 (0.09)			
		(0.428) (0.04)							−0.370 (0.08)
			−0.412 (0.05)					−0.498 (0.01)	
		−0.353 (0.07)							
			0.392 (0.06)						

The population of mid-Victorian Peel County is a case in point. Compromising when change was necessary, leaving well enough alone when it was necessary not to change, the people of Peel strove to nurture the opportunities and avoid the liabilities of time and place using the only strategies at their disposal, expressing their confidence and their misgivings equally in the forms and structures of their families and households, in the routine events associated with the ordinary circumstances of ordinary lives and, ultimately, in the intensity of their attachment to this place.

APPENDICES

1 Measuring the Marigolds: Sources and Methods

The bibliography (below) of works cited describes the range of sources consulted in the preparation of this book; but a mere list of those sources may not be especially informative to readers, particularly other scholars, who may want to understand in greater detail the data base on which this analysis rests. What follows, therefore, is a description of that data base and a brief discussion of its characteristics.

The initial task of the Peel County History Project was to construct three sets of master files — one for each of the decennial cross-sections (1851, 1861, and 1871) — adequate for the purposes of examining social change and continuity at the level of family and household through time. A survey of the available historical microdata identified two sources which were substantially complete for each of the three cross-sections: the manuscript census returns and the abstracts of deeds. A third source, the records of the probate and surrogate courts, was complete for the entire period 1840-90. Such assessment and tax collectors' rolls as existed for the county did not relate to the period for which census returns are available. Similarly, although it has been possible to make limited use of parish registers and other denominational records they proved, for the most part, to be inadequate for the purposes of this study. Consequently, the cross-sectional master files for this study were created by coding the census and real property data as discrete, machine-readable files which were then linked by an automated record linkage program to create a new composite file.

The contents of these decennial files are as follows:

1 Head of family: name, age, occupation, place of birth, religious affiliation, sex, marital status, literacy
2 Wife: name, age, place of birth, religious affiliation, literacy
3 Number of Children: 0-1 years, 2-3 years, 4-6 years, 7-9 years, 10-12 years, 13-16 years, 17-25 years (age = age on census day)
4 Number of school-age children in school

5 Type of dwelling (1851, 1861 only)
6 Number of non-family residents
7 Number of domestic servants
8 Number of non-family residents with occupations (non-domestic)
9 Number of non-family residents who appear to be resident kin
10 Number of non-family minor children
11 Second family in household
12 Occupational classification of head of household (assigned)
13 Owner or tenant (assigned by linkage)
14 Date of purchase of property
15 Purchase price of property
16 Current outstanding mortgages ($ value)
17 Interest rate and term of mortgages
18 Date of next sale
19 Market value of property
20 Total number of acres owned or occupied
21 Percentage of total acreage cultivated (1861, 1871 only)
22 Persister or transient (assigned by linkage)

Current wisdom is that these data should not be aggregated at the level of family or household, but rather collected for individuals. However, in the beginning (1971) it was neither within the means nor the defined objectives of the project to collect these data for all the 70,000 individuals who lived in Peel County in 1850-70. The principal interests of the project lay in examining the processes attendant upon the interaction between families and land in an agrarian society with particular reference to the distribution of land. Only somewhat later did it become apparent that a much broader inquiry into the boundaries of individual experience was desirable and, indeed, necessary in order to appreciate fully the effects of the processes inherent in this political economy.

In any event, the creation of these decennial files was merely the precursor of a more important step, linking these files over time in order to identify the persistent and transient populations. This was accomplished using the Russell Soundex-based automated record linkage program devised by Ian Winchester (Ontario Institute for Studies in Education) for Michael Katz's Hamilton Project. The results of the linkage program can be graphically illustrated as shown on page 165.

In addition, the 1850 Directory of Peel was linked to the 1851 master file in order to ascertain the annual level of migration.

The three new Soundex-linked master files, the decennial linked pairs, and the file of ever-present families thus formed the essential data base for this study. For the purposes of detailed family reconstitution the ever-present families of Chinguacousy Township as defined by the linkage procedure were used as the

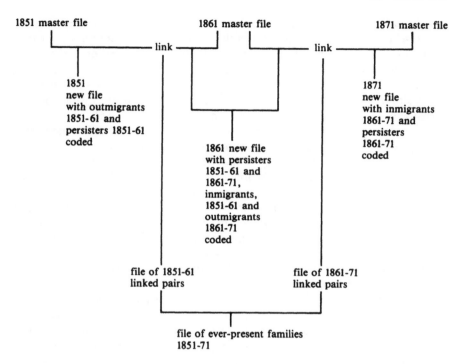

1851 master file   1861 master file   1871 master file

link   link

1851
new file
with outmigrants
1851-61 and
persisters 1851-61
coded

1871
new file
with inmigrants
1861-71 and
persisters
1861-71
coded

1861 new file
with persisters
1851-61 and
1861-71,
inmigrants,
1851-61 and
outmigrants
1861-71
coded

file of 1851-61   file of 1861-71
linked pairs   linked pairs

file of ever-present families
1851-71

basis for manual reconstruction as described in E.A. Wrigley, ed., *An Introduction to English Historical Demography*. Finally, the records of the probate and surrogate courts were employed discretely both in machine-readable form and as a literary source. They proved to be amenable to quantitative analysis primarily in a survey format designed to elicit the *intent* of the testator with respect to each of his putative heirs and the general disposition of his estate.

Without rehearsing in detail the strengths and weaknesses of these data, it is nevertheless necessary to indicate at least some of the difficulties encountered in using them. Among the census variables, literacy, the relationship of non-family residents to the head of family, and age proved to be the least reliable. The literacy columns, in fact, proved to be wholly meaningless. Relationships among the inmates of households were rarely explicit, hence our ability to distinguish only among family members, relatives of the same name, domestic servants, residents with non-domestic occupations, second families, and all other residents (within the latter group, minor children). Ironically, the linkage program reported that while men aged nine years in every decade, their wives aged only *seven* years. Aggregating acreage owned or occupied from the abstracts of deeds which are referenced only by lot, concession, and owner's name was extraordinarily difficult and links had to be manually checked against contemporary maps, directories, and agricultural census returns in order to achieve a reasonable level of accuracy. But the nineteenth-century custom of not registering titles until a sale had been effected by the payment of several years' quit-rents posed severe and sometimes insurmountable difficulties in the matter of property ownership. Acreage occupied was a more tractable problem since the 1861 agricultural census provided the figure for commercial farmers while the 1871 census provided the information for each household.

For all these reasons this analysis has been constructed to exploit the relative strengths of the data base and to minimize its shortcomings. Scholars interested in exploring nineteenth-century Canadian microdata for similar purposes should not be discouraged by the inherent constraints of admittedly imperfect data; but they would do well to examine beforehand and in some detail the sources they intend to use in order to acquire a sense of the problems they will have to confront. Among other things, the census data in particular often reveal pleasant surprises. In many townships, for example, badly informed enumerators erroneously recorded the year of marriage for each couple, presenting the historical demographer with a windfall of implicit information.

The statistical analyses which generated the tables presented in this study were accomplished using the *Statistical Package for the Social Sciences* (SPSS) almost exclusively. Given the preponderance of categorical variables and a data base which represented an entire universe rather than sample data, analysis at the level of cross-tabulation was generally adequate for most purposes. However, where multivariate analysis was desirable, both multiple classification analysis (MCA), used primarily as two-group discriminant function analysis, and the multiple regression subprogram were employed. Since the results from MCA were more amenable to an essentially descriptive level of explanation, and since the behaviour of a vast array of dichotomized variables in stepwise multiple regression presented serious problems of interpretation, I have chosen to present only the results from MCA.

Finally, it is necessary to say a word about how I have employed the accounts of nineteenth-century travellers, emigrants, and pioneers. Their stories are, in fact, an invaluable lexicon of social experience, attitudes, and behaviour, but they do not relate specifically to Peel County. Moreover, there is an ever-present temptation to use the substance of these accounts to create straw men which provide useful, but false, counterparts for the results of empirical analysis. Therefore, I have relied on these accounts principally to illustrate the generalizations which emerge from the statistical analysis in order, wherever possible, to establish the harmony of life in Peel County with the broader world of social experience represented by these printed primary sources. In the last analysis, however, the empirical evidence will not support the generally unrelieved optimism of these accounts. Clearly, as the song goes, measuring the marigolds and savouring their transitory beauty are not the same thing.

2 _Multiple Classification Analysis_

Several of the analyses presented (beginning with Tables 22 and 23) are the results of Multiple Classification Analysis. This analysis of variance compares the mean responses of particular subgroups of a population to the mean response of the entire population when the dependent variable (the thing being measured) can be expressed as an average within which there may be significant variation among subgroups. In Tables 22 and 23, for example, average household size among the families of Peel is the dependent variable. We want to know whether there was significant variation in household size from one family to another or, more importantly, between groups of families characterized by particular attributes (ethnicity, head of household's occupation, economic status), attributes which may explain significant differences within this population in the matter of household size. Moreover, we want to know how much (if at all) each broad category of predictor variables (the independent variable) contributes to the explanation of variation in household size. MCA makes this analysis possible by providing comparative responses within categories and between categories and the mean response for the entire population, by providing estimates of the net change in mean responses within categories which would occur if the population of any category represented the entire population, and by providing explicit tests of the nature and significance of the relationship between each, and all, of the categories of predictors and the dependent variable.

The F statistic and its test of significance estimate the total contribution of a cluster of individual predictors (eg, the variable 'occupational rank' is a categorical variable containing, for the purposes of MCA, six dichotomous predictors) to an explanation of variance in the dependent variable. An F score significant at the 99% level of confidence (0.01) describes a predictor the effect of which, in terms of explaining variation in the dependent variable, is highly unlikely to be the product of mere chance. Similarly, the overall F summarizes in a single statistic the collective significance of all the categories of predictors in explaining variation in the dependent variable. Two other statistics shed further light on the relationship between the dependent variable and the collective power of the predictors. The coefficient of determination, R^2, estimates the proportion of the variation in the dependent variable explained by the combined effects of the predictors on the right-hand side of the equation, in this case 0.75 or 75% in 1852, 74% in 1861, and 88% in 1871. The multiple correlation coefficient (multiple r) is a test of the association between the actual value of the dependent variable and its predicted value. In these three equations the two are highly correlated, but given the nature of the equation the strength of the correlation may be misleading.

Finally, MCA generates two statistics which help us to describe the relationship between the mean response of the entire population and the category means. The 'correlation ratio' eta is a test of the strength of association between each independent categorical variable and the dependent variable. Eta^2 describes the proportion of the variance in the dependent variable accounted for by the particular category of predictors. In this way MCA can be read as a series of cross-tabulations. The partial beta coefficients permit us to rank each category of adjusted predictors in order of importance in terms of relative ability to predict variance in the dependent variable after the confounding effects of all other predictors have been considered.

I have generally presented complete MCA documentation. It is nevertheless worth noting in passing that the F statistics and their tests of significance from regression and from MCA are comparable, and that as in regression analysis a more simplified presentation of these results consisting of category means (regression coefficients), F scores and tests of significance, multiple r and R^2 would have served equally well. In all MCA tables presented here, the assumptions that the values of the dependent variable are normally distributed and that interaction effects are present among the explanatory factors constitute the 'maintained' hypothesis.

Notes

CHAPTER 1: *Continuity, Change, and Ordinary Experience*

1 Canniff Haight, 'Country Life in Canada Fifty Years Ago' (Toronto 1885) 3
2 Since the completion of this study, the 1881 census has been opened to researchers. Unhappily, subsequent returns and provincial vital records remain effectively closed to historians.
3 The sources, methods, and conceptual basis of the Peel County History Project have been described in David Gagan and Herbert Mays, 'Historical Demography and Canadian Social History: Families and Land in Peel County, Ontario, *'Canadian Historical Review* LIV (1973) 27-47. More generally, the theoretical and methodological concerns of the new history are described and explained in a number of recent studies which include: Edward Shorter, *The Historian and the Computer: A Practical Guide* (New York 1975); Charles M. Dollar and Richard Jensen, *The Historian's Guide to Statistics: Quantitative Analysis and Historical Research* (New York 1971); Roderick Floud, *An Introduction to Quantitative Methods for Historians* (London 1973); Ian Winchester, 'The Linkage of Historical Records by Man and Computer: Techniques and Problems,' *Journal of Interdisciplinary History* I (1970) 107-24; Peter Laslett and Richard Wall, eds, *Household and Family in Past Time: Comparative Studies in the Size and Structure of the Domestic Group over the Last Three Centuries* ... (Cambridge 1972); Tamara Hareven and Maris Vinovskis, eds, *Family and Population in Nineteenth Century America* (Princeton 1978); Peter Laslett, *The World We Have Lost* (London 1965); Lawrence Stone, 'Prosopography,' *Daedalus* 100 (1971) 47-79; Tamara Hareven, 'Modernization and Family History: Perspectives on Social Change,' *Comparative Studies in the History of Culture and Society* 2 (1976) 190-206; Michael Katz, *The People of Hamilton, Canada West: Family and Class in a Mid-Nineteenth Century City* (Cambridge, MA 1975); E.A. Wrigley, ed., *An Introduction to English Historical Demography* (New York 1966); E.A. Wrigley, *Population and History* (New York 1966); E.A. Wrigley, ed, *Identifying People in the Past* (London 1973)
4 Laslett, *The World We Have Lost*, esp. ch. 10
5 See Robert Nisbet, *Social Change and History: Aspects of the Western Theory of Development* (New York 1969) esp. pp 159-88, 270-5
6 *Ibid.* 251 (italics deleted)
7 Stephan Thernstrom, *Poverty and Progress* (New York 1969) 7
8 *Literary Garland* II (1840) 401, cited in Laurence S. Fallis, Jr. 'The Ideas of Progress in the Province of Canada: A Study in the History of Ideas,' *The Shield of Achilles/Le Bouclier d'Achille*, W.L. Morton, ed. (Toronto 1968) 170
9 J. Sheridan Hogan, *Canada: An Essay* (Montreal 1855)
10 See Patrick Shirreff, *A Tour through North America Together with a Comprehensive View of Canada and the United States as Adapted for Agricultural Emigration* (Edinburgh 1835); Catharine Parr Traill, *The Canadian Settlers' Guide* (Toronto 1855); Rev. G.W. Warr, *Canada as It Is: or, The Emigrant's Friend and Guide to Upper Canada* ... (London 1847); John

Rowan, *The Emigrant and Sportsman in Canada: Some Experiences of an Old Country Settler* (London 1876); Rev. Isaac Fidler, *Observations On Professions, Literature, Manners and Emigration in the United States and Canada ... 1832* (New York 1833); William Catermole, *Emigration: The Advantages of Emigration to Canada* (London 1831); Susanna Moodie, *Life in the Clearings versus the Bush* (New York 1855); Major Samuel Strickland, *Twenty-Seven Years in Canada West* [reprint] (Edmonton 1970).

These emigration tracts and memoirs constitute only a partial list of the voluminous publications which appeared between 1835 and 1875, the heyday of the genre. Many more are referred to throughout this book, but the titles noted above are especially representative of the 'progress and improvement' school of thought.

11 Hogan, *Canada: An Essay* 9. I have discussed these and related attitudes in '"The Prose of Life": Literary Reflections of the Family, Individual Experience and Social Structure in Nineteenth-Century Canada,' *Journal of Social History* 9 (1976) 367-81.

12 G.N. Tucker, *The Canadian Commercial Revolution, 1845-51* [*reprint*] (Toronto 1964)

13 *Ibid.* See introduction by H.G.J. Aitken.

14 See J.M.S. Careless, *The Union of the Canadas: The Growth of Canadian Institutions, 1841-1857* (Toronto 1976), 170, and esp. ch. 8.

15 These developments have been explored in a number of places but see especially Jacob Spelt, *Urban Development in South-Central Ontario* (Toronto 1972), chs 3 and 4; and James M. Gilmour, *Spatial Evolution of Manufacturing, Southern Ontario, 1851-1891* (Toronto 1972) 26, 54.

16 See Vernon C. Fowke, 'The Myth of the Self-Sufficient Canadian Pioneer,' *Transactions of the Royal Society of Canada*, Series III, LIV (1962) 23-37

17 John Isbister, 'Agriculture, Balanced Growth and Social Change in Central Canada since 1850: An Interpretation,' *Economic Development and Cultural Change* 25 (1977) 679

18 M.C. Urquhart and K.A.H. Buckley, *Historical Statistics of Canada* (Toronto 1965), series L139, p 364

19 *Ibid.*, series L98, p 359; R.L. Jones, *History of Agriculture in Ontario 1613-1880* (Toronto 1948) 189-92, 204-5, 246, 325 enlarges upon this summary.

20 Isbister 'Agriculture, Balanced Growth and Social Change' 679

21 Fred Landon, *Western Ontario and the American Frontier* [reprint] (Toronto 1967) 250-1

22 Province of Canada, Legislative Assembly, *Parliamentary Debates on the Subject of Confederation of the British North American Provinces* (Quebec 1865) 10 Feb. 1865, p 158; 7 Mar. 1865, pp 788-91; 8 Mar. 1865, p 808; 9 Mar. 1865, p 892

23 Carl Berger, *The Sense of Power* (Toronto 1970) 56-9; W.L. Morton, *The Critical Years: The Union of British North America* (Toronto 1964), 232-44; P.B. Waite, *The Life and Times of Confederation* (Toronto 1962) esp. ch. 17; David Gagan, 'The Relevance of "Canada First,"' *Journal of Canadian Studies* V (1970) 36-44

24 Isbister, 'Agriculture, Balanced Growth and Change' 679; Urquhart and Buckley, *Historical Statistics of Canada* series L78, p 352; L98, p 359; L139, L143-6, p 364; S213, p 548; J165, p 305

25 Gilmour, *Spatial Evolution of Manufacturing* 26; J.H. Dales, 'Estimates of Canadian Manufacturing Output by Markets, 1870-1915,' *Papers of the CPSA Conference on Statistics, 1962 and 1968*, J. Henrepin and A. Asimakopoulos, eds (Toronto 1964) 61-91; E.J. Chambers and Gordon W. Bertram, 'Urbanization and Manufacturing in Central Canada, 1870-1890,' *Papers on Regional Studies: CPSA Conference on Statistics, 1964*, S. Ostry and T.K. Rymes, eds (Toronto 1966) 225-57

26 W.H. Smith, *Canada: Past, Present and Future. Being a Historical, Geographical, Geological and Statistical Account of Canada West I* (2 vols, Toronto 1852) 279

27 *Census of the Canadas, 1851-52* (Montreal 1856) xxxix

28 Spelt, *Urban Development* 81

29 These and other data employed here to compare Peel with other areas of the province have been computed from the aggregate data published in *Census of the Canadas, 1851-52; Census of the Canadas, 1860-61* (Quebec 1865); *Census of Canada, 1870-71* (Montreal 1875).

30 In Peel the proportion of cultivated acreage sown in wheat decreased by 30% in the 1860s. The decrease in York was 32%, in Brant 34%, and in Dundas 54%. The average decrease across the province was 15%.

CHAPTER 2: *Genesis*

1 Government of Ontario, Department of Planning and Development, *Credit Valley Conservation Report 1956* (Toronto 1956) 15-16, 55, 61-2
2 F.H. Armstrong, *Handbook of Upper Canadian Chronology and Territorial Legislation* (London 1967) 137-41; *Illustrated Atlas of Peel County ...* 1871 [reprint] (Port Elgin 1971) 56
3 Lillian Gates, *Land Policies of Upper Canada* (Toronto 1968), esp. conclusion; J.K. Johnson, 'The Businessman as Hero: The Case of William Warren Street,' *Ontario History* LXV, 5 (1973) 127-9; J. Sheridan Hogan, *Canada: An Essay* (Montreal 1855) 9
4 Gilbert C. Paterson, *Land Settlement in Upper Canada, 1783-1840: Sixteenth Report of the Department of Archives for the Province of Ontario* (Toronto 1920) 39, 115, 131, 147, 171
5 OA, CLP, Township Papers, Caledon Township Conc. III E, Lots 18, 19; Peel County, Abstracts of Deeds, Caledon Township, Conc., III E, Lots 18, 19
6 Computed by linking the lists of patentees in OA, CLP, RG I, C-I, Vols 11 and 12 with George Walton, *Directory of Toronto and the Home District* (Toronto 1837)
7 Alan Wilson, *The Clergy Reserves of Upper Canada: A Canadian Mortmain* (Toronto 1968) 127-8; Robert Gourlay, *Statistical Account of Upper Canada*, S.R. Mealing, ed. (Toronto 1974) 240-7
8 OA, CLP, RG I, A-VI-9, Vol. 16, Inspection Reports, Clergy Reserves, Albion Township, 1844-5
9 To identify these absentee speculators I have relied on a variety of sources, namely: Armstrong, *Handbook of Upper Canadian Chronology;* Henry Scadding, *Toronto of Old*, F.H. Armstrong, ed. (Toronto 1966); *Commemorative Biographical Record of the county of York, Ontario* (Toronto 1907): *Macmillan Dictionary of Canadian Biography*, W.S. Wallace, ed. (Toronto 1963): OA, CLP, R.G.1, C-I-8, Vols 11 and 12; and Township Papers for Albion, Caledon, Chinguacousy, Toronto Gore, and Toronto Townships.
10 See Alison Ewart and Julia Jarvis, 'The Personnel of the Family Compact,' *Canadian Historical Review* VI (Mar. 1926) 209-21; Robert E. Saunders, 'What was the Family Compact,' *Ontario History* XLIX (1957) 173-8.
11 Gerald Craig, ed., *Lord Durham's Report* (Toronto 1964) 78, 88-9
12 See Hugh G.J. Aitken, 'The Family Compact and the Welland Canal Company,' *Canadian Journal of Economics and Political Science* XVIII (1952) 63-76.
13 J.K. Johnson, 'The Businessman as Hero' 128
14 J.L.H. Henderson, ed., *John Strachan: Documents and Opinions* (Toronto 1969) 177; Leo Johnson, 'Land Policy, Population Growth and Social Structure in the Home District, 1793-1851,' *Ontario History* LXVII (1971) 43
15 Computed from Peel County, Abstracts of Deeds, Chinguacousy Township, and Walton, *Directory of Toronto*
16 *Credit Valley Conservation Report* (1956) 75. Citing the testimony of Hugh Black, DPS, before the Surveyor-General, in Province of Ontario, Dept of Lands and Forests, Survey Records, Letters, Vol. 11, nos. 36 and 37
17 OA, CLP, Township Papers, Albion Township, Concession IV, Lots 34, 35
18 Charles Lindsey, *The Life and Times of William Lyon Mackenzie* II (2 vols, Toronto 1862) 27-9.
19 Quoted in Gates, *Land Policies of Upper Canada* 47
20 Johnson, 'Land Policy, Population Growth and Social Structure in the Home District, 1793-1851' 41-60
21 The 1837 *Directory of the Home District* enumerates 2,140 households in a population of 12,572, an average of 5.8 persons per household. I have used this average to calculate the number of households in 1835. The average is probably too high, however, given the number of single men reputed to have been characteristic of the pioneer populations.
22 An indenture of bargain and sale was executed and a deed conveyed, in such cases, only after the full amount of the transaction had been discharged. I am indebted to Professor R.C. Risk of the University of Toronto Law School for this inference.
23 These data for Chinguacousy Township were derived by linking the following sources: Chinguacousy Township, Assessment Roll, 1842 (original in Chinguacousy Library); Walton, *Directory of Toronto and the Home District, 1837* Toronto 1837; PAC, manuscript, Census of the Canadas, 1851-2, Peel County; Chinguacousy Township, Abstract Index of Deeds [microfilm]
24 Gates, *Land Policies of Upper Canada* 239

CHAPTER 3: *Families and Land: The Mid-Century Crisis*

1 S.D. Clark, *The Developing Canadian Community*, 2nd ed. (Toronto 1968) 3-4; R.A. Billington, *America's Frontier Heritage* (New York 1966) 194

2 Billington, *America's Frontier Heritage* 25; M.H. Watkins, 'A Staple Theory of Economic Growth,' *Approaches to Canadian Economic History*, W.T. Easterbrook and M.H. Watkins, eds (Toronto 1967) 61

3 Rev. G.W. Warr, *Canada as It Is: or, The Emigrant's Friend and Guide to Upper Canada ...* (London 1847) 78

4 R.L. Jones, *History of Agriculture in Ontario 1613-1880* (Toronto 1948) 54; and see Kenneth Kelly, 'The Evaluation of Land for Wheat Cultivation in Early Nineteenth-Century Ontario,' *Ontario History* LXII (1970) 57-64

5 John Lynch, 'Agriculture and Its Advantages as a Pursuit,' *Journal and Transactions of the Board of Agriculture of Upper Canada* I (1856) 199 as quoted in Kenneth Kelly, 'The Transfer of British Ideas on Improved Farming to Ontario during the First Half of the Nineteenth Century,' *Ontario History* LXIII (1971) 103-11.

6 The coefficient of correlation, r, is 0.35, significant at 0.09.

7 Warr, *Canada as It Is* 59

8 I am indebted to a former McMaster graduate student in historical geography, Judy Hubert, for providing me with the results of her multiple regression analysis of the determinants of farm value. The land capability factor employed was derived from the *Canada Land Inventory Soil Capacity Classification for Agriculture* (Ottawa: Department of the Environment 1965). Since the inventory is premised on modern determinants of soil capacity it is difficult to say what relationship it bears to the nineteenth-century farmer's perception of soil quality.

9 The 1861 published data are incomplete insofar as they refer only to farmer-occupiers. However, by 1861, 24% of Peel's farmers occupied more than 100 acres comprising 47% of farm lands held. The data cited here for 1851 and 1871 are similarly from published aggregates.

10 Samuel Philips Day, *English America: or, Pen Pictures of Canadian Places and People* I (2 vols, London 1864) 193

11 Anna Jameson, *Winter Studies and Summer Rambles*, J.J. Talman and E.M. Murray, eds (Toronto 1943) 53; Catermole, *Emigration* 166; Thomas Conant, *Upper Canada Sketches* (Toronto 1898) 177; Patrick Shirreff, *A Tour through North America Together with a Comprehensive View of Canada and the United States ...* (Edinburgh 1835) 170

12 The 'inheritance motive' as a determinant of economic and demographic behaviour and attitudes has particularly interested historical economists in recent years. See R.M. McInnis, 'Childbearing and Land Availability: Some Evidence from Individual Household Data,' Behavioural Models in Historical Demography Conference, Philadelphia, 1974 (mimeo); Richard Easterlin, 'Does Human Fertility Adjust to the Environment?' *American Economic Review: Papers and Proceedings* LXI (1971) 399-407; and, for an interesting comparison with colonial New England, Philip Greven, jr, *Four Generations: Population, Land and Families in Colonial Andover, Massachusetts* (Ithaca 1970) esp. 222-58.

13 See table p 173.

14 Paul W. Gates, *The Farmers' Age: Agriculture 1815-1850: The Economic History of the United States* III (New York 1962) 405

15 See David Gagan, 'The Security of Land: Mortgaging in Toronto Gore Township, 1835-1885,' *Aspects of Nineteenth-Century Ontario*, F.H. Armstrong, H. Stevenson, and D.J. Wilson, eds (Toronto 1974) 148

16 *Ibid.* 137-8; and W.T. Easterbrook and Hugh G.J. Aitken, *Canadian Economic History* (Toronto 1965) 507

17 Cited in Jones, *History of Agriculture* 203

18 H.J. Habbakuk, 'Family Structure and Economic Change in Nineteenth-Century Europe,' *Journal of Economic History* XV (1955) 1, argues that this problem was faced by peasant families throughout nineteenth-century Europe. It is also clear that they frequently adopted the same inheritance systems in response. See the reference to Berkner and Mendels, below.

19 Susanna Moodie, *Life in the Clearings versus the Bush* (New York 1855) 138

Means, trend values, and three-year weighted averages for cost of land per acre, Peel County, 1840-70

Date	Mean (y) $	Units (N)	x	x^2	xy	Trend value, $	Three-year moving avg
1840	8.30	0	15	225	−124.50	13.99	
1	8.00	1	14	196	−112.00	16.18	9.15
2	11.15	2	13	169	−144.95	18.37	28.45
3	66.19	3	12	144	−794.28	20.56	30.82
4	15.13	4	11	121	−166.43	22.75	31.03
5	11.79	5	10	100	−117.90	24.94	12.31
6	10.02	6	9	81	− 90.18	27.13	12.40
7	15.40	7	8	64	−123.20	29.32	12.98
8	13.53	8	7	49	− 94.71	31.51	12.80
9	9.49	9	6	36	− 56.94	33.70	15.45
1850	23.34	10	5	25	−116.70	35.89	19.06
1	24.34	11	4	16	− 97.36	38.08	22.75
2	20.56	12	3	9	− 61.68	40.27	24.84
3	29.61	13	2	4	− 59.22	42.46	29.82
4	29.90	14	1	1	− 39.90	44.65	37.25
5	42.85	15	0	0	0	46.84	46.04
6	55.38	16	1	1	55.38	49.03	56.87
7	72.27	17	2	4	144.54	51.22	121.86
8	237.94	18	3	9	713.82	53.41	115.36
9	35.88	19	4	16	143.52	55.60	104.72
1860	40.35	20	5	25	201.75	57.79	57.29
1	95.64	21	6	36	573.84	59.98	106.33
2	183.02	22	7	49	1,281.14	62.17	102.69
3	29.42	23	8	64	235.36	64.36	82.04
4	33.69	24	9	81	303.21	66.55	45.18
5	72.44	25	10	100	724.40	68.74	50.86
6	46.45	26	11	121	510.95	70.93	56.90
7	51.82	27	12	144	621.84	73.12	48.02
8	45.79	28	13	169	595.27	75.31	45.96
9	40.28	29	14	196	563.92	77.50	49.42
1870	62.19	30	15	225	932.85	79.69	
	1,452.16	31		2,468	+7,601.79 −2,199.35		
					5,402.44		

$Y_1 = 46.84 + 2.19X_1$ $N = 1,916$

Note that the *mean* is the average value of an acre of land purchased in a given year; the trend *values* locate the straight line which best describes the long-term trend of land prices; and the *three-year moving average* is the average of the values for a given year, the year preceding it, and the year following it, and is designed to smooth out anomalous irregularities in the curve.

20 See J.F. Cooper, 'Patterns of Inheritance and Settlement by Great Landowners from the Fifteenth to the Eighteenth Centuries,' *Family and Inheritance*, J. Goody and J. Thirsk, eds (Cambridge, Eng. 1976) 197
21 This system was first described and labelled by A.R.M. Lower in *Canadians in the Making* (Toronto 1969) 336.

22 Peel County, Surrogate Court, Wills, I, 1867, will of J.V. Unless otherwise noted, data for this analysis have been computed from OA, York County, Probate Court, Wills, 1800-67; Peel County, Surrogate Court, Wills, 1867-90; OA, Home District, Probate Court, Wills, 1800-1867.

23 J. Sheridan Hogan, *Canada: An Essay* (Montreal 1855) 65-6

24 Jones, *History of Agriculture* 247 notes that the 1871 fall wheat crop in areas not affected by midge was the best in several years, and that the Franco-Prussian War had created a market for it.

25 Gagan, 'The Security of Land ...' *Aspects of Nineteenth Century Ontario* 143

26 *Ibid.*

27 OA, York County, Probate Court, 1800-67, Wills No. 13590, 264; Peel County, Surrogate Court, Wills, 1867-90, Will No. 29

28 *Ibid.*, Will of J.M., No. 66

29 *Ibid.*, Will of J.H. No. 12716

30 OA, Home District, Probate Court, Wills, 1800-67, Will of T.W., No. 09577, for example, orders that if the wife remarries the children are to be taken from her and housed elsewhere.

31 Peel County, Surrogate Court, Wills, 1867-1900, Will of N.A., No. 47

32 OA, York County, Probate Court, Wills, 1800-67, Will of J.N., No. 338

33 Moodie, *Life in the Clearings* 291

34 E.S. Dunlop, ed., *Our Forest Home: Being Extracts from the Correspondence of the Late Frances Stewart* (Toronto 1889) 80-1

35 These attitudes and other aspects of the experience of nineteenth-century Ontario farm women are discussed at length in Rosemary R. Ball, "'A Perfect Farmer's Wife': Women in Nineteenth Century Rural Ontario,' *Canada: An Historical Magazine* 3 (1975) 2-21.

36 Lutz Berkner and Franklin Mendels, 'Inheritance Systems, Family Structure and Demographic Patterns in Western Europe, 1700-1900,' *Historical Studies of Changing Fertility*, Charles Tilly, ed. (Princeton 1978) 216. As this essay makes abundantly clear, it is a misnomer to call the preferential system of inheritance found in Peel a 'Canadian' system of inheritance. Its operation was well known in Europe long before it was implemented in rural Ontario.

37 Habbakuk, 'Family Structure' 5-7

38 Berkner and Mendels, 'Inheritance Systems ...' 217

39 J. Richard Houston, *Numbering the Survivors: A History of the Standish Family of Ireland, Ontario and Alberta* (Agincourt 1979) 104-8, 118-21

40 D.A. Lawr, 'The Development of Farming in Ontario, 1870-1914: Patterns of Growth and Change,' *Ontario History* LXIV (1972) 240-51

CHAPTER 4: *Household, Family, and Individual Experience*

1 Canniff Haight, *Country Life in Canada Fifty Years Ago* (Toronto 1885) 13; Peter Laslett and Richard Wall, eds, *Household and Family in Past Time* (Cambridge, Eng. 1972) 1-73 describes and defines historical variation in household size and composition and outlines a scheme, including ideographic representations, for classifying household structures. The italicized nomenclature employed here adheres to this scheme.

2 Major Samuel Strickland, *Twenty-Seven Years in Canada West* [rpt] (Edmonton 1970) 80 (see also pp 139-40)

3 Donald V. Smiley, ed., *The Rowell-Sirois Report* ... Book I (Toronto 1963) 26

4 John Carroll, ed., *'Father Corson': or, The Old Style Canadian Itinerant Embracing the Life and Gospel Labours of the Rev. Robert Corson* (Toronto 1879) 81

5 Yasukichi Yasuba, *Birth Rates of the White Population in the United States, 1800-1860: An Economic Study* (Baltimore 1962); Frank Denton and Peter George, 'The Influence of Socio-Economic Variables on Family Size in Wentworth County, Ontario, 1871,' *Canadian Review of Sociology and Anthropology* 10 (1973) 334-45; Don Leet, 'The Determinants of Fertility Transition in Ante-Bellum Ohio,' *Journal of Economic History* 36 (1976) 359-78; R.M. McInnis, 'Childbearing and Land Availability in Nineteenth-Century Ontario,' Paper presented to Behavioural Models in Historical Demography Conference, Philadelphia, 1974 (mimeo); Richard Easterlin, 'Does Human Fertility Adjust to the Environment?' *American*

Economic Review: Papers and Proceedings LXI (1971) 399-407; Maris Vinovskis, 'Socio-Economic Determinants of Interstate Fertility Differentials in the United States in 1850 and 1860,' *Journal of Interdisciplinary History* VI (1976) 375-96; Jacques Henripin, *Trends and Factors of Fertility in Canada* (Ottawa 1972); Lorne Tepperman, 'Ethnic Variations in Marriage and Fertility: Canada, 1871,' *Canadian Review of Sociology and Anthropology* 11 (1974) 324-43

6 W.A. Armstrong, 'A Note on the Household Structure of Mid-Nineteenth Century York in Comparative Perspective,' *Household and Family in Past Time* 206-7; Edward T. Pryor, jr, 'Rhode Island Family Structure: 1875 and 1960,' *Household and Family in Past Time* 577-8; Michael Anderson, *Family Structure in Nineteenth Century Lancashire* (Cambridge, Eng. 1971) 123; Michael Katz, *The People of Hamilton: Family and Class in a Mid-Nineteenth Century City* (Cambridge Mass. 1975) 217, 233-5

7 Peter Laslett, 'Mean Household Size in England since the Sixteenth Century,' *Household and Family in Past Time* 125-58; Laslett, introduction, *Household and Family* 61, 72-3; Laslett, 'The Comparative History of Household and Family,' *Journal of Social History* IV (1970) 75-87

8 David Gagan, 'Enumerators' Instructions for the Census of Canada, 1852 and 1861,' *Social History / Histoire Sociale* 7 (1974) 355-65

9 Katz, *The People of Hamilton* 264-7

10 Strickland, *Twenty-Seven Years* 332

11 E.A. Wrigley, *Population and History* (New York 1966) 164 employs 30 months as the 'mean normal interval.' It also happens to be the average interval for all women age 15-44 in Peel's persistent population. The size of completed persistent families cited here (7.8) conforms to Henripin's estimates of total family size. See Henripin, *Trends and Factors of Fertility in Canada* 380.

12 *Ibid.* 118-19

13 See Michael Bliss, ' "Pure Books on Avoided Subjects": Pre-Freudian Sexual Ideas in Canada,' *Historical Papers 1970* (Canadian Historical Association 1971) 89-108.

14 Streetsville *Weekly Review*, 3 June 1854

15 Orangeville *Sun*, 4 Sept. 1862

16 Brampton *Progress*, 7 Nov. 1873

17 See Angus McLaren, 'Birth Control and Abortion in Canada, 1870-1920,' *Canadian Historical Review* LIX (1978) 319-40.

18 Alfred Domett, *Canadian Journal* [rpt] (London 1955) 24

19 Strickland, *Twenty-Seven Years* 320

20 N.F. Davin, *The Irishman in Canada* (Toronto 1875) 299

21 C.S. Clark, *Of Toronto the Good: A Social Study* (Montreal 1898) 125

22 Wrigley, *Population and History* 116, argues that total fertility levels among women who marry in their early twenties are at least twice as high as those of women who marry at about age 30.

23 See table p 176. These data result from an enumerator's misinterpretation of his instructions which led him to record 'age at marriage' for half the couples in one township (Toronto) in 1861.

24 Brown recounted his life to the editor of the Paisley (Scotland) *Gazette*, 20 Apr. 1870. The letter was published 14 May 1870 [OA, Miscellaneous Collection, 1870]. I have added appropriate dates from Brown's property, census, and probate records.

25 Susanna Moodie, *Roughing It in the Bush* (Toronto 1962) 235 [rpt]

26 Thomas Radcliff, ed., *Authentic Letters from Upper Canada*, James J. Talman, ed. (Toronto 1967) 122

27 Susan Houston, 'Politics, Schools and Social Change in Upper Canada,' *Canadian Historical Review* LIII (1972) 249

28 Alison Prentice, *The School Promoters: Education and Social Class in Mid-Nineteenth Century Upper Canada* (Toronto 1977) 46

29 Council Minutes, Toronto Gore Township, 13 July 1859

30 Michael Katz, 'Who Went to School,' *History of Education Quarterly* XII (1973) 438. The provincial average in 1846 was approximately 49% (Prentice, *The School Promoters* 19)

31 Prentice, *The School Promoters* 131.

32 Province of Canada, Legislative Assembly, *Journals*, 1861, Vol. 19, Paper 17

33 Strickland, *Twenty-Seven Years* 274

Trend values and three-year weighted average, age at marriage

	Men		Women	
	Trend	Moving average	Trend	Moving average
1840	23.99		20.79	
41	24.07	24.1	20.87	19.4
42	24.15	23.8	20.95	21.1
43	24.23	25.1	21.03	22.4
44	24.31	25.9	21.11	22.4
45	24.39	24.8	21.19	22.2
46	24.47	23.4	21.27	21.1
47	24.55	23.7	21.35	21.3
48	24.63	24.1	21.43	21.4
49	24.71	25.0	21.51	21.8
1850	24.79	25.4	21.59	22.2
51	24.87	25.9	21.67	22.1
52	24.95	25.5	21.75	22.3
53	25.03	24.6	21.83	21.4
54	25.11	24.3	21.91	20.9
55	25.19	24.3	21.99	21.2
56	25.27	24.2	22.07	21.3
57	25.35	24.2	22.15	20.0
58	25.43	25.2	22.23	20.8
59	25.51	26.8	22.31	21.4
1860	25.59	26.6	22.39	22.4
61	25.67	26.9	22.47	22.6
62	25.75	26.5	22.55	22.9
63	25.83	26.1	22.63	23.0
64	25.91	26.1	22.71	23.1
65	25.99	25.7	22.79	22.4
66	26.07	26.4	22.87	22.1
67	26.15	26.5	22.95	21.4
68	26.23	27.3	23.03	22.4
69	26.31	26.8	23.11	22.9
1870	26.39		23.19	

For trend value, men: $Y_1 = 25.19 + 0.08X_1$ ($N = 435$); women: $Y_1 = 21.99 + 0.08X_1$ ($N = 474$).

34 H.J. Mays and H.F. Manzl, 'Literacy and Social Structure in Nineteenth Century Ontario: An Exercise in Historical Methodology,' *Histoire Sociale / Social History* VII (1974) 344
35 Haight, *Country Life in Canada* 181
36 Ian Davey, 'Trends in Female School Attendance in Mid-Nineteenth Century Ontario,' *Histoire Sociale / Social History* VIII (1975) 240
37 Shirreff, *Tour* 168
38 Domett, *Canadian Journal* 61
39 See J.F. Kett, 'Adolescence and Youth in Nineteenth Century America,' *The Family in History*, Theodore Rabb and Robert Rotberg, eds (New York 1973) 95-110.
40 William Catermole, *Emigration: The Advantages of Emigration to Canada* (London 1831) 166
41 Radcliff, *Authentic Letters* ... 58; the birth interval for women aged 15-25, however, was 17 months.
42 See Robert V. Wells, 'Demographic Change and the Life Cycle of American Families,' *The Family in History* 88
43 Helen Chojnacka, 'Nuptiality Patterns in an Agrarian Society,' *Population Studies* 30 (1976) 205-6

44 E.S. Dunlop ed., *Our Forest Home: Being Extracts from the Correspondence of the Late Frances Stewart* (Toronto 1889) 92
45 M.C. Urquhart and K.A.H. Buckley, *Historical Statistics of Canada* (Toronto 1965) 41, Series B65-74
46 *Canada: A Memorial Volume* (Montreal 1889) 46-7
47 Mrs J.M. Wright, *The Complete Home: An Encyclopedia of Domestic Life and Affairs* (Brantford 1870) 93
48 John Rowan, *The Emigrant and Sportsman in Canada: Some Experiences of an Old Country Settler...* (London 1876) 429
49 Strickland, *Twenty-Seven Years* 299. The average birth interval, 16.8 months, among women in their twenties, 1850-70, suggests that suckling patterns had little if any effect on overall fertility.
50 The pace and timing of change in the life cycle experience of women are not amenable to short-term analysis using these data sources. It is clear from recent studies employing cohort life cycle analysis and aggregate data over an extended period of time that it took about forty years, that is, from 1850 until 1890, for the experience of women within marriage to change significantly. See Peter Uhlenberg, 'A Study of Cohort Life Cycles: Cohorts of Native Born Massachusetts Women, 1830-1920,' *Population Studies* 23 (1969) 407-20.
51 Mortality figures, particularly by birth cohort, are notoriously unreliable for nineteenth-century Canada. Nevertheless, among wives in the age 20-4 cohort of the reconstituted permanent population, the death rate during these 20 years — 200 per 1,000 — compares favourably with the rate established by Uhlenberg for early death among all women reaching age 15 in the United States, 1890-4. See Peter Uhlenberg, 'Life Cycle Experiences of US Females,' *Journal of Marriage and the Family* 36 (1974) 286.
52 Half the county's 678 widows in 1871 were under the age of 56. They represent slightly more than 17% of the total female population aged 20-30 in 1851.
53 Charlotte Clarkson to H.S. Clarkson, 15 Apr. 1859, in *Warren Clarkson of Clarkson and the Clarkson Family Letters, 1854-1859*, Betty Clarkson, ed. (unpublished ms). I am indebted to Mrs Clarkson for her permission to quote extensively from these letters.
54 Wright, *The Complete Home* 370-1
55 Tamara K. Hareven, 'Modernization and Family History: Perspectives on Social Change,' *Journal of Women in Culture and Society* 2 (1976) 198, 201
56 Harvey J. Philpot, *Guide Book to the Canadian Dominion Containing Full Information for the Emigrant, the Tourist, the Sportsman and the Small Capitalist* (London 1871) 119
57 Clarkson Letters, Charlotte Clarkson to Henry Clarkson, 12 July 1857

CHAPTER 5: *The Promise of Canadian Life*

1 See Charles F. Heller, jr and F. Stanley Moore, 'Continuity in Rural Land Ownership: Western Kalamazoo County, Michigan, 1820-1861,' *Michigan History* LVI (1972) 233-46; Merle Curti, *The Making of an American Community* (Stanford 1959) 55-83; Allen Bogue, 'Farming in the Prairie Peninsula, 1830-1890,' *Journal of Economic History*, 23 (1963) 3-29; James C. Malin, 'The Turnover of Farm Population in Kansas,' *Kansas Historical Quarterly* IV (1935) 339-72; Stephan Thernstrom, *The Other Bostonians: Poverty and Progress in the American Metropolis, 1880-1970* (Cambridge, MA 1973) 222; Michael Katz, *The People of Hamilton, Canada West: Family and Class in a Mid-Nineteenth Century City* (Cambridge, MA 1975) 119
2 John Brown to editor, Paisley *Gazette*, 20 Apr. 1870
3 E.J. Hobsbawm and George Rudé, *Captain Swing* (New York 1975) 23-4
4 *Emigration: The British Farmer's and Farm Labourer's Guide to Ontario* (Toronto 1880) 59
5 POA, James Reid Papers, Correspondence 1822-62, Reid to Thomas Reid, 27 May 1862
6 *Ibid.*, 1 Mar. 1847 and 8 Jan. 1849
7 Susanna Moodie, *Roughing It in the Bush* [reprint] (Toronto 1962) xv
8 Hobsbawm and Rudé, *Captain Swing*, esp. ch. 4
9 Geoffrey Crossick, 'The Labour Aristocracy and Its Values: A Study of Mid-Victorian Kentish London,' *Victorian Studies* XIX (1976) 301-28. This synthesis adheres to the more pessimistic side of the debate over mid-Victorian British working class standards of living. See H. Perkins, *The Origins of Modern British Society, 1780-1880* (London 1969) esp. ch. 10.

10 Figures cited are those estimated by F.M.L. Thompson, *English Landed Society in the Nineteenth Century* (London 1963) 115-17 and by Hobsbawm and Rudé, *Captain Swing* 23-4.

11 *Ibid.*

12 E.P. Thompson, *The Making of the English Working Class* (London 1965) 218-19; and see M. Blaug, 'The Myth of the Old Poor Law and the Making of the New,' *Essays in Social History*, M.W. Flinn and T.C. Smout, eds (Oxford 1974) 139-42.

13 K.H. Connell, *The Population of Ireland, 1750-1845* (Oxford 1950) 25; Robert E. Kennedy, *Irish Emigration, Marriage and Fertility* (Berkeley 1973) 28-34, 88-9; E.J. Hobsbawm, *Industry and Empire: The Pelican Economic History of Britain III* (London 1969) 103

14 John Bigsby, *The Shoe and Canoe* II (2 vols, London 1850) 131. These emigrants and their motives for emigrating have been examined in depth in Charlotte Erikson, *Invisible Immigrants: The Adaptation of English and Scottish Immigrants in Nineteenth Century America* (Coral Gables, Fla. 1972).

15 Geoffrey Best, *Mid-Victorian Britain, 1851-1875* (London 1971) 127

16 Bigsby, *Shoe and Canoe* II, 73; J. Sheridan Hogan, *Canada: An Essay* (Montreal 1855) 9; Major Samuel Strickland, *Twenty-Seven Years in Canada West* (Edmonton 1970) 265-6; N.A. *The Backwoods of Canada: Letters From the Wife of an Emigrant Officer* (London 1876) 176 [C.P. Traill]

17 Strickland, *Twenty-Seven Years* 265-6

18 *The Backwoods of Canada* 104, 46; Isabella Bird, *The Englishwoman in America* [1856] (Madison 1966) 302

19 Mrs Edward Copleston, *Canada: Why We Live in It, and Why We Like It* (London 1861) 83

20 Katz, *The People of Hamilton* 77-80

21 Thompson, *English Landed Society* 115-17

22 Lee Soltow, *Men and Wealth in the United States, 1850-1870* (New Haven 1875) 21, 28-9, 43-4

23 W.H. Wightman, 'Construction Materials in Colonial Ontario, 1831-1861,' *Aspects of Nineteenth Century Ontario*, F.H. Armstrong *et al* eds. (Toronto 1974) 124

24 See note 6, ch. 5, above.

25 Hobsbawm, *Industry and Empire* 87; Best, *Mid-Victorian Britain* 82-7, 102; Copleston, *Canada* 69; Katz, *The People of Hamilton* 27-8.

26 Moodie, *Roughing It in the Bush* 242-3; 'They can live without you and they well know that you cannot do without them.'

27 *The Backwoods Life* 271

28 *Minutes, Reports and By-Laws, Peel County, 1854-1874* (Brampton 1875) 23

29 Strickland, *Twenty-Seven Years* 140

30 Streetsville *Weekly Review*, 3 June 1854

31 Daniel Kubat and David Thornton, *A Statistical Profile of Canadian Society* (Toronto 1974) 191, Table C 11

32 Stephan Thernstrom, *Poverty and Progress: Social Mobility in a Nineteenth-Century City* 2nd ed. (Cambridge, MA 1968) 84 has put the argument for using occupation as the principal measure of social mobility in historical studies most eloquently, an argument which rests on a number of theoretical assumptions which are conveniently summarized in Gordon W. Kirk, jr, *The Promise of American Life: Social Mobility in a Nineteenth-Century Immigrant Community, Holland, Michigan, 1847-1894* (Philadelphia 1978) 58-60.

33 Katz, *The People of Hamilton* esp. Ch. 2

34 Strickland, *Twenty-Seven Years* 265

35 Bigsby, *The Shoe and Canoe* I, 91-2 quoting Arnold Guyot, *The Earth and Man* (1849)

36 Hogan, *Canada: An Essay* 39

37 Copleston, *Canada* 84

38 'Ontario,' *Canada: A Memorial Volume* (Montreal 1889) 33

39 The facts of transience and persistence presented here are derived from an analysis which employs the techniques of automated and manual linkage of historical nominal records. First, using the Soundex-based automated linkage procedure devised by Ian Winchester for Michael Katz's Canadian Social History Project, records were linked, two censuses at a time, to derive matches between individual names and characteristics.

The Soundex system itself matched surnames on the basis of comparable consonant clusters. In addition, forenames had to be consistent. Finally, the program established a binary weighting system, the scores from which established the presence of strong, possible, weak, or improbable links on the basis of several distinguishing personal characteristics assumed not to change, or to change predictably, over time: age, place of birth, and sex. We added 'township of residence' as a further check.

Once the automated linkage process was complete, the linked pairs were then checked manually against names in the same and related Soundex 'pockets' for the goodness of the match. This was chiefly necessary, as it turned out, to combat the census enumerators' penchant for phonetic spellings, and to sort out the bewildering variations on Scottish surnames. Finally, the unlinked pairs in each group were checked manually, partly in order to pick up the surviving widows of householders who had died in the intervening period, and partly, again, to link names whose peculiarities baffled the computer. Thus Greenwort and Greensword; Grenous, Grenious, Grenians, and Grenius; McDivitt, McDavitt, McDevitt, and McDade; Heron, Horan, and Harron all, for example, had to be dealt with manually by someone who knew the genealogical records well enough to make informed links, sometimes by following the enumerator around on a historical map of Peel County.

This exercise resulted in the definition of the following populations: (a) linked from 1850 directory to 1852 census and 1861 census; (b) linked from 1850 directory to 1852 census; (c) linked from 1852 census to 1861 census; (d) present 1850 directory only; (e) present 1852 census only; (f) linked from 1861 census to 1871 census; (g) present on 1861 census only; (h) present on 1871 census only; (i) linked from 1880 assessment rolls to 1871 census; (j) present 1880 only; (k) linked 1852, 1861, 1871 censuses. As the list suggests, the census links were our major preoccupation.

40 John Brown letter, and see Cecil Houston and William J. Smyth, 'The Orange Order and the Expansion of the Frontier in Ontario, 1830-1900,' *Journal of Historical Geography* 4 (1978) 251-64.

41 *Commemorative Biographical Record of The County of York Ontario* (Toronto 1907) 252

42 *Ibid.* 326

43 *Ibid.* 208

44 *Ibid.* 279, 429; William Taylor [Woodlands, Manitoba] to Editor, Brampton *Times*, 29 Aug. 1874. I am indebted to Professor George Richardson of Queen's University, who provided me with copies of his great-grandfather's correspondence.

45 W.F. Munro, *The Backwoods Life: An Interesting Story of Pioneer Days in Melancthon Township* (Shelburne 1910), originally published 1869

46 Clarkson Letters, Charlotte Clarkson to Henry Clarkson, 20 Oct. 1858, 15 Apr. 1859; George Clarkson to Henry Clarkson, 3 Nov. 1857, 14 Feb. 1859, 9 Sept. 1859

47 *Parliamentary Debates on the Subject of Confederation*, 8 Feb. 1865, 94

48 Reid Papers, James to Thomas Reid, 27 May 1862

49 The details of the group's experience in Peel are drawn from the 1871 manuscript census of Peel County and Cardwell District, particularly schedules 2-5.

50 William Taylor to Brampton Times, 29 Aug. 1874, 10 Feb. 1875, 9 Apr. 1875, 5 June 1875, 8 Feb. 1878. I have synthesized Taylor's somewhat rambling commentary.

51 US Department of State, Consular Reports, RG 59, Reel T488-2, Trade and Commerce Report for Sarnia, 17 July 1879

52 Streetsville *Weekly Review*, 4 June 1851, 8 Apr. 1855

53 Linking the most improved householders to the list of local militia officers printed in W. Perkins Bull, *From Brock to Currie: The Military Developments and Exploits of Canadians in General and of the Men of Peel in Particular, 1791 to 1930* (Toronto 1935). Appendix 13, pp 636-50 reveals that one in eight of the most improved male householders held commissions in the Peel County militia and constituted, in 1861, approximately 25% of the officers who ever held commissions in the local militia from 1846 to 1861.

CHAPTER 6: *The Urban Frontier*

1 Orangeville *Sun*, 21 Feb. 1861

2 Brampton, Town Council Minutes, 1854-72 (Genealogical Society Microfilm)

3 Orangeville *Sun*, 3 Oct. 1861, 5 Feb. 1863

4 I am indebted to three former students, John Fierheller, Chris Berry, and Stan Kutcher for undertaking this survey of commercial advertising in the Brampton press, 1856-62.

5 OA, Perkins Bull Collection, Series C, No. 3, Box 1, 'Brampton'

6 Jacob Spelt, *Urban Development in South-Central Ontario* (Toronto 1972) 148

7 James Gilmour, *Spatial Evolution of Manufacturing, Southern Ontario, 1851-1891* (Toronto 1972) 26, 50-1, 54, 60-2

8 Richard A. Easterlin, George Alter, and Gretchen Condran, 'Farms and Farm Families in Old and New Areas: The Northern States in 1860,' *Family and Population in Nineteenth Century America* (Princeton 1978) 22-84; Don R. Leet, 'Interrelations of Population Density, Urbanization, Literacy and Fertility,' *Explorations in Economic History* 14 (1977) 388-401; E.A. Wrigley, 'Family Limitation in Pre-Industrial England,' *Economic History Review* XIX (1966) 82-109 documents the effects of fertility control within marriage among the population of an English village in the seventeenth and eighteenth centuries.

9 Stanley Engerman, 'The Study of the European Fertility Decline,' *Journal of Family History* I (1976) 245-51 and see John Knodel, *The Decline of Fertility in Germany, 1871-1939* (Princeton 1974).

10 See Tamara Hareven and Maris Vinovskis, introduction, *Family and Population in Nineteenth-Century America* (Princeton 1978) 12-13.

11 Results (*F* statistics) of analysis of variance in child-woman ratios for women of various age groups, Brampton 1871:

	15-24		25-34		34-44	
	F	Sig.	*F*	Sig.	*F*	Sig.
Husband's Occupation	0.45	0.81	2.04	0.05	1.59	0.16
Religious affil. of mother	1.18	0.32	1.65	0.16	1.56	0.19
Birthplace of mother	1.25	0.30	1.40	0.21	0.98	0.42

12 See Michael Katz, *The People of Hamilton, Canada West* (Cambridge, MA 1975) 260-6; I am indebted to Dan McCaughey for this data on the residence of youths in Brampton.

13 Alison Prentice, *The School Promoters: Education and Social Class in Mid-Nineteenth Century Upper Canada* (Toronto 1977), esp. ch. 4, 'Occupations in Transition: The Danger of Downward Mobility.' There is no evidence here, in any event, that the poorest or least skilled classes in the town were disinterested in educating their children. See Michael Katz, *The Irony of Early School Reform* (Cambridge, MA 1968).

14 Richard Wade, *The Urban Frontier* (Chicago 1959) 203 notes that it took only one generation for sharply defined class divisions to emerge in the new towns and cities of the United States' trans-Appalachian frontier.

15 Again, the size, composition, relative affluence and principal attributes of Brampton's 'upper class' bear a striking resemblance to the wealthiest 10% of Hamilton's population as described by Katz, *The People of Hamilton*, chs 2 and 4.

16 In 'Migration and the Social Order in Erie County, New York: 1855,' *Journal of Interdisciplinary History* VIII (1978) 669-701 (see esp. 698), Michael Katz, Michael Doucet, and Mark Stern hypothesize that the migration / stability dichotomy had a similar effect in most mid-nineteenth-century North American urban communities.

17 See M.J. Daunton, 'Towns and Economic Growth in Eighteenth-Century England,' *Towns in Societies: Essays in Economic History and Historical Sociology*, Philip Abrams, ed. (London 1978) 254-5.

CHAPTER 7: *Peel and a Wider World*

1 OA, Reid Papers, James Reid to Thomas Reid, 4 Mar. 1826

2 *Ibid.*, James Reid to friends, 8 Jan. 1849

3 *Ibid.*

4 *Ibid.*, James Reid to Thomas Reid, 1 Mar. 1847

5 Robert Gourlay, *Statistical Account of Upper Canada* [1822], S.R. Mealing, ed. (Toronto 1974) 267

6 Philip Greven jr, *Four Generations: Population, Land and Families in Colonial Andover Massachusetts* (Ithaca, NY 1970) chs 7 and 8
7 James T. Lemon, *The Best Poor Man's Country: A Geographical Study of Early Southeastern Pennsylvania* (New York 1972) 88
8 *Ibid.*, 94-7
9 Allan G. Bogue, *From Prairie to Corn Belt: Farming on the Illinois and Iowa Prairies in the Nineteenth Century* (Chicago 1961) 22, 25-7, 52, 56
10 Michael Conzen, *Frontier Farming in an Urban Shadow: The Influence of Madison's Proximity on the Agricultural Development of Blooming Grove, Wisconsin* (Madison 1971) 48, 65-7, 87, 128
11 See Richard Easterlin, George Alter, and Gretchen Condran, 'Farms and Farm Families in Old and New Areas: The Northern States in 1860,' *Family and Population in Nineteenth-Century America* (Princeton 1978) 22-84.

Bibliography

MANUSCRIPT SOURCES

Chinguacousy Township. Assessment Roll 1840. Chinguacousy Branch, Brampton Library
Chinguacousy Township. Township Council Minutes 1857-70 (Genealogical Society Microfilm)
Christ Church (Anglican). Brampton. Marriage Registers 1855-85
Peel County, Abstracts of Deeds and Copy Books of Deeds, 1805-1900: Albion, Caledon, Chinguacousy, Toronto, and Toronto Gore Townships (Genealogical Society Microfilm)
Peel County. Surrogate Court. Wills 1867-1900 (Genealogical Society Microfilm)
Public Archives of Canada. Census of the Canadas 1851-2. Manuscript. Peel County
Public Archives of Canada. Census of the Canadas 1860-1. Manuscript. Peel County
Public Archives of Canada. Census of Canada 1870-1. Manuscript. Peel County and Cardwell District
Public Archives of Canada. Provincial Secretary's Papers, RG 5, M26 Vols I-VI
Public Archives of Canada. United States of America. Department of State. Consular Reports. RG59; Reel T488-2, Sarnia, 17 July 1879
Public Archives of Ontario. Perkins Bull Collection. Series C, No. 3, Box 1, 'Brampton'
Public Archives of Ontario. Crown Land Papers, (a) RG I, C-I-8, Vols 11-12, Land Grants 1810-35; (b) Township Papers (Peel County Townships); (c) RG I, A-VI-9, Vol. 16, Inspection Reports, Clergy Reserves
Public Archives of Ontario. Inventory of Estates Probated in the Home District 1800-67
Public Archives of Ontario. Letter, John Brown (Caledon Township) to Editor, Paisley (Scotland) Gazette, 20 Apr. 1870
Public Archives of Ontario. James Reid Papers. Correspondence 1822-62

Toronto Gore Township. Township Council Minutes 1860-73 (Genealogical Society Microfilm)
Toronto Township. Township Council Minutes 1854-60 (Genealogical Society Microfilm)
United Presbyterian Church. Brampton. Marriage Registers, 1855-85 (Genealogical Society Microfilm)
York County. Probate Court. Wills 1800-67

PRINTED PRIMARY SOURCES

Census of the Canadas 1851-52 Quebec 1853
Census of the Canadas, 1860-61 Montreal 1863
Census of Canada, 1870-71 Ottawa 1875
Commemorative Biographical Record of the County of York, Ontario Toronto 1907
County of York Directory, 1850 Toronto 1850
Ontario. Department of Planning and Development *Credit Valley Conservation Report 1956* (Toronto 1956)
Illustrated Atlas of Peel... 1871 [rpt] Port Elgin, Ontario 1971
Kubat, Daniel and David Thornton *A Statistical Profile of Canadian Society* Toronto 1974
Minutes, Reports and By-Laws, Peel County, 1854-1874 Brampton 1875
Province of Canada. Legislative Assembly *Parliamentary Debates on the Subject of Confederation of the British North American Provinces* Quebec 1865 [rpt]
Province of Canada. Legislative Assembly. Journals and Appendices 1840-67
Province of Ontario. Legislature. Sessional Papers 1871-2
Urquhart, M.C. and K.A.H. Buckley *Historical Statistics of Canada*. Toronto 1965
Walton, George *Directory of Toronto and the Home District, 1837* Toronto 1837
Warren Clarkson of Clarkson and the Clarkson Family Letters, 1854-1859 Betty Clarkson, ed. Boston Mills, Ontario 1979
W.S. Wallace, ed. *Macmillan Dictionary of Canadian Biography* Toronto 1963

NEWSPAPERS

Brampton *Herald*
Brampton *Standard*
Brampton *Times*
Orangeville *Sun*
Streetsville *Weekly Review*

THEORY, METHODS, AND COMPARATIVE STUDIES

Abrams, Phillip, ed. *Towns in Societies: Essays in Social History and Historical Sociology* London 1978

Andrews, Frank et al. *Multiple Classification Analysis: A Report on a Computer Program for Multiple Regression Using Categorical Predictors* Ann Arbor 1973

Billington, R.A. *America's Frontier Heritage* New York 1961

Bogue, Allan G. *From Prairie to Corn Belt: Farming on the Illinois and Iowa Prairies in the Nineteenth Century* Chicago 1961

Braudel, Fernand *Capitalism and Material Life, 1400-1800* New York 1973

Chirot, Daniel *Social Change in a Peripheral Society: The Creation of a Balkan Colony* New York 1976

Clark, S.D. *The Developing Canadian Community* Toronto 1968

Conzen, Michael P. *Frontier Farming in an Urban Shadow: The Influence of Madison's Proximity on the Agricultural Development of Blooming Grove, Wisconsin* Madison 1971

Curti, Merle *The Making of an American Community* Stanford 1959

Dollar, Charles M. and Richard Jensen *The Historian's Guide to Statistics: Quantitative Analysis and Historical Research* New York 1971

Floud, Roderick *An Introduction to Quantitative Methods for Historians* London 1973

Frank, André Gunder 'The Development of Underdevelopment,' *Imperialism and Underdevelopment: A Reader* R.T. Rhodes, ed. New York 1970

Gagan, David 'Enumerators' Instructions for the Census of Canada, 1852 and 1861,' *Social History / Histoire Sociale* 7 (1974) 355-65

Gates, Paul W. *The Farmer's Age: Agriculture, 1815-1860, The Economic History of the United States* III New York 1962

Hartz, Louis *The Founding of New Societies* New York 1966

Laslett, Peter *The World We Have Lost* London 1965

Lemon, James T. *The Best Poor Man's Country: A Geographical Study of Early Southeastern Pennsylvania* New York 1972

Nisbet, Robert *Social Change and History: Aspects of the Western Theory of Development* New York 1969

Shorter, Edward *The Historian and the Computer: A Practical Guide* New York 1975

Stone, Lawrence 'Prosopography' *Daedalus* 100 (1971) 47-79

Wade, Richard C. *The Urban Frontier* Chicago 1959

Warner, Sam Bass, jr and Sylvia Fleisch 'The Past of Today's Present: A Social History of America's Metropolises, 1860-1960' *Journal of Urban History* III (1976) 3-65

Winchester, Ian 'The Linkage of Historical Records by Man and Computer: Techniques and Problems' *Journal of Interdisciplinary History* I (1970) 107-24

Wrigley, E.A., ed. *Identifying People in the Past* London 1973

— *An Introduction to English Historical Demography* New York 1966

— *Population and History* New York 1966

MARRIAGE, FERTILITY, AND FAMILY SIZE

Chojnacka, Helen 'Nuptiality Patterns in An Agrarian Society' *Population Studies* 30 (1976) 203-26

Denton, Frank and Peter George 'The Influence of Socio-Economic Variables on Family Size in Wentworth County, Ontario, 1871' *Canadian Review of Sociology and Anthropology* 10 (1973) 334-45

Easterlin, Richard 'Does Human Fertility Adjust to the Environment?' *American Economic Review: Papers & Proceedings* LXI (1971) 399-407

Engerman, Stanley 'The Study of the European Fertility Decline' *Journal of Family History* I (1976) 245-51

Hareven, Tamara and Maris Vinovskis, eds *Family and Population in Nineteenth Century America* Princeton 1978

Henripin, Jacques *Trends and Factors of Fertility in Canada* Ottawa 1972

Knodel, John *The Decline of Fertility in Germany, 1871-1939* Princeton 1974

Leet, Don 'The Determinants of Fertility Transition in Ante-Bellum Ohio' *Journal of Economic History* 36 (1976) 359-78

— 'Interrelations of Population Density, Urbanization, Literacy, and Fertility' *Explorations in Economic History* 14 (1977) 388-401

McLaren, Angus 'Birth Control and Abortion in Canada, 1870-1920' *Canadian Historical Review* LIX (1978) 319-40

McInnis, R.M. 'Childbearing and Land Availability: Some Evidence from Individual Household Data' Behavioural Models in Historical Demography Conference, Philadelphia 1974 (mimeo)

Tepperman, Lorne 'Ethnic Variations in Marriage and Fertility: Canada, 1871' *Canadian Review of Sociology and Anthropology* II (1974) 324-43

Vinovskis, Maris 'Socio-Economic Determinants of Interstate Fertility Differentials in the United States in 1850 and 1860' *Journal of Interdisciplinary History* VI (1976) 375-96

Wrigley, E.A. 'Family Limitation in Pre-Industrial England,' *Economic History Review* XIX (1966) 82-109

Yasuba, Yasukichi *Birth Rates of the White Population in the United States 1800-1860: An Economic Study* Baltimore 1962

THE STRUCTURE OF HOUSEHOLDS AND FAMILIES

Anderson, Michael *Family Structure in Nineteenth Century Lancashire* Cambridge, Eng. 1971

Berkner, Lutz and Franklin Mendels 'Inheritance Systems, Family Structure and Demographic Patterns in Western Europe, 1700-1900' *Historical Studies of Changing Fertility* Charles Tilley, ed. Princeton 1978. Pp 209-23

Cooper, J.F. 'Patterns of Inheritance and Settlement by Great Landowners from the Fifteenth to the Eighteenth Centuries' *Family and Inheritance* J. Goody and J. Thirsk, eds Cambridge, Eng. 1976

Greven, Philip, jr *Four Generations: Population, Land and Families in Colonial Andover, Massachusetts* Ithaca NY 1970

Habbakuk, H.J. 'Family Structure and Economic Change in Nineteenth Century Europe' *Journal of Economic History* XV (1955) 1-12

Laslett, Peter 'The Comparative History of Household and Family' *Journal of Social History* IV (1970) 75-87

Lasslett, Peter and Richard Wall, eds *Household and Family in Past Time: Comparative Studies in the Size and Structure of the Domestic Group over the Last Three Centuries...* Cambridge, Eng. 1972

THE LIFE CYCLE

Ball, Rosemary R. ' "A Perfect Farmer's Wife": Women in 19th Century Rural Ontario' *Canada: An Historical Magazine* 3 (1975) 2-21

Davey, Ian 'Trends in Female School Attendance in Mid-Nineteenth Century Ontario' *Histoire Sociale / Social History* VIII (1975) 238-54

Gagan, David ' "The Prose of Life': Literary Reflections of the Family, Individual Experience and Social Structure in Nineteenth-Century Canada' *Journal of Social History* 9 (1976) 367-81

Hareven, Tamara 'Modernization and Family History: Perspectives on Social Change' *Comparative Studies in the History of Culture and Society* 2 (1976) 190-206

Katz, Michael *The Irony of Early School Reform* Cambridge, MA 1968

— 'Who Went to School' *History of Education Quarterly* XII (1972) 432-54

Kett, J.F. 'Adolescence and Youth in Nineteenth Century America' *The Family in History* Theodore Rabb and Robert Rotberg, eds New York 1973. Pp 95-110

Prentice, Alison *The School Promoters: Education and Social Class in Mid-Nineteenth Century Upper Canada* Toronto 1977

Uhlenberg, Peter 'Life Cycle Experiences of US Females' *Journal of Marriage and the Family* 36 (1974) 284-92

— 'A Study of Cohort Life Cycles: Cohorts of Native Born Massachusetts Women, 1830-1920' *Population Studies* 23 (1969) 407-20

Wells, Robert V. 'Demographic Change and the Life Cycle of American Families' *The Family in History* Theodore Rabb and Robert Rotberg, eds New York 1971 Pp 85-94

GEOGRAPHICAL AND SOCIAL MOBILITY

Bogue, Allen G. 'Farming in the Prairie Peninsula, 1830-1890' *Journal of Economic History* 23 (1963) 3-29

Erickson, Charlotte *Invisible Immigrants: The Adaptation of English and Scottish Immigrants in Nineteenth Century America* Coral Gables, Fla. 1972

Gagan, David and Herbert Mays 'Historical Demography and Canadian Social History: Families and Land in Peel County, Ontario' *Canadian Historical Review* LIV (1973) 27-47

Heller, Charles F. and F. Stanley Moore 'Continuity in Rural Land Ownership: Western Kalamazoo County, Michigan, 1820-1861' *Michigan History* LVI 233-46

Katz, Michael *The People of Hamilton, Canada West: Family and Class in a Mid-Nineteenth Century City* Cambridge, MA 1975

Katz, Michael, Michael Doucet, and Mark Stern 'Migration and the Social Order in Erie County, New York: 1855' *Journal of Interdisciplinary History* VIII (1978) 669-701

Kirk, Gordon W., jr *The Promise of American Life: Social Mobility in a Nineteenth-Century American Community...* Philadelphia 1978

Knights, Peter *The Plain People of Boston, 1830-1860: A Study in City Growth* New York 1971

Mays, H.J. and H.I. Manzl 'Literacy and Social Structure in Nineteenth Century Ontario: An Exercise in Historical Methodology' *Histoire Sociale / Social History* VII (1974)

Soltow, Lee *Men and Wealth in the United States, 1850-1870* New Haven 1975

Thernstrom, Stephan *The Other Bostonians: Poverty and Progress in the American Metropolis, 1880-1970* Cambridge, MA 1973

— *Poverty and Progress* New York 1969

THE SOCIETY AND ECONOMY OF CANADA WEST/ONTARIO

Aitken, Hugh G.J. 'The Family Compact and the Welland Canal Company' *Canadian Journal of Economics and Political Science* XVIII (1952) 63-76

Armstrong, F.H., ed. *Handbook of Upper Canadian Chronology and Territorial Legislation* London, Ont. 1967

Berger, Carl *The Sense of Power* Toronto 1970

Bliss, Michael ' "Pure Books on Avoided Subjects": Pre-Freudian Sexual Ideas in Canada' *Historical Papers 1970* (Canadian Historical Association 1971) 89-108

Burnet, Jean *Ethnic Groups in Upper Canada* Toronto 1972

Careless, J.M.S. *The Union of the Canadas: The Growth of Canadian Institutions 1841-1857* Toronto 1967

Chambers, E.J. and Gordon Bertram 'Urbanization and Manufacturing in Central Canada, 1870-1890' *Papers on Regional Studies: CPSA Conference on Statistics, 1964* S. Ostry and T.K. Rymes, eds Toronto 1966. Pp 225-57

Craig, Gerald, ed. *Lord Durham's Report* Toronto 1964

Cudmore, S.A. 'Rural Depopulation in Southern Ontario' *Transactions of the Royal Canadian Institute* IX (1913) 261-7

Dales, J.H. 'Estimates of Canadian Manufacturing Output by Markets, 1870-1915' *Papers: CPSA Conference on Statistics 1962 and 1963* J. Henrepin and A. Asimakopoulos, eds Ottawa 1964 Pp 61-91

Easterbrook, W.T. and Hugh G.J. Aitken *Canadian Economic History* Toronto 1965

Ewart, Alison and Julia Jarvis 'The Personnel of the Family Compact' *Canadian Historical Review* VI (Mar. 1926) 209-21

Fowke, Vernon C. 'The Myth of the Self-Sufficient Canadian Pioneer' *Transactions of the Royal Society of Canada* Series III, LIV (1962) 28-37

Gagan, David 'Land, Population, and Social Change: The "Critical Years" in Rural Canada West' *Canadian Historical Review* LIX (1978) 293-318

— 'The Relevance of "Canada First"' *Journal of Canadian Studies* V (1970) 36-44

— 'The Security of Land: Mortgaging in Toronto Gore Township, 1835-1885' *Aspects of Nineteenth Century Ontario* F.H. Armstrong et al. eds Toronto 1974 Pp 35-153

Gates, Lillian *Land Policies of Upper Canada* Toronto 1968

Gilmour, James M. *Spatial Evolution of Manufacturing, Southern Ontario, 1851-1891* Toronto 1972

Henderson, J.L.H., ed. *John Strachan: Documents and Opinions* Toronto 1969

Houston, Cecil and William Smyth 'The Orange Order and the Expansion of the Frontier in Ontario, 1830-1900' *Journal of Historical Geography* 4 (1978) 251-64

Houston, Susan 'Politics, Schools and Social Change' *Canadian Historical Review* LIII (1972) 249-71

Innis, H.A. *Essays in Canadian Economic History* M.Q. Innis, ed. Toronto 1956

Isbister, John 'Agriculture, Balanced Growth and Social Change in Central Canada since 1850: An Interpretation,' *Economic Development and Cultural Change* 25 (July 1977) 673-97.

Johnson, J.K. 'The Businessman as Hero: The Case of William Warren Street' *Ontario History* LXV (1973) 125-32

Johnson, Leo 'Land Policy, Population Growth and Social Structure in the Home District, 1793-1851' *Ontario History* LXVII (1971) 32-57

Jones, R.L. *History of Agriculture in Ontario 1613-1880* Toronto 1948

Kelly, Kenneth 'The Evaluation of Land for Wheat Cultivation in Early Nineteenth-Century Ontario' *Ontario History* LXII (1970) 57-64

— 'The Transfer of British Ideas on Improved Farming to Ontario during the First Half of the Nineteenth Century' *Ontario History* LXIII (1971) 103-11

Landon, Fred *Western Ontario and the American Frontier* [rpt] Toronto 1967

Lawr, D.A. 'The Development of Farming in Ontario, 1870-1914: Patterns of Growth and Change' *Ontario History* LXIV (1972) 240-51

Lower, A.R.M. *Canadians in the Making* Toronto 1955

Morton, W.L. *The Critical Years: The Union of British North America* Toronto 1964

— ed. *The Shield of Achilles / Le Bouclier d'Achille* Toronto 1968

Paterson, Gilbert C. *Land Settlement in Upper Canada, 1783-1840: Sixteenth Report of the Department of Archives for the Province of Ontario* Toronto 1920

Saunders, Robert E. 'What Was the Family Compact,' *Ontario History* LXIX (1957) 173-8

Smiley, Donald V., ed. *The Rowell-Sirois Report ... Book I* [rpt] Toronto 1963

Smith, Allan 'The Myth of the Self-Made Man in English Canada, 1850-1914' *Canadian Historical Review* LIX (1978) 189-218

Spelt, Jacob *Urban Development in South-Central Ontario* Toronto 1972

Tucker, G.N. *The Canadian Commercial Revolution, 1845-1851* [rpt] Toronto 1964
Waite, P.B. *The Life and Times of Confederation* Toronto 1962
Watkins, M.H. 'A Staple Theory of Economic Growth' *Approaches to Canadian Economic History* W.T. Easterbrook and M.H. Watkins, eds Toronto 1967 Pp 49-73
Wightman, W.R. 'Construction Materials in Colonial Ontario, 1831-1861' *Aspects of Nineteenth Century Ontario* F.H. Armstrong, et al. eds Toronto 1974 Pp 114-34
Wilson, Alan *The Clergy Reserves of Upper Canada: A Canadian Mortmain* Toronto 1968

MID-VICTORIAN BRITAIN

Best, Geoffrey *Mid-Victorian Britain, 1851-1875* London 1971
Blaug, M. 'The Myth of the Old Poor Law and the Making of the New' *Essays in Social History* M.W. Flinn and T.C. Smout, eds Oxford 1974 Pp 123-53
Connell, K.H. *The Population of Ireland 1750-1845* Oxford 1950
Grossick, Geoffrey 'The Labour Aristocracy and Its Values: A Study of Mid-Victorian Kentish London' *Victorian Studies* XLX (1976) 301-28
Hobsbawm, E.J. *Industry and Empire. The Pelican Economic History of Britain* III London 1969
– 'The Tramping Artisans' *Labouring Men: Studies in the History of Labour* London 1968 Pp 24-63
– and George Rudé *Captain Swing* New York 1975
Kennedy, Robert E. *Irish Emigration, Marriage and Fertility* Berkeley, CA 1973
Meacham, Standish *A Life Apart: The English Working Class 1890-1914* Cambridge, MA 1977
Thompson, E.P. *The Making of the English Working Class* London 1965
Thompson, F.M.L. *English Landed Society in the Nineteenth Century* London 1963

NINETEENTH-CENTURY EMIGRATION TRACTS, ESSAYS, AND MEMOIRS

N.A. [Catharine Parr Traill] *The Backwoods of Canada: Letters from the Wife of an Emigrant Officer* London 1876
Bigsby, John *The Shoe and Canoe* II, 2 vols London 1850
Bird, Isabella *The Englishwoman in America* [1856] Madison 1966
Canada: A Memorial Volume (Montreal 1889)
Carroll, John, ed. *'Father Corson': or the Old Style Canadian Itinerant, Embracing the Life and Gospel Labours of the Rev. Robert Corson* Toronto 1879
Catermole, William *Emigration: The Advantages of Emigration to Canada* London 1831
Clark, C.S. *Of Toronto the Good: A Social Study* Montreal 1898
Conant, Thomas *Upper Canada Sketches* Toronto 1898
Copleston, Mrs Edward *Canada: Why We Live in It, and Why We Like It* London 1861

Davin, Nicholas F. *The Irishman in Canada* Toronto 1875

Day, Samuel P. *English America: or, Pen Pictures of Canadian Places and People I* 2 vols London 1864

Domett, Alfred *Canadian Journal* [rpt] London, Ontario 1955

Dunlop, E.S., ed. *Our Forest Home: Being Extracts from the Correspondence of the late Frances Stewart* Toronto 1889

Emigration: The British Farmer's and Farm Labourer's Guide to Ontario Toronto 1880

Fidler, Rev. Isaac *Observations on Professions, Literature, Manners and Emigration in the United States and Canada... 1832* New York 1833

Gourlay, Robert *Statistical Account of Upper Canada* S.R. Mealing, ed. Toronto 1974

Haight, Canniff *Country Life in Canada Fifty Years Ago* Toronto 1885

Hogan, J. Sheridan *Canada: An Essay* Montreal 1855

Jameson, Anna *Winter Studies and Summer Rambles* J.J. Talman and E.M. Murray, eds Toronto 1943

Lindsay, Charles *The Life and Times of William Lyon Mackenzie* II 2 vols Toronto 1862

Moodie, Susanna *Life in the Clearings versus the Bush* New York 1855

— *Roughing It in the Bush* [rpt] Toronto 1962

Radcliff, Thomas, ed. *Authentic Letters from Upper Canada* James J. Talman ed. Toronto 1967

Munro, W.F. *The Backwoods Life: An Interesting Story of Pioneer Days in Melancthon Township* Shelburne, Ont. 1869

Philpot, Harvey J. *Guide Book to the Canadian Dominion Containing Information for the Emigrant, the Tourist, the Sportsman, and the Small Capitalist* London 1871

Preston, R.A., ed. *For Friends at Home: A Scottish Emigrant's Letters from Canada, California and the Cariboo, 1844-1864* Montreal 1974

Rowan, John *The Emigrant and Sportsman in Canada: Some Experiences of an Old Country Settler...* London 1876

Scadding, Henry *Toronto of Old* F.H. Armstrong, ed. Toronto 1966

Shirreff, Patrick *A Tour through North America Together with a Comprehensive View of Canada and the United States as Adapted for Agricultural Emigration* Edinburgh 1835

Smith, W.H. *Canada: Past, Present and Future: Being a Historical, Geographical, Geological and Statistical Account of Canada West* I 2 vols Toronto 1852

Strickland, Major Samuel *Twenty-Seven Years in Canada West* [rpt] Edmonton 1970

Traill, Catharine Parr *The Canadian Settlers' Guide* Toronto 1855

Warr, Rev. G.A. *Canada as It Is: or, the Emigrant's Friend and Guide to Upper Canada...* London 1847

Wright, Mrs J.M. *The Complete Home: An Encyclopedia of Domestic Life and Affairs* Brantford 1870

Index

THE ONTARIO HISTORICAL STUDIES SERIES

The Ontario Historical Studies Series is a comprehensive history of Ontario from 1791 to the present, which will include several biographies of former premiers, numerous volumes on the economic, social, political, and cultural development of the province, and a general history incorporating the insights and conclusions of the other works in the series. The purpose of the series is to enable the general reader and the scholar to understand better the distinctive features of Ontario as one of the principal regions within Canada.

Published

Olga B. Bishop, Barbara I. Irwin, Clara G. Miller, eds *Bibliography of Ontario History, 1867–1976: Cultural, Economic, Political, Social*, 2 volumes (1980)
J.M.S. Careless, ed *The Pre-Confederation Premiers: Ontario Government Leaders, 1841–1867* (1980)
Peter Oliver *G. Howard Ferguson: Ontario Tory* (1977)
Christopher Armstrong *The Politics of Federalism: Ontario's Relations with the Federal Government, 1867–1942* (1981)
David Gagan *Hopeful Travellers: Families, Land, and Social Change in Mid-Victorian Peel County, Canada West* (1981)

Forthcoming

Roger Graham *Hon. Leslie M. Frost* (Premier, 1949–1961)
A.K. McDougall *Hon. John P. Robarts* (Premier, 1961–1971)
R.M. Stamp *The Schools of Ontario, 1876–1976*

Lightning Source UK Ltd.
Milton Keynes UK
UKHW010002210722
406167UK00001B/209